THE ASIAN AMERICAN EXPERIENCE

Series Editor
Roger Daniels, University of Cincinnati

RACE AND POLITICS

Asian Americans, Latinos, and Whites
in a Los Angeles Suburb

Leland T. Saito

Foreword by Roger Daniels

University of Illinois Press
Urbana and Chicago

1 2 3 4 5 C P 5 4 3 2 1

This book is printed on acid-free paper.

Library of Congress Cataloging-in-Publication Data
Saito, Leland T., 1955–
Race and politics : Asian Americans, Latinos, and whites in a Los
Angeles suburb / Leland T. Saito ; foreword by Roger Daniels.
p.   cm. — (The Asian American experience)
Includes bibliographical references (p.   ) and index.
ISBN 0-252-02413-3 (cloth : acid-free paper). —
ISBN 0-252-06720-7 (pbk. : acid-free paper)
1. Monterey Park (Calif.)—Race relations. 2. Monterey Park
(Calif.)—Politics and government. 3. Asian Americans—
California—Monterey Park. 4. Hispanic Americans—
California—Monterey Park. 5. Whites—California—
Monterey Park. I. Title. II. Series.
F869.M7S25   1998
305.8'009794'93—dc21   97-45435
CIP

To my parents, George and Clara Saito

CONTENTS

Roger Daniels

Although the word *Chinatown* has been in the English language for almost 150 years, the suburban Chinatowns that have developed since the 1960s are quite different from the traditional central-city Chinatowns that characterized the first century of Chinese American urban life and still exist.[1] The latter, like many downtown neighborhoods, tended to be cramped, dilapidated, and noisome, although they were also vibrant communities and, at least in part, tourist attractions. The new suburban Chinatowns tend to be undifferentiated in housing stock from the areas that surround them; their residents, most of them recent immigrants from either the People's Republic (particularly Hong Kong), Taiwan, or the Chinese diaspora in Southeast Asia, have often displaced middle- and lower-middle-class whites.

Monterey Park, a city of some sixty thousand in Los Angeles County's San Gabriel Valley, is the outstanding example of this new phenomenon and has received a good deal of scholarly attention.[2] The major contribution of Leland Saito's work is that it provides a vivid, participant-observer view of how the politics of multiculturalism operate in such an environment. His analysis, based on much observation and study over a number of years, provides important insights into what will be an increasingly important aspect of California politics for the foreseeable future. It is a story of effective grass-roots coalition-building and empowerment at the local level. Saito emphasizes the significance of ethnic and racial identities, not just in politics but in everyday life, and demonstrates that these identities are deeply rooted and manifest themselves in a number of ways.

Although some of the dynamics of the San Gabriel Valley's ethnic politics are like those that have characterized American politics since Pennsylvania political "boss" Ben Franklin complained about the German vote, there are other aspects that are quite different. The major element in Monterey Park's situation is that the "whites" are the minority there. Not only is there an Asian American majority—57 percent at the 1990 census—but there is also a sizable Latino population, which makes for a complex political equation. Yet, as Saito shows, mere numbers do not automatically translate into political power, and diverse Asian American groups do not always see eye-to-eye on each issue. Consciousness has to be raised, coalitions have to be built, and, even in Monterey Park, money, the mother's milk of American politics, must be raked in, albeit in relatively modest amounts.

The political success of local Asian American candidates in the San Gabriel Valley is quite different from the better known successes of other West Coast Asian American politicians. The elections of Asian Indian, Japanese, and Korean American congressional candidates in California and of Gary Locke, the Chinese American governor of Washington State, have not been based on ethnic bloc voting, although ethnic money-raising has been important. In Monterey Park the situation is different: Most candidates there are clearly aiming their campaigns at ethnic voters, as ethnic politicians have been doing since the eighteenth century. But in Monterey Park and elsewhere in the San Gabriel Valley, candidates such as Judy Chu, while basing themselves on an ethnic bloc, cannot win by focusing on one ethnic group or race. They must attract votes from groups that are not Asian American.

Saito shows how and on what issues local Asian American politicians have successfully campaigned. Much of the scholarly literature about Asian Americans, for obvious reasons, focuses on what was done to them. Although prejudice and discrimination are all too present, even in Monterey Park, Saito describes what is clearly an Asian American success story.

ACKNOWLEDGMENTS

This study is based on my observations as I listened to, watched, and participated in the public and private political lives of the people in this book. Although they knew that I was a researcher gathering data, it was my identity as a local resident and activist that shaped our interactions, and I was continually surprised by, and grateful for, their remarkably candid and detailed discussions of their biographies and understandings of local politics. As a conversation at a board meeting of the West San Gabriel Valley Asian Pacific Democratic Club—the major Asian American political organization in the region at the time—clearly revealed, however, we occasionally broke from our role as political activists and became observer and observed. Mike Eng (the club's founding president) was talking about the upcoming Monterey Park City Council elections when he suddenly stopped, turned to me, and said, in a voice filled with mock horror, "What are you doing, writing down everything I say?" "He's a spy," laughed Janet Lim, president of the group. Another member added, "We're all going to appear in his book."

A number of years have passed since that exchange in 1989, and those at that meeting are indeed part of this book. This work represents a journey into the world of politics in the San Gabriel Valley. I am deeply indebted to the following for their counsel and guidance on that trip: Eleanor Chow, Judy Chu, George Ige, Sam Kiang, Joe Vasquez, and Sophie Wong, all elected officials, and Jose Calderon, Mike Eng, Janet Lim, Bob McClosky, and Jeff Su, community activists. Through their selfless hard work dedicated to political equality, they were civil rights crusaders and an inspiration to me. I thank them, as well as the countless others who allowed access to their lives, for their wonderful patience and candor. I grew up and lived in this community and continue to maintain contact with the individuals there. I hope that I have accurately and fairly represented their story. I also thank Aimee Arakawa and her coworkers for quickly and meticulously responding to my many requests for information from the Monterey Park City Clerk's office.

This book developed in two stages. First, while I was a graduate student at UCLA, I had the good fortune to work as a research assistant on a community study of Monterey Park with John Horton, the principal investigator, and Linda Shaw, Mary Pardo, Jose Calderon, and Yen Fen Tseng, the collaborators. Horton proved to be a valuable and exemplary mentor, not only for his scholarly counsel but also as a model of how a professor can treat students with respect, dignity, and kindness. Mary Pardo and Jose Calderon were fellow students who have turned into supportive colleagues and friends. I thank Linda Shaw for her invaluable training on ethnography, which started me on the path of fieldwork, and Yen Fen Tseng's insightful discussions on immigrant Chinese that opened a new world to me, a Yonsei (fourth-generation Japanese American). These individuals have established a large body of work that provides a critical perspective on multiracial communities and continues to inform my work. David Lopez, Don Nakanishi, and Paul Ong provided intellectual guidance when this work began and offered collegial support as the project reached completion. They were also excellent models, demonstrating how scholarly research can be effectively combined with worthwhile community projects. I also thank Charles Choy Wong and Tim Fong, the pioneers in research on Monterey Park, whose work formed an invaluable foundation for my project.

When the UCLA group project ended, the second stage began. I continued fieldwork for several more years, joined the faculty at the University of California, San Diego, and began reworking my manuscript. My colleagues have created an intellectually stimulating environment. George Lipsitz has offered insightful critiques of my work. Yen Espiritu, Lisa Lowe, and Stephen Cornell have provided critical suggestions at key points. Ramon Gutierrez has provided wise counsel, and Paule Cruz Takash has been the perpetual sounding board for my political analysis. Thanks also to Amy Bridges, Steven Erie, Leslie Sebastian, Ralph Lewin, and Benita Roth for their help on all of my projects, and I appreciate Ivonne Avila's and Chris Diani's computer skills.

I am grateful for research support from the UCLA Asian American Studies Center, American Sociological Association Minority Fellowship Program, Rockefeller Foundation, UCSD Academic Senate, and the California Policy Seminar. Shirley Hune, the UCLA Institute of American Cultures, and the Chicano Studies Center provided a postdoctoral fellowship that provided time to complete a major portion of this book. Russell Leong and Glenn Omatsu shared their visions of Asian American studies; Roger Daniels has been a dedicated, patient, and encouraging editor in guiding the project along; and Karen Hewitt at the University of Illinois Press has been particularly helpful.

I especially thank my parents, George and Clara Saito, for the love and support that has sustained me through the many stages of my life and career. I also thank my sisters, Nadine Tateoka and Wendy Saito Lew, and their husbands and children—Paul, Benjamin, Elise, and Joseph Tateoka and Albert Lew—for their constant encouragement and kindness and for providing a warm and caring family.

RACE AND POLITICS

Race, Ethnicity, and Politics

Asian Americans and Latinos are the two fastest-growing groups in the United States, and the political, economic, and cultural implications of this growth are clearly visible in the San Gabriel Valley of Los Angeles County. Located fifteen minutes by freeway east of downtown Los Angeles, the region is undergoing dramatic demographic changes due to international and domestic migration. As a result, the economic and political dominance of whites has rapidly declined as their population has dropped from an overwhelming majority in 1970 to a minority in 1990.[1] Latinos are the largest group and have become the most powerful politically at the regional level, holding all higher elected offices in 1996.[2] The conspicuous emergence of Chinese immigrant entrepreneurs in the region's business and manufacturing districts adds to the complexity of interethnic relationships. Since the mid-1970s a large infusion of Chinese immigrants and capital has made the San Gabriel Valley the home of the largest Chinese ethnic economy in the nation in terms of the number of ethnically owned businesses.

Using this complex and dynamic case of demographic, economic, and political restructuring, I examine the bitter conflicts that emerged in the 1980s and 1990s among Latinos, Asian Americans, and whites around issues of political representation, economic development, urbanization, and definitions of who and what is "American." I also describe how long-term residents of the region—native-born Japanese, Chinese, Mexican Americans, and whites—worked to overcome their initial antagonism and developed political alliances to address these issues. African Americans are nearly invisible in the region, only about 1 percent of the total population.

I analyze what these events reveal about the construction of racial and ethnic identities, in particular the development of panethnic identities. By "panethnic identities," I mean the ties and cooperation among groups of different national origins, such as Japanese and Chinese Americans, that lead to the formation of more inclusive identities—in this case, as Asian Americans (Espiritu 1992). I also examine how race and ethnicity are used for political mobilization, interethnic and interracial political relationships, and how the need to acquire resources and establish networks and organizations to participate in politics effectively plays a central role in these processes (Morris 1984).[3] And I explore how cultural construction (Nagel 1994)—establishing a common culture as part of the process of developing a political identity—emerges from everyday events and provides a key element for the development of ethnic identities and political alliances.

The population growth among Latinos and Asian Americans in California surpasses national patterns, and both groups outnumber African Americans in the state (table 1).[4] Because Latinos and Asian Americans are the dominant groups at the local level in the San Gabriel Valley, both numerically and politically, rather than the minorities they are in other areas of the United States, politics there moves beyond the African American–white focus of traditional studies on minority-majority race relations and demonstrates other configurations of multiracial community politics as the United States enters a new demographic and political era.

Table 1. Racial and Ethnic Composition, California and the United States, 1980 and 1990

| | Number and Percentage of Population | | |
Race/Ethnicity	1980	1990	Growth
California			
African American	1,818,660 (7.7)	2,198,766 (7.4)	20.9%
Asian and Pacific Islander	1,312,973 (5.6)	2,847,835 (9.6)	116.9
Latino	4,393,908 (18.6)	7,317,389 (24.6)	66.5
Native American	231,702 (1.0)	248,929 (0.8)	7.4
White	15,850,775 (67.0)	17,093,961 (57.4)	7.8
	23,667,902	29,760,021	25.7
United States			
African American	26,482,349 (11.7)	29,930,524 (12.0)	13.0
Asian and Pacific Islander	3,726,440 (1.6)	7,226,986 (2.9)	93.9
Latino	13,935,827 (6.2)	20,873,141 (8.4)	49.8
Native American	1,534,336 (0.7)	2,015,143 (0.8)	31.3
White	180,602,838 (79.7)	188,424,773 (75.8)	4.3
	226,545,805	248,709,873	9.8

Sources: U.S. Department of Commerce, Bureau of the Census (1983); U.S. Census Bureau (1990a, 1990b).

Race, ethnicity, and politics have been intertwined throughout U.S. history. Government policies have defined and reflected racial categories and have heavily influenced the social, political, and economic consequences of those categories. For example, government policies toward Native American lands and labor, immigration and naturalization practices, and slavery created or reinforced racial hierarchies and privileges based on race. Recognizing the material consequences of racial categories, groups have organized politically along racial and ethnic lines to contest the boundaries of such categories and express and fight for economic and social interests through politics.

Political mobilization along racial and ethnic lines has been extremely important for groups that lack other forms of power and resources to protect and promote their interests. The Irish political machines of the late 1800s and early 1900s (Erie 1988) and the African American civil rights movement (McAdam 1982; Morris 1984) are examples of political efforts by groups that have either contested policies of exclusion that have limited their access to resources the government generates and controls or have used tactics, such as economic boycotts, to address discrimination in society directly.

Recognizing the need for developing networks, organizations, and resources for political power, racial and ethnic coalitions have had a long history in U.S. urban politics. Timothy D. "Big Tim" Sullivan's political machine in New York City elected him, an Irish American, to the state assembly in the 1890s, with the help of Germans, Jews, Italians, and Greeks (Czitrom 1991). A white ethnic coalition of southern and eastern Europeans helped to elect Anton Cermak, a Czech immigrant, as mayor of Chicago in 1931 (Cohen 1990). Edward Roybal, a Mexican American, also built a coalition of Mexicans, Jews, Asians, and African Americans to become a member of the Los Angeles City Council in 1949 (Underwood 1992). And Tom Bradley, an African American, depended heavily on Jews and African Americans in the campaigns that elected him to the Los Angeles City Council in the 1960s and to the mayor's office from the 1970s and through the early 1990s (Sonenshein 1993).

Research on racial and ethnic formation recognizes that identities are fluid and highly contested rather than static and fixed because individuals and groups challenge boundaries and the privileges or discrimination marked by such boundaries (Omi and Winant 1986). The change in identity of eastern, central, and southern Europeans from "black" to "white" in the United States is an example of shifting identities and economic and political gains (Lieberson 1980). With the institutionalization of white-ness—racial hierarchy and white racial privilege—whites need not invoke their racial identity to reap the benefits of whiteness because everyday in-stitutional activities and practices embed and support their advantages (Lipsitz 1995). As a result, whites understand the contemporary expres-sion of European American ethnicity as largely symbolic, linked to factors such as food and holidays with little self-consciously acknowledged polit-ical or economic consequences (Waters 1990).[5] By their participation in the unmarked practices that support whiteness, whites who sincerely be-lieve that they are not racist maintain and profit from the benefits of ra-cial privilege. For example, they accumulate capital aided by financial in-stitutions' discriminatory lending practices, purchase homes from realtors who use discriminatory tactics to ensure segregated neighborhoods, find jobs through employment networks that exclude racial minorities, and take advantage of federal tax policies that enhance the value of past and present forms of discrimination that favor them (Feagin and Vera 1994; Jackson 1985; Massey and Denton 1993; Oliver and Shapiro 1995).

In contrast, to challenge white racial privilege that systematically gen-erates and supports benefits for whites and disadvantages for racial mi-norities, those of Asian, Latin American, and African ancestry must bring attention to race and reveal how the practice of symbolic ethnicity disguises the ways in which whiteness permeates U.S. society. California's passage of the 1996 anti-affirmative action Proposition 209 by a clear majority of white voters although strongly opposed by Latinos, Asian Americans, and African Americans demonstrated two opposing views on the way race influences one's life chances. Although research on whiteness examines racial privilege and racial identities, the connection between whiteness and the construction of identities among racial minorities—and how such iden-tities are used in politics—is largely overlooked. Explicating that connec-tion is a major goal of this book.

Rather than being simply volitional, racial and ethnic identities—and their social costs—may be imposed by others. The attempt of Japanese Americans to "assimilate into the mainstream" and act and think of them-selves as American, for example, was judged a failure by the U.S. govern-ment and public when Japanese Americans were singled out, labeled a security threat, and put into concentration camps during World War II, although almost all Italian and German Americans remained free (Daniels 1986; Ichioka 1988). At the same time, ethnicity is neither unvarying nor monolithic throughout the United States. Rather, as Micaela Di Leonar-do (1984) points out in her study of Italian Americans in California, ethnicity varies from region to region and is shaped by local history, politics, and demographics. As research on panethnicity demonstrates, individuals possess more than one identity, and multiple levels exist simultaneously. A person can identify as Okinawan (Kobashigawa 1985–86), Japanese American, and Asian American, for example. Lisa Lowe (1991, p. 28) emphasizes the "heterogeneity, hybridity, and multiplicity" of racial identities through time and among individuals and groups and the ways historical and regional context, class, and gender texture and influence such identities (Espiritu 1997).

Whiteness and the imposition of racial identities belies the American ideal of being recognized as individuals and evaluated by individual merits. I document the experiences of Latinos and Asian Americans who moved to the San Gabriel Valley and wished to be thought of simply as Americans without regard to race. Despite their sincere and diligent efforts to be accepted as good neighbors and citizens, their histories have been marked by racial discrimination against a backdrop of white privilege. I show how these Latinos and Asian Americans became "reluctant ethnics" and cognizant of their racialization by whites and how politics became a critical site of struggle as they negotiated the meaning and material consequences of race.

Constructing Race, Ethnicity, and Political Alliances

Traditionally, research on racial and ethnic politics either has taken identities as a given or has characterized identities as being in a state of decline because of cultural assimilation (Browning, Marshall, and Tabb 1984; Gordon 1964), ignoring the way that people construct and give meaning to ethnic and racial identities. Research on panethnicity corrects that oversight by studying the development of ethnic identities on multiple levels and increasing levels of inclusiveness. Such research considers the structural factors that generate the need for ever-larger groupings for political purposes (such as the increasing organizational scale required for effective participation in electoral politics) and the historical context that create common interests (such as U.S. government policies on naturalization, immigration, and census procedures).

With an emphasis on structural factors, however, both research on ethnic and racial politics and panethnicity pay little attention to the details of everyday life that illustrate how individuals interpret and give meaning to events at the local, regional, national, and global level. The lived experiences of everyday life are a critical site of observation. They link the micro-level with the macro-level and reveal how institutional structures such as politics, work, and race relationships enter into and affect daily life and, in turn, how people understand, accept, and/or contest such social structures. Macro-level analysis also overlooks how personal and local events contribute to the formation of ethnic and racial identities and political activism. I discuss the range of meanings, and the varying levels of importance and commitment, that individuals attach to their ethnic identities, expressed through different forms of political activity in a community setting. Research that emphasizes structural factors overlooks these details and variations.

Entering the community, I initially concentrated on the views of Japanese Americans, long-term residents of the San Gabriel Valley, about the influx of Chinese immigrants and the region's rapid demographic changes. At a Monterey Park City Planning Commission meeting on the use of foreign languages (primarily Chinese) on business signs in November 1988, a brief incident occurred that illustrated the negative feelings some Nisei (second-generation Japanese Americans) have about the Chinese immigrants and the way ethnic identities are continually reaffirmed and reconstructed in interaction with local and regional events.

During the meeting, I went into the lobby to get something to drink from a vending machine. When I realized I had no change, I looked around, noticed a woman (around fifty-five, who I later found out was Japanese American) sitting nearby, and asked whether there was a change machine in the building. She said no, and when I mentioned that I had change in my car she said that she would give me the money. "You're Japanese aren't you?" she asked after handing it to me. I said that I was. Then she replied firmly, "You're not Chinese." Judging from her facial expression and tone of voice, I believed she meant that she would not have given me the money if I were Chinese, a feeling supported by the conversation that followed. Why, she asked, was I attending the meeting? When I explained that I was there to listen to the discussion on the language issue, she replied that only English should be allowed on signs and that people should be "American." She added that she did not like some of the Chinese immigrants because of their rude public behavior.

After that exchange we talked for a few minutes, and she mentioned that as a child she had been in a concentration camp with Harry Kitano, a professor at UCLA. The World War II camp experience is one of the defining moments of Japanese American ethnicity, and by invoking its memory and mentioning Kitano, the Japanese American professor, she emphasized our link as Japanese American. The bond was further strengthened during the conversation when she repeatedly used *Nihonjin* (Japanese) to refer to Japanese Americans.

Nisei in the community often said *Nihonjin* and *Hakujin* (white) in conversations with me. They used those words without any prompting on my part, assuming that I would understand; usually they were the only Japanese words used. Because they referred to race and ethnicity, their use tacitly acknowledged our bond as Japanese Americans. The woman's earlier suggestion that only English should be allowed on signs because people should be American, as well as her use of Japanese words and mention of the camps, clearly ethnic markers, were not contradictory. They conformed to the belief expressed by many Japanese Americans in the community about what was proper for public display, such as business signs, and for private behavior, such as personal conversations (Ichioka 1988).

The woman's reference to the camps and discussion of American ways indicate that history and experiences in the United States are important elements for constructing a Japanese American identity. The Japanese language and culture have rapidly vanished among those born in the United States, reduced, in the case of language, to a handful of words (Bonacich and Modell 1980). What is "proper" behavior is learned not only through the experience of one's group in relation to whites but also through observation of the experiences of other racial and ethnic groups with whites—in this case, Chinese immigrants.

The woman's resentment of Chinese immigrants was rooted in local and national events and corresponds with the history of many Japanese Americans in the region. Leaving the camps after World War II, many Japanese Americans settled in low-income urban ethnic neighborhoods. In the 1950s Japanese Americans began entering Monterey Park (fig. 1), then a predominantly white, middle-class suburban community considered a step up from their previous ethnic neighborhoods on the east side of Los Angeles. They had to contend, however, with restrictive covenants—written agreements between individual buyers and sellers about who could buy or rent property—that banned the sale of homes to racial minorities. Successfully fighting these covenants, Japanese Americans became active in city events and struggled to integrate themselves into community affairs. Eventually, they were accepted, in the words of one Nisei, as "good neighbors and citizens," symbolized by the election of George Ige, a Japanese American, to the city council in 1970. An upsurge of discriminatory acts in the San Gabriel Valley directed at the new Chinese immigrants, however, also af-

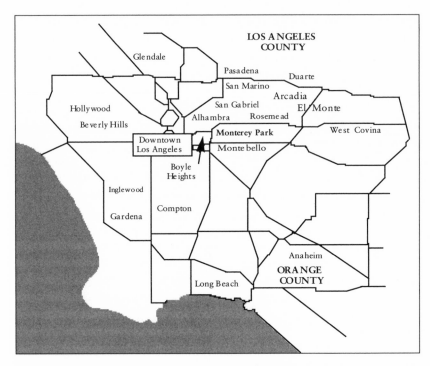

Figure 1. Monterey Park, Surrounding Region, and Freeway System

fected Japanese Americans. Many non-Asians cannot, or do not, make distinctions among those of Asian ancestry, reversing the acceptance Japanese Americans thought they had achieved.

In a reaction to the recent increase in racially motivated hate crimes in the area, the Nisei woman adhered to a traditional view of assimilation and actively separated herself from the Chinese immigrants. In doing so, she demonstrated how ethnicity was constructed partly out of difference with others in reaction to local events, a theme emerging from many interviews with local Japanese Americans.[6] As a Nisei man explained, "I think it's kind of a bad thing for us, that the Caucasian categorizes us as Chinese. I would like the Caucasian people to think that there is a difference between the Japanese and the Chinese, but they don't do it here in Monterey Park because they see me, they think, hey, here's another Chinese."[7]

Alliances within an ethnic group do not happen automatically, and the factors that divided the Nisei from the new immigrants were also a source of tension for native-born, long-term Chinese American residents of the city. They, too, expressed concerns about the behavior and wealth of some of the new Chinese immigrants and the negative impact, "Asian flack," that resulted. As one Chinese American woman mentioned, "We get this 'Asian flack' from the upper class Asians here. You know that the upper-class Asians flaunt their money and drive around in Mercedes. Now, all the Asians look alike [to non-Asians] so they think every Asian they see is rich. See, I am second generation but they don't see the difference" (Pardo 1990a, p. 329).

Despite the tensions, in 1990, two years after my conversation with the Nisei woman at the city hall vending machine, native-born Japanese and Chinese Americans were helping a Chinese immigrant, Sam Kiang, in his successful campaign for a seat on the Monterey Park City Council. That support moved the expression of race and ethnicity from the private domain to the most public of domains, politics. Fourteen Japanese American community leaders signed a letter and sent it to Japanese American voters in the city. They recognized the resentment that some Japanese Americans might feel toward the Chinese immigrants. One of the persons who organized the letter campaign explained that when they talked to many Japanese Americans about Kiang the "first thing they ask: Is he an ABC?"—an American-born Chinese. With that in mind, the committee crafted a letter that emphasized Kiang's strong educational credentials but did not mention his immigrant background, a demonstration of information being used selectively to build alliances across ethnic lines.

The Japanese American community leaders saw the discrimination aimed at the recent immigrants as the root of the problem, with the immigrants as the target. Realizing the futility of distancing themselves from the immigrants, they viewed discrimination as something that bound the groups together, and effective opposition to discrimination required the combined efforts of Chinese and Japanese Americans to elect qualified and competent Asian Americans. A numerical minority among a new Asian American majority, the leaders recognized clear differences between themselves and the Chinese immigrants. They also understood that combining numbers and resources with established Chinese Americans and new Chinese immigrants—acknowledging common interests as Asian Americans toward electing a Chinese American immigrant to the city council—would also benefit Japanese Americans. An Asian American on the council would help offset the blatantly anti-Chinese immigrant policies and rhetoric of white council members, which affected all Asian Americans through hate crimes and "Asian flack."

Similar to the Nisei, Latinos were established residents of the San Gabriel Valley, and some felt that the growing Asian American population—Latinos generally did not distinguish among Asian ethnic groups—was intruding on "their" territory. The growing electoral success of Asian Americans on local school boards and city councils was viewed as a threat to the recent electoral gains of Latinos. When the Southwest Voter Registration Education Project (SVREP), an organization concerned with Latino political issues, held one of the first voter registration drives in the area for Asian Americans, some Latinos complained about it and argued that the organization's resources should be used only for Latinos (Calderon 1991).

The San Gabriel Valley is important to both Latinos and Asian Americans because, as Leo Estrada, a demographer and political analyst, has explained (1991), the region has been an "incubator" for ethnic politics. Historically, the valley has been a training ground for minority politicians who have started careers locally and gone on to state and federal (in the case of Latinos) offices. Creating political districts through redistricting and reapportionment is a critical factor affecting political power; drawing new district lines can consolidate or fragment a group's political influence.

Redistricting is an extremely contentious process in which groups—especially as defined by political partisanship, race, and class—often compete to represent specific interests. Despite these conflicts, on August 30, 1991, Latinos and Asian Americans held a press conference in Monterey Park to announce the formation of an alliance to work together on the redistricting and reapportionment process in the San Gabriel Valley.

Overcoming their initial position as competitors, they agreed in principle about district plans for the west San Gabriel Valley, illustrating how changing political circumstances and strategies contribute to the dynamic and shifting character of race relations. The tremendous resource requirements of redistricting served as a powerful impetus for panethnic alliances among Asian Americans and interracial alliances between Asian Americans and Latinos. The two groups recognized the advantages of pooling technical and legal resources, especially in light of their common concerns about issues that included bilingual education, immigration policy, and employment discrimination. Equally important, the groups recognized their common histories of political fragmentation and disfranchisement, which linked their histories and legitimated their participation in the redistricting process along racial lines.

Research Methods

In gathering the material for this volume, I primarily use data from ethnographic fieldwork and interviews collected between 1988 and 1992.

Other major sources of data include two exit polls of Monterey Park City Council elections, the 1980 and 1990 U.S. Census, candidate campaign contribution statements, and election results.[8]

Through ethnography—sustained, full participation in the events under study—I have attempted to capture the range and complexity of participants' perceptions and understandings of the events and how those perceptions have changed in response to new circumstances. Ethnographic fieldwork was critical for documenting and analyzing the construction of racial and ethnic identities and political alliances through the intimate details that are revealed as people conduct their everyday lives, emerging from historical and contemporary factors rooted in the context of Los Angeles County. Recognizing the personal reality expressed through narratives and also the partial and subjective character of any representation, the narratives are combined with historical and sociological information. They are meant to provide an understanding of how factors on a number of levels influence the development of racial and ethnic identities and political alliances. My work examines the range of perspectives in a community setting that emerges from the lives of individuals, where factors such as gender, class, and nativity intersect with political and economic systems that influence and texture the range of racial experiences. Racial and ethnic identities are not simply volitional; they are formed through a process of continual negotiation through interaction with others carried out in a particular community context.

My deep involvement with the community raises the long-standing insider-versus-outsider debate over the advantages and disadvantages of a researcher's identity and background for ethnographic research (Gerth and Mills 1946; Merton 1972; Zinn 1979). Questions of distance and objectivity that arise from my involvement should be weighed against increased access to people and events and the possible insight that comes from in-depth knowledge. One assumption driving the debate, however, is that knowledge is a concrete, objective fact, waiting to be uncovered and documented.

My approach is based on critical ethnography, in which meaning is recognized as socially constructed and highly subjective. Events do not have a single, objective meaning. Instead, meaning emerges from an event as it unfolds, and each participant brings to the event (and takes from it) a personal understanding of what has occurred. As sociologist Robert M. Emerson (1983, p. vii) asserts, fieldwork is an "interpretive enterprise," that is, "'facts' and 'data' are understood not as 'objective entities,' but rather as social meanings attributed by social actors—including the fieldworker—in interaction with others." A fieldworker is not a neutral tool used merely in the collection of data. Rather, data are processed by field-workers, and collection and analysis are affected by this action.

Aware of the risks and problems associated with such deep involvement and immersion, I nevertheless embraced it. It was the only way that would allow the kind of access I was striving to achieve to people and events. Ethnographic fieldwork enabled me to examine events as they unfolded, to view people's actions, listen to their conversations, and question par-ticipants about their understanding of events as the events occurred. As Max Weber pointed out, although we may strive for value-free research in which personal presuppositions and values are absent, the very acts of conducting research and the selection of topics and particular methodol-ogies bring personal values into play (Gerth and Mills 1946). Weber sug-gested that perhaps the best researchers can do is explain their ideologies, choices, and procedures as clearly as possible so readers may evaluate where personal understandings of events enter someone's work.

My history is similar to that of many Japanese Americans in the area. My parents were born and raised in Hawaii, and after my father complet-ed college in Utah, where I was born, my family moved to the Boyle Heights area of East Los Angeles, which had a large number of Japanese Ameri-cans mixed among the dominant Latino population. When I was seven, my family moved to Alhambra, then to Montebello, cities to the north and south of Monterey Park, respectively. When I asked my parents about their move into the San Gabriel Valley, they explained that when they would enter field offices at the sites of tract houses under construction in the ear-ly 1960s they would be ignored by builders' representatives. Unable to by a new home, they purchased a used home in one of those tracts several years later. I lived in Montebello and attended public schools until I moved to northern California to attend college. I then returned to live in Monte-bello during the period of the study.

As I examined how matters of race and politics emerge and are influenced by day-to-day interaction among residents of the community, my experi-ences became an integral part of my awareness and influenced how I in-terpreted the ways in which race and ethnicity enter people's lives. Despite social scientists' emphasis on the civil rights gains made by middle-class African Americans, discrimination in public places remains a significant factor for them (Feagin 1991). The same is true for Asian Americans and Latinos. Widespread problems persist; for example, hate crimes and the employment discrimination documented by the 1992 U.S. Commission on Civil Rights report.

For me, one incident vividly and forcefully demonstrated the hostility some whites feel toward Chinese immigrants and Asian Americans and the crude and arbitrary differences they perceive and use to distinguish one Asian American group from another. One afternoon I went to the American Legion Post in Monterey Park to inquire about a Nisei veterans' group that regularly met there. As I walked in, I saw a white man seated at a bar along the left wall, a drink in front of him. The only other person in the room was the bartender at the far end of the bar. As I started to walk toward the bartender I could see in the mirror behind the bar that the seated man was looking at me closely. I felt that because it was his clubhouse, and I was an intruder there, I should introduce myself. I stopped, turned, and told him my name, mentioning that I lived in Montebello and was working on a study of the city with a research group at UCLA. He said that he had gone to school there. "Good, maybe we have something in common," I thought. But then he added, "It was a good school before all you people started going there. Just like Monterey Park." Looking at the man, I tried to figure out whether he was serious or joking. He closed one of his eyes, but I was unsure whether he intended a friendly wink or a menacing glare, or perhaps he had some sort of tic.

I asked about the meaning of his remark. "UCLA must be 90 percent Chinese," he said. "I'm Japanese," I responded. When he replied "killed my first one [Japanese] in 1942," I realized he was seriously anti-Asian. When he talked, strong emotions were apparent. He said things with energy, not loudly but earnestly. I worked hard to control my expression, tone of voice, and questions. Meanwhile, the bartender had moved toward us and said something like "Oh, come on," as if trying to defuse an uncomfortable situation. I took the opportunity to introduce myself to the bartender and tell him I was looking for information about the Japanese American group that I heard met there.

The incident illustrates one episode in a lifetime of discriminatory events I have experienced, as have many other racial minorities in the United States. It is a part of one's personal life as a racial minority that most whites do not know exists. Rather than being an isolated incident, the event fit a pattern of other events in my life and in the systematic and institutionalized forms of discrimination that exist in the United States.

The encounter reveals individual conceptions about the existence of racism in everyday life and how people think they should respond when incidents occur. Feagin (1991) documented instances when middle-class African Americans with power and resources were able to address a situation—such as being ignored in a restaurant—and change the offending

practices. My reaction was different. At first I wanted to ignore and forget the incident, thinking of it as just another unpleasant reminder of the
number of times I had been called a "Jap" or told "I hate foreigners."

I thought it useless to confront the man at the American Legion Post;
after all, what happened was nothing new. Yet I also realized that it was
data and could have value in illustrating a common but important way in
which race is brought up in everyday life. When I discussed the story, which
I had included in my fieldnotes, with a UCLA research group, the white
members were shocked at the blatant racism of the event and surprised
that it had occurred. The Asian American and Latino members, however,
merely rolled their eyes and shook their heads, recognizing a commonplace
event. A professor at California State University Los Angeles has mentioned
to me that the reaction had been similar when her students discussed the
brutal beating of Rodney King, an African American, by white Los Angeles police officers, an event that preceded the 1992 civil unrest in Los
Angeles. Most white students were surprised and outraged that the event
had occurred. Latino and African American students, however, were all
too aware of similar beatings in their respective communities.

In the insider-versus-outsider debate, another problem for those who
study their own communities is whether certain events and processes es-
cape critical observation and analysis because of taken-for-granted assump-
tions. What might attract an outsider is commonplace for an insider. Suggesting that this might happen, however, is part of an essentializing
discourse that portrays Asian Americans or any other racial group as homogeneous. Within a community, contrasting opinions and interpretations
of events constantly emerge, challenging any one point of view. For example, because of my background in Asian American electoral politics and
experience working with panethnic coalitions I mistakenly assumed that
Japanese Americans in Monterey Park would actively build political links
with the recent Chinese immigrants. I was disabused of such notions quickly as I learned of the range of views that existed concerning possible political relationships, not only between those two groups but also between
Chinese Americans who were long-term residents of the city and the new
Chinese immigrants.

I began the study by regularly attending the meetings of three Monterey
Park civic boards: the city council, design review board, and planning
commission, each of which met two times a month. Although city hall
continued to be a valuable place to follow issues and talk to residents, my
involvement shifted to other events and organizations after nearly a year.
The other activities were richer sites for my research because they allowed

greater access to the dialogue and activities surrounding the construction of racial and ethnic identities and political alliances.

I regularly attended meetings of the region's political groups, including the West San Gabriel Valley Asian Pacific Democratic Club, the United Democratic Club (composed primarily of white members), and the League of United Latin American Citizens (LULAC). I was a member of the Coalition of Asian Pacific Americans for Fair Reapportionment, the statewide organization formed to participate in the redistricting process following the 1990 census and its regional affiliate in the San Gabriel Valley.

Local political campaigns provided valuable opportunities to see how racial and ethnic issues were defined and the extent of support candidates received among various ethnic communities. Doing a variety of activities, including precinct-walking, office work, and staffing telephone banks, I volunteered for a number of campaigns of Latino and Asian American candidates.[9]

My research follows a natural history of events in the region and analyzes the development and transformation of racial and ethnic identities, political mobilization, and political relationships within and among Asian American, Latino, and white communities. I examine the process whereby groups with initially antagonistic relationships and apparently conflicting interests form political alliances that lead to greater levels of inclusiveness. In particular, I explore interracial political conflict and cooperation among Asian Americans, Latinos, and whites and the construction of an Asian American identity among diverse ethnic groups.

Monterey Park and the San Gabriel Valley:
Regional, National, and International Trends

Metropolitan Los Angeles has been transformed since the 1960s into a world city, competing with San Francisco as the center of financial and corporate headquarters for the western United States and the Asian-Pacific region and surpassing New York in industrial output and manufacturing jobs (Ong 1989; Soja 1989). Reflecting the strength of the high-technology industries in the region and the increasing importance of trade with Asian-Pacific countries relative to Europe, the dollar value of trade through the Los Angeles Customs District surpassed that of New York in 1994 (Claremont McKenna College and *TradeWeek* 1996).[1] The 1994 ranking of Hong Kong and Singapore as the top two container ports in the world (the combined volume of the Los Angeles and Long Beach ports ranks as third) indicates the importance of Asia and Southern California in the world trade network (Newton 1995).

Yet these signs of economic growth and industrial diversification conceal a much more complex picture of expansion and contraction in Los Angeles. With an abundant supply of oil, space, and labor, in its early years and through the two world wars the Los Angeles economy was driven by agriculture and the production of movies, aircraft, automobiles, and related industries (Soja and Scott 1996). After World War II, the city continued to benefit from government spending in defense- and aerospace-related activities and became one of the major high-technology regions in the world.

Since the 1970s, however, the regional economy has undergone fundamental changes in a process of deindustrialization and reindustrialization (Soja and Scott 1996). Growing international competition, the flexibility and mobility of the production process, and the pursuit of cheaper labor and fewer regulations have resulted in manufacturers leaving the United States, and traditional smokestack industries such as those involving automobiles, tires, and steel have abandoned Los Angeles. The dismantling of the former Soviet Union and a growing U.S. budget deficit also contributed to massive cuts in spending for defense- and aerospace-related industries, resulting in the closure or downsizing of businesses and factories in the region.

Edward Soja (1989, p. 210) explains, however, that in tandem with deindustrialization, Los Angeles has been revitalized by the "centralization, concentration, and internationalization of industrial and finance capital that has marked the contemporary restructuring of the world economy." It has become a major center for financial and corporate headquarters as well as for government employment. Contributing to new employment opportunities are expanding segments within manufacturing, such as the garment industry, and service industries. These jobs, however, offer primarily low-wage, part-time work that takes advantage of the availability of cheap immigrant labor. Bennett Harrison and Barry Bluestone (1988, p. 28) have described the process of deindustrialization as a "hollowing of America."[2] Growth at the top and the bottom but a hollowing out of the middle, with the loss of unionized manufacturing jobs that offered a livable wage and benefits, is a major reason for the "widening divide" of "increasing income inequality and poverty" in Los Angeles (Ong 1989, p. 1).

Major demographic changes have accompanied those produced by economic restructuring. Since Mexican settlers established Los Angeles in 1781 the city has always had a diverse population influenced by internal and international migration. The Chinese community gained a foothold during the 1870s, the Japanese in the 1890s, and the African American population grew rapidly due to migration in the 1940s.

Between 1970 and 1990 Los Angeles County experienced another transformation. The number of whites during that period declined, and the population changed from a majority to a minority white one. Largely due to immigration, Latinos tripled in number, while Asian Americans quadrupled their population during the same period. The African American population grew steadily, albeit at a much slower rate than the previous two groups, and migration to the suburbs and back to the southern part of the nation also increased during the 1980s (table 2).

Beginning in 1943 with the repeal of the Chinese Exclusion Acts and continuing through the 1965 Immigration Act, restrictive U.S. immigration policies, with quotas favoring Europe, have gradually changed. Whereas Europe had been the main region of origin for immigrants entering the United States before 1965, immigrants from Asia and Latin America have become the two major groups entering the country. Los Angeles's large,

Table 2. Racial and Ethnic Composition of Los Angeles County, 1970–90

| Race/Ethnicity | Number and Percentage of County Population | | |
	1970	1980	1990
African American	747,000 (10.8)	929,000 (12.7)	993,000 (11.2)
Asian and Pacific Islander[a]	234,000 (3.4)	645,000 (8.8)	954,000 (10.8)
Latino	1,024,000 (14.9)	1,918,000 (26.1)	3,230,000 (36.4)
White	4,885,000 (70.9)	3,849,000 (52.4)	3,619,000 (40.8)

Sources: Ong (1989, 1991).
a. Includes Other.

diverse economy and long-standing ethnic populations have made it a major settlement point for immigrants. Because of economic incentives, established networks, and proximity to Mexico, it is the primary U.S. destination point of Mexican immigrants.[3]

The greater concentration of Asian Americans and Latinos in Los Angeles County compared to California is shown by population figures for the state (table 1); an even larger difference is shown by the population figures for the United States in the same table. Whereas 8.4 percent of the U.S. population in 1990 was Latino, they composed 24.6 percent of the California population and 36.4 percent of the population of Los Angeles County. Asian Americans made up 2.9 of the U.S. population, 9.6 percent of the California population, and 10.8 of the population of Los Angeles County.

The San Gabriel Valley

While financial institutions, corporate headquarters, and government employment have tended to cluster in downtown Los Angeles, the region has had a pattern of polynucleated and decentralized development characterized by industrial growth and residential settlement in outlying regions (Soja 1989). With the growing economies of foreign countries, foreign investment, in terms of purchasing real estate and establishing businesses, is a major influence in Los Angeles.

Foreign investment, immigration, and settlement in Los Angeles's suburbs is epitomized by the Chinese experience in the San Gabriel Valley. Located several miles to the east of downtown Los Angeles, the San Gabriel Valley is directly tied into the Los Angeles economy and has been transformed by international and regional trends.

Most residents in the San Gabriel Valley were working- or middle-class whites until freeways were built during the 1950s and 1960s and provided quick and easy access to the region. With downtown Los Angeles only fifteen minutes away, suburban communities in the San Gabriel Valley, with their new housing tracts offered at affordable prices, good schools, and proximity to the ethnic communities of Little Tokyo, Chinatown, and East Los Angeles, became an attractive destination for upwardly mobile Asian Americans and Latinos. Beginning in the 1970s, international immigration created the next wave of change as the valley became a major destination point for Chinese immigrants from Hong Kong, Taiwan, and the People's Republic of China. The end of British rule and the return of Hong Kong to China in 1997, as well as the uncertain relationship between Taiwan and China, have been the major impetuses for the movement of people and capital from those locations to the United States (Tseng 1994a).

Measured by number of businesses, Los Angeles County has become the site of the largest Chinese ethnic economy in the United States, surpassing those in San Francisco and New York (Tseng 1994a, 1994b). Unlike settlement patterns for New York Chinese immigrants, who tend to cluster in New York City, those entering the Los Angeles region have tended to settle in the suburbs.

The San Gabriel Valley has become the focal point of what Yen Fen Tseng (1994b, p. 171) characterizes as a "transnational business enclave" linked with the immigrants' countries of origin and ethnic Chinese communities in other cities, such as Sydney and Vancouver. The valley offers a well-developed infrastructure that includes interstate highways, proximity to airports and shipping ports, and lower land and office space costs than downtown areas. Abundant low-wage immigrant labor, highly educated and skilled technicians and engineers, and the synergistic effect of clustering among research centers and industries in Southern California have also contributed to the valley's appeal and development.

The Chinese ethnic economy in the valley includes the traditional mix of low-wage workers in the secondary labor market (such as garment factories and the service industries) found in traditional urban ethnic economies of earlier periods and in contemporary Los Angeles and New York (Kwong 1996; Waldinger and Bozorgmehr 1996; Zhou 1992).[4] The valley's Chinese economy represents a fundamental change in scale, however, from traditional ethnic economies. Not only are the new entrepreneurs engaged in a much broader range of enterprises but they are also involved in ones that require high levels of capital investment and technological skills: aircraft and computer manufacturing, financial institutions, real estate development, and medical facilities. In another departure from the traditional model of urban ethnic enterprise where family members or co-ethnics are the primary source of labor (Portes and Bach 1985), wage laborers in many businesses such as restaurants and supermarkets are Latin American immigrants.

Some businesses, spin-offs from the region's aerospace and computer industries, have been created by entrepreneurs who left major U.S. companies to capitalize on the need for subcontractors who can respond quickly to the demand for highly specialized products incorporating recent technological innovations. Other businesses are directly linked to the growing Asian economy and involved in the trade of finished products, such as apparel.

The computer industry is an example of the international character of trade in high-technology equipment (Tseng 1994b). Dealing primarily with personal computer products manufactured in Hong Kong and Taiwan, an estimated 65 percent of the $750 million worth of personal computer products imported in 1991 entered the country through Los Angeles and were controlled by Chinese businesspeople. Nearly 55 percent of the approximately 350 Chinese computer distribution and assembly enterprises in Los Angeles are headquartered in the San Gabriel Valley.

That range of enterprise is possible because recent immigrants are highly educated, well financed, and generally have business experience before immigration. The group is augmented by a segment of Chinese immigrants who have obtained graduate degrees from U.S. schools and experience and training from major U.S. high-technology companies such as IBM, McDonnell Douglas, and Lockheed. As an indication of the massive global flow of capital between the Asian-Pacific region and Los Angeles, between 1985 and 1987 the Taiwanese government estimated that more than $1.5 billion moved into the Los Angeles area from Taiwan (Tseng 1994b).[5]

The rise of the San Gabriel Valley Chinese economy is partly the result of the varied backgrounds and settlement patterns of Chinese immigrants. Rather than a homogeneous stream of migrants entering the United States, Roger Waldinger and Yen Fen Tseng (1992) have found that the immigrants who settled in Los Angeles differed greatly in terms of professional background and pre-immigration work histories compared to those who settled in New York, greatly affecting the economic development of the respective settlement communities. Two particularly significant parts of the 1965 Immigration Act for Asians are the occupational preference category, which favors highly skilled professionals, and the family unification provisions that allow relatives to migrate and are often used to bring family members to the United States who would be otherwise ineligible under the occupational preference category because of lower levels of education and job skills.

Los Angeles was the major destination point in 1990 for Taiwanese, 42 percent of whom entered under the occupational preference category. That same year, New York was the favored place for immigrants from the People's Republic of China, 83 percent of whom entered under the family preference category. Of those from the People's Republic of China who had previous work experience, 60 percent were in "blue-collar, agricultural, or service jobs" compared to 15 percent of the Taiwanese (Waldinger and Tseng 1992, p. 94). Even among immigrants from the same areas (China, Hong Kong, and Taiwan), the differentiated pattern of class, occupational background, and place of settlement was evident.

Although the degree of entrepreneurship among Chinese in both cities is high, the growing ethnic economies in New York and Los Angeles have developed in different directions, in part as the result of migrants' varying class backgrounds. In New York, the concentration of restaurants and garment factories is higher, whereas the Los Angeles ethnic economy is more diversified and has larger segments composed of high-technology industries, financial services, real estate development, and health services. Comparing Koreans, another Asian group with high levels of entrepreneurship, with Chinese immigrants, Tseng (1994a) has found the same relationships between the business trajectory of the U.S. immigrant enterprise and pre-immigration economic and professional backgrounds. Tseng suggests that greater access to capital, prior entrepreneurial expertise, and more developed transnational networks explain the higher level of Chinese enterprises compared to those of Koreans.[6]

Chinese entrepreneurs have placed the San Gabriel Valley directly in the global economy. With the flow of capital, products, and people, the region has become a major node of production and distribution.

Monterey Park, Alhambra, San Gabriel, and Rosemead

Monterey Park, with a population of 60,738 in 1990, is at the center of the rapid demographic and economic restructuring in the valley. During the 1970s the city suffered from a declining tax base and a deteriorating commercial district, in part due to competition from major shopping malls built in surrounding communities. Deindustrialization also directly affected the region, with vacant manufacturing-related space such as warehouses and offices and through diminished wages and investment.

Recognizing the potential appeal of Monterey Park to the new wave of Chinese immigrants because of its proximity to downtown Los Angeles and much lower property prices than Los Angeles's Chinatown area, Chinese immigrant realtors and developers bought—and heavily marketed—

land in the city. One of the pioneers was Frederic Hsieh, who was born in China and lived in Hong Kong before immigrating to the United States, where he became a citizen in 1970. During the 1970s he bought property in the city and advertised it in Taiwan and Hong Kong as the "Chinese Beverly Hills" (Fong 1994, p. 29).

The success of these real estate tactics and the effects of immigration are clearly demonstrated by the rapid demographic changes that followed (table 3). The percentage of whites dropped dramatically, from 85.4 percent in 1960 to 11.7 percent in 1990. At the same time, the percentage of Latinos climbed from 11.6 to 29.6, and the percentage of Asian Americans increased from 2.9 to 57.5. Monterey Park became the only city outside of Hawaii with an Asian American majority population.

As the Chinese community grew, it eclipsed the original Asian American residents, the Japanese Americans who entered during the first period of population change (table 4). The numbers of Korean, Vietnamese, and Filipino immigrants also increased.

Table 3. Racial Composition of Monterey Park, 1960–90

Race	Percentage of City Population			
	1960	1970	1980	1990
African American	0.003	0.2	1.2	0.6
Asian American	2.9	15.0	34.8	57.5
Latino	11.6	34.0	37.8	29.6
White	85.4	50.5	25.5	11.7
Population	37,821	49,166	54,338	60,738

Sources: Monterey Park Planning Department (1974); U.S. Bureau of the Census (1983, 1990c).

Table 4. Monterey Park's Changing Asian American Population, from Japanese to Chinese, 1970–90

	Population			Percentage of Asian American Population		
	1970	1980	1990	1970	1980	1990
Chinese	2,202	7,735 (251.3)[a]	21,971 (184.1)	29.2	40.9	63.0
Japanese	4,627	7,528 (62.7)	6,081 (−19.2)	61.4	39.9	17.4
Korean	118	1,180 (900.0)	1,220 (3.4)	1.6	6.2	3.5
Vietnamese	n.a.	862 (n.a.)	2,736 (217.4)	n.a.	4.6	7.8
Filipino	481	807 (67.8)	1,067 (32.2)	6.4	4.3	3.1
Pacific Islander/ Other	112	778 (594.6)	1,823 (134.3)	1.5	4.1	5.2

Sources: Monterey Park Planning Department (1974); U.S. Bureau of the Census (1983, 1990d).
a. The percentage change from the preceding decade is given in parentheses.

The transformation of the commercial areas is immediately apparent to valley residents as they travel major traffic arteries, although many business and manufacturing enterprises and activities go unnoticed because of their location in industrial areas and business parks. The region has become the business, service, and entertainment center for Los Angeles County's Chinese immigrant population, and businesses whose signs are in Chinese dominate Monterey Park's main commercial streets: financial institutions, supermarkets, restaurants, realtors, real estate developers, travel agencies, doctors, attorneys, insurance agencies, and medical centers.

As the center of Asian American residential, commercial, and political growth, Monterey Park is the focus of my research. Its importance is magnified, however, by the growth of the Asian American community in the region, and its politics are strongly linked to issues and trends in the valley. The Chinese population and businesses have spread beyond the borders of Monterey Park to include other parts of the San Gabriel Valley, especially along the east-west corridors formed by Interstate 10 along the northern border and the Pomona Freeway along the southern border of the city. Monterey Park and the contiguous cities of Alhambra, San Gabriel, and Rosemead represent the core of the Asian American population in the valley, the cities with the largest and fastest-growing Asian American populations. Monterey Park, Alhambra, and Rosemead rank among the top six U.S. cities listed on immigration applications as destinations for Chinese immigrants (Fong 1994).[7] The cities also rank as the third, eighteenth, and twenty-fifth most popular destinations, respectively, for all Asian immigrants.

The cities also represent the center of the 11,034 businesses in Los Angeles's Chinese economy. In terms of the number of enterprises, Tseng's (1994b) calculations for 1992 show that Monterey Park, Alhambra, and San Gabriel are the top three, in that order, with 12, 10, and 7 percent of the Los Angeles area total, respectively. Los Angeles's Chinatown, Industry, and El Monte, with 6, 5, and 4 percent, contain the three next-largest concentrations.

Linkages among San Gabriel Valley communities are built and strengthened by this business presence through the networks and ties developed by people who live, shop, or own businesses in the region. They are connected politically by the Alhambra School District and its elected school board. The 1990–91 demographic profile of students in the Alhambra School District (1990)—which includes Monterey Park, Alhambra, San Gabriel, and Rosemead—suggests population changes occurring in the region. The student population, representing younger, child-bearing families, is replacing aging, established residents. According to the profile, 51.02 percent of high school students are Asian American, 38.15 percent are Latino, 10.16 are white or other, and .84 percent are African American. Figures are similar for elementary school students.

The Politics of Exclusion and Segregation

Even though Chinese immigrants may be the most visible group in Monterey Park, the city's multiracial history began during the 1950s with the migration of native-born Latinos (primarily of Mexican ancestry) and Japanese Americans from East Los Angeles, an unincorporated area of Los Angeles County that shares Monterey Park's western border. It is not a coincidence that Latinos and Asian Americans shared the same geographic and political space in East Los Angeles and repeat the pattern in the San Gabriel Valley. Rather, it is the result of economic and political practices of segregation that have limited and shaped residential choices and generated efforts for social change as World War II veterans and others sought to dismantle exclusionary barriers.

The politics of exclusion and segregation are part of a long history of discrimination racial groups in the United States have faced, a fact made vividly clear when Japanese American and African American veterans of World War II and Jewish survivors of Dachau gathered in a community center in Los Angeles's Little Tokyo in December 1991 to discuss, for the first time in a public setting, their wartime meeting. They told of Japanese American soldiers, many of whom were drafted from U.S. concentration camps where their families remained imprisoned, fighting in a segregated military unit run by white officers and liberating Jews incarcerated by Nazis, the allies of Imperial Japan.[8] The participation of the African Americans, who discussed their role in the camp's liberation, emphasized the irony of the liberation of Dachau: they and the Japanese Americans had fought to give Europeans the human rights the troops did not enjoy at home.

Recounting the event, a Nisei veteran described how they had shot the lock off the camp's gate, driven in, and seen row upon row of black, tar-paper barracks. He had cried at the sight, reminded of his parents locked up in Heart Mountain concentration camp in the United States. The irony of Nisei soldiers liberating Jews while their own families were imprisoned at home was expressed by one of the liberators, Clarence Matsumura: "I had to think, what the heck am I doing here? My family was still behind barbed wire in Wyoming" (Nakayama 1991).

Nearly four hundred people attended the discussion. They sat in amazement, a largely Japanese American audience hearing for the first time a fragment of concentration camp history. Janina Cywinska described her moment of liberation. She had been blindfolded and was standing against a wall, surrounded by dead bodies and waiting to be shot, when suddenly a man pulled off her blindfold and told her, "We are liberating you—you are free." Confused at the sight of a Japanese American soldier, she wondered who he was, thinking of the wartime alliance between Germany and Japan. Finally, she understood that the U.S. military had arrived. Her dance training had been interrupted by the war, but she returned to it afterward and runs a ballet school in the United States. Her voice filled with emotion that night in Little Tokyo as she thanked the Nisei for the chance to dance again.[9]

Then, near the end of the meeting, three African American veterans stood in the audience and told their story, adding to the remarkable uncovering of history. Seeing an announcement about the event in a local newspaper, they had come to share their memories. Part of the U.S. military medical unit, it was their belief that they had been chosen to examine Dachau in advance of the main group because white officers were worried about the danger of disease and did not want to send in white medics.

Jewish, African, and Japanese Americans were united in Little Tokyo that evening by events that had taken place forty-six years earlier. They were also joined by the fundamental importance of race in the United States. Since the earliest history of the nation, when voting rights were limited to white men of property, privileges have been circumscribed by gender, race, and class. Political practices in the United States have always had racial consequences, particularly in the way such practices have been rooted in privileged access to power, rewards, and opportunities for whites (Lipsitz 1995). These practices have resulted, as George Lipsitz suggests, "through systematic efforts from colonial times to the present to create a possessive investment in whiteness for European Americans" (p. 371), establishing an identity for European Americans that is based in part on racial privilege. Much research and discussion on race that emphasizes the consequences of government policies for racial and ethnic groups, especially in the post–civil rights era—as if policies with racial implications are a recent phenomenon—ignores the legacy of white racial privilege embedded in such policies (D'Souza 1991; Rodriguez 1982; Schlesinger 1991; Steele 1990).

African Americans and Japanese Americans fighting for human rights that they themselves lacked at home constitute one of the many stunning paradoxes in U.S. history. American ideals such as equality and justice run counter to the reality of a long history of discrimination that supports white privilege. Immigration laws, for example, favored European immigrants while limiting immigration from other areas. "Give me your tired, your poor, your huddled masses yearning to breathe free," declared Emma Lazarus in a poem inscribed on the Statue of Liberty. The gift from France to the United States has been embraced by Americans as a symbol of the country's openness, freedom, and equality, echoing the judgment of Alexis de Tocqueville (1960) in his classic nineteenth-century *Democracy in America*. Yet when the statue was put into place a half-century after Tocqueville wrote his work, the United States had already passed the Chinese Exclusion Act of 1882, which banned the immigration of Chinese laborers, and would enact additional laws prohibiting the immigration of other Asians.[10]

The Chinese Exclusion Act of 1882 and the Gentlemen's Agreement of 1907–8, focusing on the Japanese, cut off segments, primarily laborers, within the early Asian immigrant groups and marked Asians as the only racial group in U.S. history specifically banned from immigration. Those who did manage to immigrate faced discriminatory policies created specifically to curtail their rights while protecting the economic, social, and political privileges of whites. In 1790 Congress limited the right of naturalization to "free white persons," and in 1870 that was modified to include those of African descent. Asian immigrants attempted to gain the right of naturalization through the courts, but those efforts failed when the Supreme Court ruled against the Japanese in 1922 and the Asian Indians in 1923. Those rulings were in effect until various laws were passed during the 1940s and 1950s to make Asian groups eligible for naturalization (Chuman 1981).[11]

Other laws that protected the privileged position of whites included the California Alien Land Laws of 1913 and 1920, which were aimed at preventing Asians from owning or leasing land. The purpose of the legislation was to reduce competition from Japanese immigrant farmers who were highly successful in agricultural niches involving fruits and vegetables. As Ivan Light (1972) suggests, the Alien Land Laws were also intended to keep the Japanese out of self-employment to maintain a cheap labor force for harvesting crops.[12]

A tax on foreign miners established in California in 1850 was primarily targeted at the Chinese. The Criminal Proceedings Act prohibited court testimony against whites from African Americans and Native Americans, and in 1854 the California supreme court also ruled that Asians could not testify against whites until 1872 (Chan 1991). Across the nation, violence, economic intimidation, and anti-miscegenation laws were other forms of enforcing segregation and white privilege. In fact, anti-Asian violence encouraged the development of ethnic enclaves as Asians gathered for self-protection (Kwong 1996).

The protection of white privilege extended across class and ideological lines (Roediger 1994; Saxton 1971). Anti-Asian rhetoric and policies were used by trade, craft, and unskilled labor unions in their early efforts to organize and protect the interests of white workers. Karl Yoneda, a Japanese American and a long-time member of the American Communist Party, has written that during World War II the Party suspended its members of Japanese ancestry "in the name of 'National Unity' in the fight against Japanese imperialism" and that he was "stunned and speechless" when he heard this news (1983, pp. 115–16).[13]

When Jewish, African, Mexican, and Japanese American veterans returned from war, they believed that their participation as soldiers had "earned" them the right to live where they wanted (Acuna 1988; Hosokawa 1969). Their lives were again linked, however, as they faced a country where segregation continued unabated, supported by government policies and practices.

Residential segregation is an example of how federal and local governments create broad policies and procedures that are interpreted and acted on in communities and that affect people's lives on the most basic level—where they are able to purchase a home, for example. As Lipsitz (1995) points out, such policies are a prime example of how whites need not consciously invoke their race in daily life. To the general public, the policies seem race-neutral and whites remain unmarked, yet billions of government-controlled dollars were reserved for whites through government and private housing practices.

The Supreme Court found in *Buchanan v. Warley* (1917) that city zoning ordinances requiring housing segregation by race were unconstitutional. Restrictive covenants came into widespread use following the decision and were employed to continue segregation. Although the Court ruled in *Shelley v. Kraemer* (1948) that restrictive covenants were unconstitutional, their use continued into the 1950s.[14]

As the U.S. Commission on Civil Rights (1975) noted, the Court's rulings were not so much judgments in favor of racial equality as they were decisions upholding the right of property owners to sell their property without such restraints as zoning ordinances or court enforcement of restrictive covenants. With an emphasis on the rights of property owners, racial segregation continued unabated in housing and was supported by the practices of the real estate industry.[15]

The Federal Housing Administration (FHA) mortgage insurance program was established in 1934, and the Federal National Mortgage Association ("Fannie Mae") in 1938. Those programs dramatically transformed the housing credit process and made credit more available and affordable. The "federal housing agencies were staffed by industry representatives and, as a result, the discriminatory practices of the industry became established Federal policy," however (U.S. Commission on Civil Rights 1973, pp. 4–5). The Federal Home Loan Bank Board's guidelines on rating neighborhoods stated, for example, that minority areas should be given low ratings and white areas should be given high ratings, and the FHA Underwriting Manual cautioned against "inharmonious racial groups" and supported restrictive covenants. In the post–World War II building boom, financial institutions would not loan money to construction companies that planned to offer homes on an integrated basis, and many did not offer mortgages to either African Americans or those whites who wished to move into non-white neighborhoods.

As a result of these practices, by 1959, more than twenty years after the programs were established, fewer than 2 percent of FHA-insured housing constructed since the war was available to racial minorities. The issue is critical because home ownership is one of the major ways for low- and middle-income families to accumulate capital (U.S. Commission on Civil Rights 1973, 1975). In addition, where a person lives has important consequences in terms of access to employment and public schools.

Congress enacted the Federal Fair Housing Law (Title VIII) in 1968, and the Supreme Court ruled in *Jones v. Mayer* (1968) against racial discrimination in the sale or rental of property. Yet government agencies could investigate claims, not generate them. Therefore, individuals who press claims bear the burden of enforcement and the possibility of expensive and protracted legal battles. As a result, few complaints have been filed.[16]

Discrimination in housing continued but in a more covert manner after the passage of federal legislation and Supreme Court decisions against discrimination. Some realtors continued to steer people to particular neighborhoods based on race and some financial institutions continued to redline neighborhoods, affecting patterns of home ownership and residential segregation. After World War II, movement into segregated suburbs, aided by federal and state-funded infrastructure construction, including highway, sewer, and water system construction, aided whites and increased ethnic and racial minority concentration in the centers of cities.[17]

As immigrants seeking low-cost housing and access to jobs, Mexican and Japanese Americans have a history of sharing communities in Los Ange-

les County. A major destination point was Boyle Heights—an unincorporated area of East Los Angeles near downtown Los Angeles that offered
access to employment, services, and low-cost housing.[18] Home ownership
created disparities in wealth along racial and ethnic lines that were exacerbated by FHA policies that refused mortgages in such racially heterogeneous areas (Lipsitz 1995).

White middle- and upper-class neighborhoods are attractive places of
residence, not only because of the amenities provided by the tax bases the
communities' wealth generate but also because of the disproportionate
amount of money that regional, state, and federal sources have invested
in infrastructure and services. Communities composed primarily of racial
minorities have been neglected, and those minorities that can afford to do
so have sought out suburban areas and contested exclusionary barriers.

Monterey Park

One of the first Asian American realtors working in Monterey Park, a
Japanese American who eventually moved there in 1963, mentioned to me
that the major white brokers who controlled the city's housing market used
a number of methods to block the entrance of Latinos and Asian Americans. He explained that he was denied access to the main sources of listings and had to go door-to-door to find people willing to sell homes to his
Asian American clients.

Despite the 1948 Supreme Court ruling that declared restrictive covenants unconstitutional, they remained in widespread use, as Latinos and
Asian Americans discovered when they attempted to purchase homes in
Monterey Park. Japanese Americans described how they used third parties to sign the paperwork to get around restrictive covenants. An early
resident recalled how that was done when he moved to Monterey Park in
1953: "At that time, there were restrictive covenants, so I had to buy
through a third party, a *Hakujin* (white). I went through a Japanese American realtor, he set up a third party. It had to be bought in a *Hakujin*'s name
and then there was just a paper transaction." When I asked why he wanted to move to a place where there was opposition to his presence, he as-
serted that he had earned the right to live where he wanted after fighting
in World War II: "I was one of the first Japanese Americans in Monterey
Park. I just felt at the time that I fought in the war, what the hell, I put my
life on the line. I went in here with the intent that if it came to a legal battle, we'd fight. I think it was just a continuation of what went on during
the war. We hadn't won all our rights."

Latinos and Japanese Americans shared the experience of battling seg-regation, and because they were neighbors and friends they were also linked intimately and emotionally to the major events in each other's lives. Lati-nos, too, were affected by the tragedy of the camps. A man in his sixties described his experiences with restrictive covenants and Japanese Ameri-can neighbors. He explained that on his block, which was originally part of East Los Angeles before it was annexed by Monterey Park, people had owned homes for a long time because "nobody sells their home." When he first moved there, "Only Anglos could buy houses, but we fought it and could move into these two blocks. There is a Japanese American family at the other end of the block, and they had been here a long time, too." He talked about the land behind his house, now covered by a low-income housing project, and the Japanese American family who used to farm it until being sent to the camps. "Before there were houses, there were Jap-anese gardens there. Japanese used to grow watermelons and things there. We use to help them sometimes and we would get some free fruit. They had the place up until about 1942, and then they had to go to the camps. My wife's best friend had to go and my wife drove her to the train, they cried. We still have some pictures of her."

The man's thoughts returned to contemporary issues, and he talked about the increasing demographic complexity of the region and the unique his-tories and cultures not recognized by whites, leading to instances of abuse caused by racial discrimination and occasions where ethnic identities are blurred and ignored.

> I don't like the way everyone is grouped together as Latinos. We are different groups, from different countries. Puerto Ricans, Mexicans, Cubans. People [whites] forget that. I know a Japanese American woman who works at the college there [East Los Angeles Community College, located a block away from his house]. One day when she was driving to work, someone yelled at her, "Get out of the way you Chink." She was so upset, she didn't even look at them, she was crying. [By the way he was shaking his head, it was obvious that he was very upset by the event.]

Restrictive covenants, poignant memories of the camps, and more re-cent episodes of discrimination are some of the factors that have tied Lati-nos and Asian Americans together in the region.[19] Although the Mexican American man was proud of his unique ethnic heritage, which disappeared in the generic category "Latino," he also understood that discriminatory practices linked to essentializing discourses that negate differences within panethnic categories also affected his Japanese American friends and neigh-bors and created a shared experience among Latinos and Asian Americans.

The enforcement of segregated neighborhoods slowly waned in the face of economic forces and legal challenges. As one Asian American realtor explained, new housing tracts were being developed, and brokers and developers were forced to deal with Latinos and Asian Americans as whites began to move away from the city to communities in Orange County to the south. Realtors were reluctant to change their practices, however, and it took organized protest to hasten the process. A Chinese American remembered being refused a house when he first tried to buy one in Monterey Park. Ironically, an African American protested the exclusion of racial groups but later complained about the number of Chinese immigrants entering the city.

> When I first tried to buy a home in Monterey Park, in the Highlands, the real estate person said that he would rather wait to sell us a home, until after some other homes were sold because if he sold us a home first, no one [whites] would buy the surrounding homes. A black man was the one to challenge that. He got the NAACP involved, and they complained and had demonstrations. Ironically, some years later he went down to city hall to try to get some sort of regulation passed to prevent Chinese from moving in. He thought that there were getting to be too many in Monterey Park. He said that he didn't move from a black ghetto to live in an Oriental ghetto.

Despite such early discrimination problems, however, Monterey Park represented a suburban community that had affordable housing near downtown employment and ethnic communities. Asian Americans and Latinos represented 14.5 percent of the city's population by 1960, and overt racism was muted in comparison to the city's early history. Also in 1960, Alfred Song, a Korean American, became the first Asian American elected to the city council. One Japanese American resident, discussing her move to Monterey Park in 1967, mentioned the welcoming atmosphere of the community and its suburban character.

> Well, we did look all over for a home. We went as far as Glendale [a city to the northwest of Monterey Park]. We would walk into real estate offices, and they would look at us but wouldn't talk to us because we were Japanese. And so we decided, well this is not the kind of neighborhood I would like to raise my children in. And so that was the reason why we moved to this area. People were very friendly who we had come in contact with, you know, the neighbors and the real estate agents and we thought this was a good place for us. So that's the reason why I thought it was very nice. The community atmosphere, I liked the open space, and it wasn't too crowded.

In a decade when racial tensions in the United States were expressed through riots and demonstrations, Monterey Park was well on its way to becoming a multiracial city. Characterized more by grudging acceptance than enthusiastic support, it achieved a degree of racial and ethnic diversity and cooperation with the election of three Asian Americans (Alfred Song, George Ige, who was Japanese American, and G. Monty Manibog, a Filipino) and one Latino (Matthew Martinez) to the city council during the 1960s and 1970s. In 1985 the National Municipal League and *USA Today* selected Monterey Park as one of the nation's eight "All-America" cities and noted local efforts to develop innovative programs to establish English-as-a-second-language courses and bilingual services to immigrants (Monterey Park Seventy-fifth Anniversary Committee, p. 49).

Although resistance against further "Asianization" remained among some long-established residents, Asian Americans were actively courted by builders and real estate agents in a Southern California housing market that had experienced a strong downturn in the early 1990s and showed only weak signs of recovery by the middle of the decade. Major construction and real estate companies targeted Asian Americans by adding such features to new homes as large bins for rice storage and stoves that had optional built-in wok-holders. They also followed the principles of *feng shui* in the placement of doors, staircases, trees, and lampposts, and the full-page advertisements they placed in the San Gabriel Valley real estate listings of the *Los Angeles Times* featured a large, four-color photograph of a young Asian American couple (Hamilton 1995; *Los Angeles Times* 1995).

The Slow Growth Movement in Monterey Park

During the 1970s and 1980s, movements opposing growth proliferated in cities throughout California. Reflecting patterns in other parts of Los Angeles County, the San Gabriel Valley experienced rapid urbanization and increased building density, traffic, and pollution. In Monterey Park, single-family houses were torn down and replaced by condominiums and apartment complexes, traffic congestion and mini-malls proliferated, and demands on city services created bitter public debate over regulations on development. John Logan and Harvey Molotch (1987, pp. 32–34) describe this conflict as a confrontation between entrepreneurs who see the city as a "growth machine," where profits and the free market should guide land use, and residents concerned with quality-of-life issues and controlling growth. Influencing the land use policies of city hall is a key battle between those pursuing profits and those seeking a congenial environment in which to live and raise a family.

A strong slow-growth movement emerged in Monterey Park, and the grass-roots populism of the movement followed the broad outline of Joe R. Feagin's and Stella M. Capek's (1991) discussion of contemporary examples of community organizing, including a focus on issues and pragmatism, alliances across class lines, and a minimum of ideology. The movement involved local activists rather than the traditional political and economic elite linked to development. A number of propositions dealing with development were introduced during the 1980s, and voting overwhelmingly favored controlled growth. Voters signaled their concern about development clearly, and in 1986 the city council declared a moratorium on building.[20]

Activism in the city can be partly explained by a large segment of middle-class residents, many of whom owned property.[21] In addition, Mary Pardo's (1990a) study of two successful grass-roots women's movements in the region demonstrated the importance of mediating institutions that influenced and structured the type of politics that occurred (Lamphere 1992). Pardo examined residents in Monterey Park who organized to remove a parole office located near a school and residential area. She compared that effort with an incident in neighboring East Los Angeles, where residents organized to block the placement of a prison in the community. Pardo noted that Monterey Park is a predominantly middle-class city where a variety of institutionalized programs—regular public hearings and commissions staffed by residents—allow resident involvement in city policies. Women are able to use those channels. In contrast, in the unincorporated area of neighboring East Los Angeles, which is administered by the county of Los Angeles and provides few opportunities for involvement, women had to stage protests and elicit the help of the media to apply pressure.

The economic transformation of Monterey Park has brought about substantial changes in the lives of its residents, and the responses of long-term residents must be understood in that context. They are not merely a reaction to racial differences in the population and owners of businesses; they are responses rooted in concrete changes that involve a loss of services and disruptions in everyday routines. These changes have particularly affected older residents who may be retired, living on fixed incomes, and lacking mobility. They also may have an impact on those who have financial means but do not want to go through the uprooting experience of moving to another city.

One area of change frequently mentioned by established white residents revolves around differences in behavior of the new Chinese immigrant shopkeepers compared to the ones they replaced. Although language barriers exist, the main problems the residents cite focus on what is interpreted as rude behavior stemming from a lack of interest in non-Chinese shoppers.

An example is the case of a white woman in her sixties. She spoke in a soft voice as she described such cherished daily routines as buying thread or socializing with shopkeepers, which had been disturbed because of the change in shopkeepers at stores she frequented. Although she was guarded in talking to a stranger, she looked into my eyes and discussed matters straightforwardly.

A resident of Monterey Park for thirty-four years, she was unable to drive and preferred walking to stores a short distance from her home. I could appreciate her frustration at having the simple, everyday things she had enjoyed turned into unpleasant experiences. She used to be a seamstress, working at home, and missed the stores at which she used to shop: J. C. Penney and the supermarkets. It was convenient having them nearby; now they were gone. "Sounds like little things," she said, "but I like to be able to dash out when I need something."

She had gone to a store run by an immigrant Chinese man to look at sewing machines. When she asked the price of one, he abruptly said, "Tell you when you are ready to buy." She believed the response meant that he was not interested in her, only her money. In the stores run by old residents, workers would say hello, try to help you, and be friendly. That's the "American way," she said. She added that she felt that the immigrant Chinese were trying to push her out of the city. They wanted her house.

Established whites were not the only ones who talked about the changes. Established Nisei also complained about the disappearance of familiar stores and the search for new ones that offered good, friendly service. What was once a five-minute jaunt to a local shop had turned into a forty-minute ordeal across Los Angeles freeways.

The changes in store ownership are clear, what is less obvious is the interpretation of the behavior of the store personnel. Whereas some established residents may feel that non-Chinese are treated rudely or receive indifferent service, Chinese immigrants disagree and note that being Chinese does not guarantee receiving good service. One Cantonese-speaking resident mentioned that when she goes into shops and tries to talk with the workers some of the Mandarin-speaking ones ignore her or treat her rudely. Another added that "in China such treatment is normal and people should not be upset by it because workers act that way to everyone, Chinese or white."

It seems from these conversations that what is often interpreted by non-Chinese as rude behavior is often merely business as usual, depending on

one's frame of reference. For example, while having dinner in one of the
large, elaborately decorated, Hong Kong–style restaurants in the city, one
Chinese immigrant provided his theory about restaurant help and service:
"You get the best service in restaurants run by people from Hong Kong.
Good service is part of the business in Hong Kong. You get the worst ser-
vice from people from China. Taiwan is somewhere in between."

In addition to the racial changes in the business sector, development has
brought problems associated with increasing urbanization, for example,
air pollution and disappearing park land and open space. Working to attract businesses, generate tax revenue, and increase employment opportunities, Monterey Park's city government has developed business parks
on some of the major portions of open land. A Nisei couple reminiscing
about the changes in their neighborhood talked about this change: "Mc-
Caslin Park [an industrial complex], that was all vacant and my kids use
to go up there and collect lizards and snakes. It was really nice, hills, but
now it's all buildings."

Another Nisei resident talked about the pollution caused by the heavy
traffic on the Pomona Freeway, which had been built several blocks from
her home after she moved to the city. She led me into her backyard as she
complained that everything was now covered with a thick layer of black,
sticky, soot: "It was so nice and quiet and clean before the freeway. Now,
everything looks so dusty. In my back yard, the bushes back there, you touch
something, your hands turn black. Come over here. Look at it, see how
unhealthy it looks? When I go to pick lemons, my hands turn black. Any-
way, see that bush over there. . . . That's a pomegranate one, and it's covered
with that stuff. And that persimmon tree, it used to be such a healthy tree.
And then, ever since the freeway, and the black stuff, it's not the same."

As dramatic and visible as the demographic changes, the transformation
of the business districts of Monterey Park and contiguous cities attests to
the region's economic restructuring, as Asian immigrants emerge as major investors. Grass-roots movements can be progressive in terms of growing class, racial, and political inclusiveness, or they can be reactionary,
driven by the defense of privilege or territory, and exclusionary in outlook
(Feagin and Capek 1991). Faced with declining political and economic
power, the slow-growth movement in Monterey Park represented a nativist effort on the part of some whites to preserve their diminishing power
(Horton 1989). Because whites encouraged the development of white-
owned businesses while discouraging those that were Asian-owned, the
movement was not explainable solely through class differences.

The Residents Association of Monterey Park (RAMP) emerged as a major grass-roots political force in the city during the 1980s. It took a strong position against development and backed city council candidates in favor of slow growth. Yet support for candidates who had strong anti-immigrant views, such as Barry Hatch, ostensibly because of their equally strong stands against development, opened the group to criticism for mixing anti-Chinese issues with those that were anti-growth. Slow-growth activists claimed they were concerned only with the quality of new development and that developers were using race as a smokescreen to draw attention away from shoddy development.

Pardo's (1990a, p. 326) study of women activists in Monterey Park, however, clearly documents how anti-Chinese sentiment was part of the slow-growth movement. Leaving RAMP, a Latina explained, "At the time I also felt the Chinese were invading us and I would attend meetings with the RAMP group. They would call me up and tell me you better come to the council meeting because the chinks will be there. I began to think, if they say that about them, what do they say about me: I was the only Latina. Then, one day at a city council meeting they started in on David Almada—jeering and laughing at him, the Latino on the council. That hurt me because he is Latino. So, I broke away from the group."

Similarly, a Latino formerly on the Monterey Park City Council was asked whether the issue was growth rather than Asian immigration. He recalled the work that some of his family had carried out over a growth initiative in 1981 and some of the responses they received while placing telephone calls to voters. Linking the recent experiences of the Chinese immigrants with the housing discrimination that Asian Americans and Latinos had faced during the 1950s, he said, "Baloney. . . . They would say, 'We don't want any more Goddamn Chinks.' At one time there was a similar attitude about Hispanics: 'They come in and they take over.' Jesus Christ, these are Americans talking!" (Fong 1990).

The slow-growth movement peaked with the city council election of 1986, when three incumbents linked to growth lost and three RAMP-supported candidates won. The winners—Chris Houseman, Barry Hatch, and Patricia Reichenberger—were white, whereas the losers—Lily Lee Chen, David Almada, and Rudy Peralta—were Chinese American and Latino. Hatch's slow-growth platform was linked with his nativist views on Official English and immigrants. As Almada explained, "It [the election] was a backlash primarily against the Asians and ethnic people in general" (Fong 1994, p. 122).

Immigrant scapegoating, a common political tactic throughout U.S. history, played a prominent role in Monterey Park politics. During the 1980s, growth and the new immigrants merged in a number of anti-Asian, anti-immigrant activities by the city government and residents. Rather than working to overcome conflict and providing leadership, for example, by examining the roots and regional context of problems such as traffic and pollution, some members of the city's government aggravated racial tension by blaming immigrants for a wide range of the city's problems. Between 1986 and 1990, Barry Hatch, a member of the city council and then mayor, used his positions as platforms to give speeches during council meetings. "Immigration built America, and immigration will destroy America unless controlled," he would declare. He also tried to ban the use of foreign languages on commercial signs in the city and led the council's drive to pass a resolution in 1986 (which has since been rescinded) declaring English as the city's official language.[22]

Grass-roots activism, racism, and city politics combined in the slow-growth movement, and, as Horton (1995) points out, it became the task of progressive individuals and groups to disentangle nativist and racist elements from genuine slow-growth issues. Although important in the way it demonstrated the strength of populist activities in the city, the slow-growth movement was politically significant in that it emphasized the racialized context in which individuals and groups operated. "Development" became a code word for Chinese immigrants, and nativist sentiments became politically respectable behind the cover of defending the community against uncontrolled development. Slow-growth issues raised in the political arena, and the tacit approval of discriminatory rhetoric and acts, became catalysts for political mobilization in Asian American and Latino communities.

Racism in the political arena over development was important not only in itself but also because it represented, and was linked to, the discriminatory activities people encountered daily and throughout their histories in the region. Rather than being an aberrant occurrence that would fade away as economic development balanced with quality-of-life issues, discrimination was tied to a long pattern of such activities in U.S. history.

Reasserting Whiteness: Racial Privilege and
the Transformation of History and Architecture

The redevelopment of a shopping mall in the San Gabriel Valley provided an opportunity to study the local circumstances and everyday activities that supported white privilege, racial hierarchies, and how the emergence of white ethnicity was strongly rooted in the transformation of the political and economic structure. A case in point, the rebuilding of a shopping mall, Atlantic Square in Monterey Park, showed how ethnicity and history rooted in local, Asian, Latin American, and European sources were expressed, contrasted, and manipulated. Fundamental conceptions of community and the contours of membership were highly contested, configured by race and ethnicity, and tied to personal interactions and systems of social relationships.

In the study of race in the United States, whites are often left unexamined. As Ruth Frankenberg (1993) asserts, that lack of attention is linked to, and reinforces, the position of whites and whiteness as the unexamined norm in society against which other groups are compared and marginalized in the process. In order to dismantle the authority and power supporting racial privilege, David Roediger (1994) points out the need to expose, examine, and catalogue whiteness, by which he means racial privilege and hierarchy and the cultural practices that support them.

The discussion of Atlantic Square's redevelopment revealed two types of narratives. First, a general theme that permeated U.S. society and was implicitly acknowledged was that Americanness equates whiteness. That focus on systemic racial hierarchy and privilege contrasts with the symbolic conception of white ethnicity that Mary Waters (1990) and Richard Alba (1990) found when whites were the majority population and remained the dominant political and economic force (see also Gans 1979). Waters and Alba explain that the contemporary expression of European American ethnicity is largely symbolic, linked to factors such as food and holidays, and of little political or economic consequence. In contrast to identities imposed on members of racial minorities, ethnic identities for middle-class whites are freely chosen and unacknowledged in most aspects of their lives.

The second topic revealed in the redevelopment discussion was how whiteness is experienced and expressed in the culture and language of everyday life when the defense and reassertion of whiteness becomes explicit, challenged by the growing demographic and economic presence of Chinese immigrants. As Waters suggests, in some situations the rise of white ethnicity may be a response to a threatening of economic and political privileges by racial minorities demanding increased access to resources. Instead of remaining in its customary, unstated position as a norm, at this moment when whiteness is losing its primacy, it is explicitly expressed.

I focused on the process through which residents, developers, elected officials, and city hall staff debated the issues and decided on the architectural style of the shopping center and the mix of tenants who would be encouraged to locate there. Chinese immigrants were rarely mentioned specifically but were invoked through code words or signifiers and replaced whites as the immediate, practical backdrop against which the discussion was framed. Using ethnography, I concentrated on the everyday activities, stories, and explanations revealed through the work of a group of established local residents (primarily Latino and white) who mobilized to intervene in the process. The group developed the name Citizens for Atlantic Square Restoration (CARE), and I attended their private and public meetings and followed their participation in city hearings from April 1989 to September 1989.

Atlantic Square: Background

In the midst of the slow-growth movement and resident charges of poorly planned and haphazard development, the Monterey Park City Council declared a moratorium on building in 1986. The city hired two private companies—Sedway Cooke Associates and the Arroyo Group—to work with city staff, and a resident community design advisory committee was formed to develop plans for the city's business districts.[1] A key topic discussed in the planning guides was development of an identity for each area so that a "sense of arrival" or place was established (Sedway Cooke Associates 1987, pp. 3–4).

Contradictions emerged from the discussion of the city's past, present, and future. The importance of Asian influences was noted in the general report: "Monterey Park is fortunate to have established a unique identity not only in Los Angeles or Southern California, but literally half way around the world. The City has become identified as a land of opportunity for Asians interested in investing in and emigration to the United States" (Sedway Cooke Associates 1987, p. 6). Yet rather than taking advantage of that identity, the plan specifically recommended avoiding it. Acknowledging that a "vital commercial environment" existed, the plan sought to correct what its authors judged to be "visually chaotic" (p. 7). The city should "devise architectural standards to encourage more common architectural treatments, based not upon a particular style (such as 'Spanish' or 'Chinese') but rather upon functional characteristics of the building and district" (p. 13).

Similarly, the Arroyo Group stressed the multiethnic character of the Monterey Park population. What began as a statement of multiculturalism, however, and a recognition of the long history of ethnic diversity in the city, became an affirmation of Anglo primacy: "The purpose of the Area-wide Identity Program is to implement the multi-cultural theme. . . . This theme is characterized by subtle abstractions of forms found in Asian, Hispanic and Anglo Cultures. . . . Contemporary English graphics and the blending of elements reflects the eclecticism of our Anglo culture" (Arroyo Group 1987, p. 29). At a point when Asian immigrants were establishing a place in the region, the Arroyo Group's plan proposed to enfold that space within "our Anglo culture." Anglo culture, they suggested, is what defines America, not recognizing the way new influences transform and expand conceptions of American.

Built in the 1950s, the physical structure of Atlantic Square was deteriorating, and major businesses were leaving for new malls built in surrounding communities. The shopping center was a high priority for redevelopment in a city faced with declining tax revenues. Major portions were to be torn down and new buildings erected.

After a competition, the city council and staff chose Champion Development Company for the project. A white person who had worked closely with council members and staff expressed concern about that choice, noting the council and staff's preference for white developers. During a break in a public hearing, the person asked me, "Do you know why they chose Champion Development Company for the Atlantic Square project? If the company was run by any other group of people, they would not have the support of the city staff that they now had." "You mean if the company was run by guys, for example, by the name of Wong that they would have more problems?" I responded. "Right" was the reply.

The defense of whiteness went beyond the symbolic value of architectural style. Business opportunities for Chinese immigrants were lacking in a mall where the emphasis was on American businesses as defined by nativist whites. There was also material support for white developers in the form of city subsidies and a supportive city staff during the permit process and the lack of the same for Chinese immigrant developers. Preferential treatment was corroborated by the experience of a Chinese developer interested in building a shopping center in the city (Tseng 1994a, pp. 167–68). He had received no financial assistance from the city, whereas Champion Development had received substantial subsidies.

> When we submitted our project plan (a $20 million shopping center) to the city government, they asked us to raise the proportion of American businesses from 30 to 60 percent. They told us that if we followed this proportion, the city government would help to finance the whole project. If we didn't then there would be no financial aid. For my clients (the investors), it makes no sense at all. The whole point of investing in this project is because the Chinese market is there and without enough Chinese businesses in the center, it is not going to be profitable. So we went ahead with the original plan entirely on our own.[2]

Judging from the list of developers who submitted proposals for the redevelopment of Atlantic Square, it appears that none of the firms were owned by Asians.[3] The situation was ambiguous, however. It is possible that perceptions about the city's preferences for white developers—a serious allegation that is difficult to prove or disprove—were completely false. Perhaps no Asian developers were interested in a complex project involving the city's redevelopment agency and the added complications of a project involving public funds. The critical point, however, was that some people believed the city to be not as favorable toward Asian development companies as it was toward white companies.

The Citizens for Atlantic Square Restoration

Although community residents were involved in the process of forging general guidelines for development in the city, they were not involved in the specific discussion surrounding Atlantic Square until they actively inserted themselves into the process.

The residents' participation followed a tradition of heavy community activism in the San Gabriel Valley (Horton 1995; Lo 1990; Pardo 1990a). In contrast to the strong state and regional economy that framed the early period of the slow-growth movement, however, economic recession and a declining tax base created a new climate in which activists exercised political influence. Residents became involved in Atlantic Square because they wanted to ensure that a plan that incorporated community interests was created, not because they were against development. Concerned about the proposed architecture, sites of buildings, type of stores and restaurants, and lack of community input in the process, those who lived around Atlantic Square organized a group called Citizens for Atlantic Square Restoration. By following the group and its private planning sessions, public forums, and participation in city hall meetings, the issues that concerned established white and Latino residents became clear.

One concern was that the city council did not form a resident group to provide recommendations on the project and the city staff had not actively solicited input, leading residents to believe that the city wanted to build as quickly as possible without their involvement. That was made clear during one of CARE's early meetings when one person asked, "What was the first thing you remember which upset you about the Atlantic Square project?" Another replied that he had been upset because he was not notified of the cancellation of a design review board meeting. He added, "The sign on the door said that it was postponed indefinitely, which will give them just enough time to . . ." "Build it," another person interjected (before residents could be involved in what was happening). The group broke into heavy laughter.

Some organizers were involved because they lived next to the center and were concerned about initial proposals that would have directly affected them. For example, one part of the Atlantic Square forms a right angle to the rest of the development. Within that angle is a city street and a house. One of the early plans would have extended the parking lot to incorporate the street into the parking lot, bringing the project up to the edge of the property line of the house and blocking street access to the house's garage. The house was owned by a retired Latino couple who held one of the group's first meetings in their home. The host appeared for a few minutes during the meeting to say hello to everyone, trailing an oxygen tank connected by a nose-tube.

One of the first to become involved in CARE was Mike Hamner, white and in his early thirties. He had grown up in the community, worked as an architect, and was a member of the city's design review board. "When I first started talking to people about Atlantic Square," he commented, "I came to this house because I thought that it would be natural that they would be involved. But then I met Mr. R, he walks around with oxygen, just like my mother. But I left a card, and I got a call from their son. I was pretty surprised at that." I asked if the son was doing this to help his parents. He said, "Yes. Look how close things are right now. The street, which now acts as a buffer, will be gone and things will be right up against the house." The son, who had to battle traffic to reach Monterey Park from his home on the far side of Los Angeles, helped the group mobilize and establish goals.

Early in the process, CARE organized two community forums in a local church auditorium. Nearly eighty people, primarily Latinos and whites, showed up each time, a good turnout for a Monterey Park community meeting. Organizers stressed that residents had to become involved in the process. Lucy Ammeian—an Armenian American who had moved to Monterey Park in the mid-1950s when Atlantic Square was built and worked for years at J. C. Penney before it relocated to a new mall in Montebello—spoke words of encouragement. "I've been fighting since day one," she recalled of her successful battles to bring services to the city and block unwanted development. "Look what we've accomplished. We wanted a pool at the park, we got one. We wanted to stop the helicopter pad, we stopped it. We wanted to stop the tower, we stopped it. You have to fight in this town."

CARE became heavily involved in the process of developing plans for the new center, and its actions resulted in a number of public hearings in conjunction with the review boards and city council. Plans begin with the city's staff and then move through two boards (the design review board and the planning commission) of residents appointed by the city council and responsible for review projects and generating recommendations for it, which makes the final decision. CARE members monitored city meetings and notified residents when the project was on the agenda. And on June 29, 1989, the group submitted a petition to city hall, stating on its delivery that the document carried 1,087 signatures, that the "people wanted to be included" in decisions about Atlantic Square, and that the "basic concept plan is not acceptable."[4]

Public Discussion: A Place to Feel at Home

As participants, Asian immigrants were conspicuous by their absence in the public debate. Only a few Asians and occasionally a reporter for a Chinese-language newspaper attended the hearings. The increasing economic and demographic dominance of the new immigrants provided a backdrop, however, for discussion of the plans for Atlantic Square—a reversal of the more common white dominance. Some residents, for example, believed the Chinese were "buying up the town" and blamed them for the problems of Atlantic Square, such as unrented stores and graffiti. A long-term resident who had a business in town before retiring and was a member of the Chamber of Commerce said, "Atlantic Square is dead. The Chinese raised the rents too high." Atlantic Square, however, was owned by a white person.

In the public forums, speakers established the legitimacy of their views by invoking their many years of residence in the city, a tactic based on individual biographies grounded in traditional ideas of community in terms of rootedness or a sense of belonging as a result of time in a place. It was something that established white and Latino residents could declare—and a claim developers, city staff, and new immigrants were unable to match.

Mike Hamner talked of his early days in the city. He had been pushed around Atlantic Square in a stroller, like the three-year-old son now held by his wife, a Japanese American, in the back of the auditorium. "Although some of you may disagree," he said, "I probably kept Bill's Toys going." There was laughter from the audience.

Chris Houseman, a city council member and a strong critic of the redevelopment plans, was an accomplished public speaker who had a good ear for small-town nostalgia. He used the word *we* when he talked, including the audience who shared those memories but excluding those who did not: "Many of us are from that section of the city. We have many memories of Atlantic Square. We share memories of Lawson's Jewelry and Bill's Toys. It used to be a big adventure when I was a kid to go there on a Saturday. A few friends and I would walk from one end to the other. We would get thrown out of the shops because we had no money to spend."

Length of time in the city and knowledge of the area were measures used to question the credentials of those involved with the project. At a community meeting organized by CARE, Keith Breskin, director of economic development for Monterey Park and one of the key city staff members involved with the project, was questioned by Houseman:

Houseman: How long have you worked for the city?
Breskin: Since October [of the previous year].
[A loud, negative OOOOHH!!! came from the crowd.]
Breskin: But before that, I lived in the city for five years.
Houseman: People at city hall, on the city council, are people who just blew into town. We grew up here, it's part of our history. The city manager, he just got here in September or October of last year.

Latinos and whites, using the one resource they had in abundance—their many years in the city—insisted that the new shopping center should reflect the history of the area. Their concerns were based on real changes in their daily lives. Familiar stores and needed services, long-established routines, and the small-town feeling of the area were disappearing as the city experienced rapid development fueled primarily by Chinese immigrant capital. They argued for a place where, as they put it, "We can shop and eat and feel comfortable," "a place where we could go to have a cup of coffee and talk."

At one of the community meetings, a Latina talked to those sitting around her about shopping, naming places that were links to the past and not yet dominated by Asian stores: "There are only three places in Monterey Park where I shop," she said, "Atlantic Square, Prado, and Hughes Market. If Atlantic Square turns into another Chinese mini-mall, I'll just go to Montebello [which borders Monterey Park to the south]." "Me too," a Latino man a few seats away responded. "It's the last frontier."

The majority of Montebello's population is Latino. For Monterey Park's established residents, the Chinese immigrants do not represent the so-called civilizing influence implied in the manifest destiny of colonial or imperial powers encroaching on the mythical native naturalness of the last frontier, but the invading force of a foreign economic power.

Although whites have not completely disappeared from Monterey Park, their numbers and power are shrinking, and Asian Americans are aware of their resentment. In 1989, at the grand opening of a social service agency for young Asian Americans, one Chinese immigrant, a reporter for a Chinese-language daily newspaper headquartered in Monterey Park, told me of a story circulating among city employees. Because of the city's budget problems, council member Barry Hatch had been having little success in soliciting city and private help to erect a statue of George Washington in front of city hall. Perhaps worried that she might offend some of the whites present at the event, the reporter nervously looked around before telling me, in a low voice, an ironic tale of racial succession: "They [white city employees] are saying that in the future, residents of Monterey Park will take their kids to look at the Washington statue if it is built and will tell their kids that this is George Washington, the father of this country, and ten or twenty years ago, white people like this lived here [in Monterey Park]. It will be like the whites talking about the Indians in the U.S."

Whitening History and Architecture

The efforts of whites and Latinos to preserve a part of the city for non-Asians emerged and was expressed repeatedly in the form of two issues:

architectural style and type of restaurants. One white resident, discussing the architectural theme of Atlantic Square, proposed looking to the past for possible ideas. Analyzing the developer's proposed plans, he asked, "What is the theme? Things have changed so fast that our roots are blurred. We have to go back to the history of the town. Some of the streets have Spanish names and wrought iron poles were used for lamps." The planners had suggested a Mediterranean style for certain business areas. In terms of architecture, however, much of what is considered Mediterranean is actually Mexican, because Southern California was once part of Mexico. More recently, architectural styles have been brought north or reinterpreted by Mexicans and others in the United States.

To frame the discourse without specifically rejecting Chinese influences, history was invoked that included the Mexican past of the region. Mexicans and Mexican Americans were momentarily elevated from being a target of suspicion to being appreciated and used to counter the influence of the Chinese, temporarily displacing concerns over undocumented immigrants from Mexico and the media focus on Mexican American gang activity in nearby East Los Angeles.

In the process of reconstructing their history to suit their purposes, the area's Mexican past was "whitened" in its translation into an architectural style for the remodeling of the shopping center, becoming Spanish, and, finally, Mediterranean, demonstrating the shrinking white population's continued power in its control of public discourse.

Architecturally, the terms *Mexican* and *Spanish* were merged and became synonymous during discussions on the center. After summoning historical references to legitimate a non-Chinese theme, "Mexican" or "Spanish" became too specific and too ethnic, as mentioned in the Sedway Cooke report. Eventually, talk of "Spanish" turned to the more generic *Mediterranean,* and community leaders gently encouraged the use of that term. For example, during one of the community forums a woman said, "This is a Spanish town, it should have a Spanish look." One of the organizers said, "Mediterranean." The woman replied, "yes," nodding her head in agreement.

Not everyone thought that the decision to adopt a Mediterranean theme for Atlantic Square was a good one, however. In the lobby of city hall during the city council meeting when the decision was made, a Latina in her forties expressed her displeasure with the idea. She shook her head from side to side and pointed to an old black and white photo of an adobe building in Monterey Park. "Look at that," she said, "that's what they want. You know why? Because it's cheap to build. I would have preferred something contemporary, let's move forward, not backward." Hamner, an architect, shook his head in disapproval, noting the popularity of that style in Southern California and the cookie-cutter approach that makes it less expensive for development companies to build similar projects in different locations.

The city council approved a Mediterranean style for the center, however, and instructed the developer to use colors, building materials, and design elements to reflect that theme.[5] Asian immigrants and capital had become major factors influencing social and economic life in the city. Countering that change, Latinos momentarily became more acceptable to mainstream whites, but only in a whitened, Europeanized form.

What Are "Good" Restaurants?

The dense concentration of Chinese restaurants lining Monterey Park's commercial areas represented more than a major physical presence. They symbolized the economic and demographic transformation of the region. Discussion about what type of restaurants should be encouraged to move into the new Atlantic Square clearly illustrated the attempt of whites and Latinos to define and judge what was considered American and therefore desirable.

More than a symbol of ethnicity, restaurants represented control over cultural and economic matters. Design review board discussion about an acceptable restaurant for Atlantic Square was instructive. Bob Champion, head of the development company, said, "I heard that you have around 120 restaurants in the city." "We could use a few *good* restaurants," a resident called out. Another echoed his words, saying softly to herself, "Yes, a few good ones." What residents meant by "good" was made clear when a white woman from the audience interrupted, "At Atlantic and Garvey [a major intersection in a commercial area] they were supposed to put in nice restaurants like the Velvet Turtle [the audience laughed], but it ended up being totally Oriental."

Monterey Park had good restaurants, attracting people from the entire Los Angeles County area, a fact ignored by residents and Champion, who mentioned that there were "no regional draws in your community" at a 1989 design review board meeting. In fact, the complaint over the restaurant at Atlantic and Garvey involved a place that a *Los Angeles Times* restaurant critic had rated as one of the top thirty restaurants— of any kind—in the county. The restaurant served Chinese food, however. For Atlantic Square, white and Latino residents suggested popular chain restaurants such as the Red Onion, Velvet Turtle, or Soup Plantation, which are in the low to medium-high price range and serve "American" food.

The issue was not quality of food; many local restaurants easily surpassed the chain restaurants in that respect. Rather, the issue was type of food, and beyond that type of restaurant. The food and service of Monterey Park's new Chinese establishments is geared to an immigrant clientele; those unfamiliar with such restaurants might find eating in one uncomfortable and daunting rather than relaxing and enjoyable. Some well-known local spots are very large and have main dining rooms capable of seating two to four hundred. Although restaurant workers try to be helpful, many speak limited English, and menu items are often puzzling to non-Chinese.

The image of a Chinese restaurant for some residents was that of a small, family-run neighborhood eatery. Entering one of the huge, ornately decorated palaces with large tanks of fish lining the walls, seeing hundreds of people eating, hearing them speaking enthusiastically in Chinese, and encountering the large waiter staff on duty constitutes a major change in ambiance as well as food. One white person mentioned a comment by a native-born Chinese American friend who jokingly said, "Just as restaurants have smoking and nonsmoking sections, they should have English and non-English sections." A white woman in her sixties mentioned her preference for Chinese restaurants that cater to non-Chinese: "When my husband and I go to eat Chinese food we go to a restaurant in Montebello, not Monterey Park. We go to Chinese Gardens, it's been there for twenty or thirty years. I don't like the Chinese restaurants in Monterey Park. I don't like Cantonese and other types of food. I like American-style Chinese food." Restaurants like the one she described serve familiar items such as sweet and sour pork and fortune cookies. Although many whites and Latinos associate those items with Chinese food, they are often not served in Chinese restaurants in Monterey Park that cater to an immigrant Chinese population.

"Just like being in China" is a seemingly innocent phrase often used by people describing a visit along the streets or in a restaurant in the San Gabriel Valley. It is certainly accurate in terms of the people there and the printing on business signs and the conversation that fills the air. Yet what is the generic "China" expressed in this phrase—Hong Kong, Taiwan, or the People's Republic of China? In the case of restaurants, their proprietors try to create an environment that removes customers from the urban traffic and noise just outside the doors. Categorizing such places as foreign, however, negates the immigrant history of the United States and presence of such ethnic places throughout the country. It also ignores the

uniquely American features of the restaurants: the Latino immigrant laborers in the kitchens, the heavy use of such places as fund-raising sites
for Asian American politicians, and the occasional nod to customs such
as fortune cookies.

During a council meeting discussing the business tenants the city would
try to bring to Atlantic Square, a white council member, the owner of a
small business, declared, "I know one thing, we don't need anymore restaurants or banks." It was not necessary for her to say "Chinese restaurants or banks"; her meaning was clear. I mentioned her statement the next
day to a Chinese immigrant who had a successful real estate business in
the region. He, too, knew what she meant, and he shook his head from
side to side, frowning. "Was she talking about Chinese banks and restaurants?" I asked. "Yes, definitely," he replied. "It's a shame, she is supposed
to represent everyone in the city."

What white and Latino residents expressed was concern over the material and symbolic control of public places. Part of the discomfort some
whites experience in Chinese restaurants is that the eating places clearly
cater to Chinese immigrants and—usually for the first time in their lives—
the whites feel economically superfluous and culturally marginal.

White Culture and Whiteness

Racial and ethnic identities can flow from an attachment to a geographic
place, and cultural elements such as history and memories create a sense
of rootedness, as expressed by those who wanted a place where "they could
feel at home" once again. A very different matter, however, is the way identities tied to a place can also be used as a form of entitlement, supporting
racial privilege and hierarchy.

La Maravilla (1993), Alfredo Vea's novel of life in a tiny, predominantly Latino town in Arizona, contains a wonderfully evocative scene in which
a grandfather talks about identity when his grandson asks, "Is it true I am
an American?" "You are Spanish and Yaqui," the grandfather explains,
"you are a mestizo from Aztlan, this land, right here where the Nahua
people began. . . . you know where your blood has been for the last ten
thousand years, *mijo*. There are words and songs, *palabras y canciones*,
that tell you and explain to you. You do not become American, no, no.
Shit, no. America becomes you, *mijo*" (pp. 35–36). In contrast, "It's only
the gringos that become! . . . those people on earth who do not know where
they belong. . . . They have no stories. They have no tribe. Their camp fire
is the goddamn television" (p. 35).

A similar theme is found in David Roediger's (1994, p. 13) work on the construction of whiteness: "Whiteness describes, from Little Big Horn to Simi Valley, not a culture but precisely the absence of culture. It is the empty and therefore terrifying attempt to build an identity based on what one isn't and on whom one can hold back." Like Vea, Roediger points out the richness contained in ethnic cultures and "the increasing suspicion of the emptiness of whiteness among white American youth" (p. 126).

Roediger (1991, 1994) uses that point in his larger argument on how whiteness is constructed to support a racial hierarchy that can and should be dismantled. His major assertion is that social structures supported and constructed by racism are empty because of the false premises incorporated in racist ideology. As Frankenberg (1993) also points out, whites have the power to define America with themselves at its center. Cultures become ethnic in comparison to whiteness, and what is on the surface an appreciation for the richness of another culture is in reality a reflection of racial hierarchies.

Rather than promoting equality, cultural celebrations leave racial hierarchies unexamined and in place if the power and legitimacy of culture and cultural practices to establish norms in U.S. society is overlooked and culture is conceived simply as food, clothing, and music (Frankenberg 1993). At a multicultural celebration that included dances from around the world and square dancing and clogging from the United States, a Chinese immigrant told Monterey Park's white mayor, "This is a good thing because many Asians don't think that Americans have any traditional things. This gives them a chance to see the dances."[6] Although a criticism of the supposed lack of culture in white America, the remark ignores the way "white" culture (recognizing that it is not monolithic) has been accepted as the norm and passes unnoticed unless some of its more unusual elements, such as clogging, are emphasized.

In contrast to the way whiteness supports racial hierarchies, white culture has another purpose—unacknowledged in Roediger's argument—in the way it anchors people to what is familiar, comforting, and everyday.[7] The daily routine of leaving the house to engage in conversation with a friendly shopkeeper as one buys thread; dropping by a local restaurant after a city council meeting for a cup of coffee and a rehash of the evening's topics; and a special dinner at a small, neighborhood Chinese restaurant run by a helpful Chinese American family are everyday activities situated in a life enriched by many forms of culture associated with whites.

One evening in the mid-1980s in a bar in Athens, Greece, I witnessed the two sides of white culture—racial privilege and hierarchy and an emotional connection to place. The bar was frequented primarily by military personnel stationed at the U.S. Air Force base in the city. Similar to the whites in Monterey Park who were working hard to preserve "a place where they could feel at home," the crowd in Athens, primarily white Americans, gathered to create a home away from home, and they sang along to Bruce Springsteen's "Born in the USA" with wild enthusiasm. The moment demonstrated the deeply felt memories of home, family, and country that can be connected to, but are often separated from, the frustration and ambivalence of the failed U.S. military effort in Vietnam and the imperialism that guided it.

Asserting the emptiness of white culture, as Vea and Roediger imply, underestimates the power, the resiliency, and the meaning such music has for whites. Not ignoring that much of this music has appropriated elements from other cultures and supports racial hierarchies, some of it is also finely crafted, artistically inspired, and rich in the way it evokes and creates feelings and memories. To develop strategies to dismantle the racial privileges of whiteness the affirmative and beneficial aspects of white culture must be recognized.

Conclusion

Protests against the loss of the familiar were apparent during the discussion of the redevelopment of Atlantic Square, as long-term residents discussed the real changes in their daily lives brought about by rapid development and urbanization. Well-known stores, needed services, and long-established routines were disrupted and made to disappear. Established residents believed that the new Chinese immigrants displayed little interest in their history and concerns—or those of the city.

The way in which those concerns were expressed and defended, however, clearly crosses into the support and reaffirmation of a racial hierarchy, with whites at the top and a momentary redefinition of the image and position of Asian and Latino. Discussion of "Mediterranean" architecture mixed with the beliefs that immigrants should "adapt to the ways of America" and that "good" restaurants were important revealed the struggle to retain a narrow, discriminatory vision of what properly belongs in the United States and where it should be located.

A clearly exclusionary declaration of who belonged in the category "American" was proclaimed in a sign placed in a vacant gas station: "Will the last American leaving Monterey Park please take down the American flag" (Arax 1985, p. 1). The message restricted citizenship to whites abandoning the city, and Asian Americans and Latinos were once again characterized as outsiders in their own neighborhoods and country. Even though Chinese have been in the United States for more than a century, they still seem foreign to many whites who find it uncomfortable to see business signs they cannot read and hear a language they do not understand. It seems that such things are acceptable if they are confined to the quaint preserves of urban Chinatowns, where they can be visited and left behind at will, but not if they penetrate the suburbs and become a part of everyday life.

Nativist forces have complained about business signs covered with Chinese characters, citing the signs as evidence that the immigrants did not want to become a part of America but rather to create a "Hong Kong of the West" and have responded by trying to regulate the use of foreign languages on signs. Revealing the Eurocentric character of their beliefs, the same people who claim that "this is America" and that foreigners should adopt to "our ways" feel it perfectly acceptable to demand a Mediterranean architectural design for the redevelopment of Atlantic Square.[8] The unstated message is that although Mediterranean is foreign it is acceptable because it is European. The immigrant history of Europeans and the cultural items and habits they have brought to the United States, which inform the country's culture and institutions, are ignored or go unnoticed throughout the discussion. Whiteness forms the backdrop of public discourse, and a double standard is applied to immigrants from Asia and Latin America.

In a predominantly middle-class community with institutionalized means for resident involvement and a long history of local activism, the active dialogue among residents, city staff, development company, and council members was not unusual. What was remarkable about the events that led to the adoption of a Mediterranean design was a conspicuous lack of conflict. Problems and controversies among residents and council members concerned questions of design and fiscal risk rather than the bias embedded in the discourse, demonstrating how events were framed by the national and local dominance of whiteness.[9] Supported by community design plans that called for an avoidance of ethnic themes and a celebration of "our Anglo culture," a city staff and council that demanded "American" businesses, reasserting whiteness in Monterey Park, received institutional support in the form of generous city subsidies and strong backing from the city council.

The new Atlantic Square opened for business in stages during the early 1990s and by 1996 had an occupancy rate comparable to similar developments in the region. As a council member noted, since the opening of center she had not received a single complaint from long-term residents about the need for a place to shop. In terms of restaurants, the familiar fast-food places that saturate Southern California—Pizza Hut, El Pollo Loco, Subway, Boston Market, International House of Pancakes, See's Candies, and Fatburger—have found a home in the new shopping center. In the end, residents' discussions about a place that would reflect the distinctive history of Monterey Park and the developer's assurances that such things would be considered in the finished project produced a mall that looks like many other light-colored stucco and red-tile-roofed shopping malls across the Southwest. Although Asian Americans were quiet on the Atlantic Square issue, some individuals and groups did organize to participate in city politics and challenge racial privilege (chapter 3).

Asian American Politics:
Identity and Political Mobilization

Historical and contemporary conditions in the San Gabriel Valley create a shifting series of contexts in which racial and ethnic identities are formed and translated into political activity. The restrictive covenants of the 1950s gave way to builders and real estate agents who actively courted Asian American buyers in the 1990s. The climate is changing, yet a racial hierarchy supports whiteness; the Atlantic Square project, for example, demonstrates the persistence and multiple forms of discrimination.

To capture the range of sites and activities that constitute the basis of racial and ethnic politics, and the conditions that shape their form and content, Don Nakanishi (1991, p. 31) proposes that an "expanded conceptual framework" is needed. Concentrating exclusively on electoral activities such as voting or running for office conceptualizes racial categories as static—unchanging classifications in which interests may divide members but boundaries around groups are viewed as unproblematical. A broader framework takes into account the relationship between the construction of racial and ethnic identities, the development of political activity, and the range of nonelectoral political activities that Asian Americans use.[1]

Local Context and Racial, Ethnic, and Panethnic Identities

Some residents of Asian ancestry identify themselves simply as unhyphenated Americans, shorn of all racial and ethnic traces. Such attempts at self-identification, however, are negated when racial and ethnic identities are assigned to individuals by others and discriminatory activities are based on such labels. Immigrant Chinese are the focus of a climate of anti-Chinese, anti-immigrant rhetoric and actions in the defense of whiteness. And, because some non-Asian Americans treat Asian Americans as a single group and ignore differences in ethnicity and nativity, all individuals of East Asian ancestry become potential targets of abuse.

The alarming number of hate crimes that have occurred against Asian Americans in the San Gabriel Valley and Los Angeles County reflects a nationwide trend and illustrates the way varying ethnic groups are lumped together (Los Angeles County Commission on Human Relations 1994; NAPALC 1994). Crosses have been burned on lawns of Asian American homes, and swastikas and anti-Asian slogans have been painted on public buildings they use, including schools and churches. A flyer was left on the doorstep of a Chinese family's home with "a drawing of an Asian person choking, and a message telling the family to 'get out of the country'" (Chang 1991, p. J1). In Arcadia, a city northwest of Monterey Park, a Japanese American man and Chinese American woman built a home in a distinctly Asian architectural style, with a "blue tile roof, a Buddhist shrine and a red bridge." Within two years the "front windows [had] been broken more than twenty times with rocks or BBs," and the family had been verbally assaulted by "passers-by yell[ing], 'Japs, go home!' almost daily" (Arax 1987a, p. A1).

The desire to think of oneself as a person, without regard to race, is thwarted by incidents that intrude on such efforts of self-identification, and these encounters were reflected in the interviews I carried out in the region. For example, one afternoon I sat in the home of a Japanese American woman (U.S.-born, sixty years old) as she discussed her feelings and the memories she had of many years in the valley. I noticed that she talked about herself as an unhyphenated American, and the room was absent of any "ethnic" items. The private world of her living room is left behind, however, as she makes her daily rounds and memories of World War II and her incarceration in a U.S. concentration camp linger and mix with public life. She described being attacked by a white woman in a fabric store. As a result, her arm was in a cast for a month. She said, her voice rising with emotion and becoming louder and higher pitched, "I got attacked in 1986. I mean, I was just sitting in the store, just looking at stuff. Kcccch [she imitated the sound of her wrist being twisted]. She grabbed me, turned the thing where it's not supposed to turn, you know. Right after she did it, she says, 'Go back to China where you belong!' And she zoomed out of the store."

The narrative reveals how the woman strives to think of herself as an American and yet others may impose, inaccurately in this case, ethnicity and place of birth on her. Her account illustrates that ethnic identities are not simply volitional, but are formed through a process of continual negotiation through interaction with others. The impact of the incident is magnified by her knowledge that it was not a rare, isolated act but part of a larger pattern in her life and the lives of her friends in the region. When asked if she knew of similar events, she answered, "Well, one other incident happened when I was driving. There was a car full of Caucasians, you know, fair-skinned, blonde guys. They must have seen me, and they decided that they were going to harass me. And so first they went by me, making remarks and sticking their fingers at me. And then when there was an opening ahead of me, they got ahead of me, then braked so that I had to suddenly stop. And they kept harassing me."

She then spoke of an incident that happened to a Japanese American couple she knew:

> But I was thinking, well, that's not as bad as what has happened to another lady. She was driving. Her husband was sitting in the seat next to her, but he was tired so he was sort of laying in the seat. She was going on Valley [a main street in the commercial region of the San Gabriel Valley]. And this car came by her side, the guy looked at her, and then the guy went and cut her off, and stopped the car and got out of the car with a switch blade. He was deciding to cut her up, something like that. And she said, "Wake up! Wake up!" and her husband sat up. Then the guy said, "uh oh." He turned around and went back to his car and drove away.

She explicitly placed responsibility for these hate crimes on whites who were against the recent immigration of Asians, and she recognized the crimes as linking Asians and other targeted groups. When I asked what she thought had motivated such actions, she replied, "This is what they call the yellow backlash. And we've got plenty of that yellow backlash here after they came [Chinese immigrants]. People that consider themselves the Aryan Nation, they think that the U.S. should be only for the whites. I mean they don't think the Indians, or the Jews, or the Latins, or the Orientals, or the blacks belong here. They said that it should be strictly all white. And so they're doing their best, trying to eliminate [Asians] or to get people to leave."

Although the Japanese American woman explicitly recognized racism as the root of such attacks and members of racial and ethnic minorities as the targets, that knowledge did not automatically translate into political activity, joining her and others who experience discrimination. In fact, her response was to flee the city, and she expressed a desire to move to another state where such crimes were uncommon. In her view of the region, hate crimes melt into a larger scene of massive change as urbanization and immigration rapidly transform the town.

The woman's understanding of events in the region and her attempts to distance herself from Chinese immigrants and hate crimes are informed by her experiences and those of her Nisei generation. The patterns of Nisei adaptation to Monterey Park were created during a period of intense discrimination. Leaving concentration camps a brief decade before moving into the city during the 1950s from nearby ethnic ghettos, in a sense they experienced a "second migration" into white America as they struggled to overcome restrictive covenants (Saito 1989, 1993a).

Acutely aware of white hostility, the Nisei kept their ethnicity private; Japanese American culture was kept in the home and among themselves. Dubbed the "quiet Americans" by Bill Hosokawa (1969), also a Nisei, in his account of that generation, the Nisei worked hard to be accepted as good neighbors and citizens. They were polite in public, kept their homes and yards neat and clean, and participated in community activities such as the PTA. They were also active in city politics. A number were appointed to city commissions, and when Nisei George Ige was elected to the Monterey Park City Council in 1970 it was a sign for many that they had achieved some level of acceptance.

The idea that ethnic culture should remain a private rather than a public affair was supported in a conversation with a Nisei who bitterly opposed the inclusion of Chinese-language books in the city's library. He maintained that city funds should not be used to maintain collections that would also be used by people who did not live in the city. When "we [Japanese Americans] want to read books in Japanese," he said, "we go to Little Tokyo and go to the center." Similarly, council member Barry Hatch, listening to former council member David Almada speaking at a 1989 Cinco de Mayo festival in Monterey Park, remarked that Almada constantly stressed his Mexican culture. Although allowing that it was fine to celebrate it on occasion, Hatch believed that Almada should then "put it away" and not stress his Mexican roots "twenty-four hours a day."

Although the Nisei believed that discrimination had greatly decreased as they experienced political and social integration in the community, in fact, the rise in hate crimes demonstrated that public expression of racism had only temporarily retreated in an era of civil rights reform, resurfacing with the influx of the new Chinese immigrants.

Compared with the experiences and memories of the first Asian immigrants to the United States, more recent Chinese immigrants entered under entirely different circumstances. Immigration policies have been liberalized from the strict earlier bans on Asian immigrants, naturalization is possible, and the most egregious barriers to social and political access have been struck down by federal policies and Supreme Court rulings. Because large segments of their population are highly educated, politically astute, experienced in business affairs, and possess large amounts of capital, the new immigrants have been able to create an economy "from the top" (Tseng 1994a). A more traditional route has been to work up from the bottom. As *Los Angeles Times* reporter Mark Arax declared in a series of articles on Monterey Park, the immigrants created the "nation's first suburban Chinatown" (1987b, p. A1).

Similar to the feelings of displacement and loss of control of Latino and white established residents, during an interview a Nisei also expressed dismay with the demographic and economic changes that had occurred in the community. He quoted what his son had said upon returning to Monterey Park after several years of overseas military service: "Goddamn dad, where the hell did all these Chinese come from? Shit, this isn't even our town anymore."

The nativist and racist tendencies in the slow-growth movement and the defense of racial privilege contained in whiteness are evident in the concept I call the "good immigrant." Established residents—including Asian American, Latinos, and whites—try to regain social and political control of a community by invoking a mythical image of how good immigrants should conduct themselves in the United States—working to blend in and adapt to the ways of America. They certainly did not remake the city in their image to create a "Hong Kong of the West" or a "Little Taipei." Of course, that ignores the history of immigrants in the United States and the ethnic enclaves formed by Europeans, Latin Americans, and Asians; ethnic holidays such as Octoberfest and Lunar New Year; or Saint Patrick's Day celebrations.

The racism and forms of coercion embedded in social relationships that structured and limited the forms of adaptation of earlier immigrants and their descendants in what became the American way of doing things remains unrecognized. From their point of view, the residents' use of the concept of the good immigrant is not racist. They define racism as individual acts committed against someone or some group based on race, such as verbal or physical attacks or employment discrimination. Suggesting that the new immigrants act like good immigrants is not racist according to this definition because what is requested is behavior defined as American—the way "everyone has done it in the past." What is missing is the recognition of an enduring Eurocentric bias throughout U.S. history that allows for the support of Mediterranean architecture for Atlantic Square but not Chinese architecture.

The strong emotions and opinions about demographic and economic change and the way people believe that immigrants should adapt to the United States, rooted in real or imaginary images of one's own family, were expressed during a telephone conversation I had with a Latino man while I volunteered on Xavier Becerra's 1990 assembly campaign.

> The fucking yellow people are taking over the city. It's a goddamn shame. You go down Garvey [a major commercial street] and you see all those stores, Lim Fuck-Suck liquor store. VC restaurants. All the grease plugging up the sewers, and those asses cause fires. They're forcing older people to pay protection. They own those goddamn banks, funnel gang and drug money. The American people are fine. I'm talking about some of the immigrants. It's not that I'm against it, but when my family left Mexico, they spoke Spanish. They learned English. I'm for English Only. If you are Vietnamese, Taiwanese, and that includes Hispanics, you should speak English.

Racism and the acts such as hate crimes it provokes make racial identities—Asian as well as white—explicit. They compel persons of Japanese ancestry to recognize their identity as Japanese Americans and their links with other Asian Americans. Discrimination does not automatically lead, however, to the development of more encompassing ethnic identities. Instead, Japanese Americans developed a range of responses toward Chinese immigrants. The woman attacked in a store remembered (with an embarrassed laugh) her indignation as an eleven-year-old, saying "it wasn't fair" back then that they were put into camps while Italian and German Americans remained free. She believed the answer to hate crimes lay in fleeing the city.

Racial lumping—treating different ethnic groups as one—can also lead to disidentification with Chinese immigrants. Reacting to the anti-Chinese sentiment in the city, one Nisei, a long-term resident of the city, pointed out some of the differences he had found between Japanese and Chinese Americans: "I think we probably behave better in public than they do, we're not as boisterous in public, we're not as pushy in public as the Chinese are, I mean you don't see a Japanese person crowding in line or talking at the top of his voice." As another Nisei jokingly said, "[We] should wear buttons saying, 'I'm Japanese, not Chinese,' just like some Chinese who wore buttons during World War II which declared, 'I'm Chinese.'" Going beyond disassociation to active hostility, some Chinese Americans even wore buttons that declared "I Hate Japs Worse than You Do" (Daniels 1988, p. 205).

Constructing a Chinese American identity is also problematic, considering differences such as language, region of origin, nativity, and historical enmities. Tension might exist between Taiwanese and those from the

People's Republic of China or be created by the effects of the Chinese diaspora and the fact that Chinese immigrants in the San Gabriel Valley may be from Malaysia and Vietnam as well as from Hong Kong, Taiwan, and China or the differences of language that exist among speakers of Cantonese, Mandarin, or one of the many other Chinese dialects.

A major division exists between Chinese immigrants and the native-born. The term *ABC* (American-born Chinese) is sometimes used in a friendly, joking manner, yet at other times it is meant to be mocking and derisive, meaning that the U.S.-born have lost their culture. In a study of politics in New York's Chinatown, Peter Kwong describes some immigrants' resentment of U.S.-born Chinese professionals who have "little knowledge of or contact with the community" and are sometimes called "juk-shen (the 'heart of a hollow bamboo stick'), implying that American-born Chinese often lack Chinese soul" (1996, pp. 132–33).

Revealing differences based on class and nativity, native-born Chinese Americans complain of the "Asian flack" they receive because of the rich Chinese immigrants who "flaunt" their wealth by driving expensive automobiles, are "rude and arrogant in public," and construct large homes that dwarf others in the city. Fleeing the city, disidentification, and invoking the image of the good immigrant are possible responses to the new Chinese immigrants. Given such differences among Asian Americans, the question is, What events and circumstances in the history of the United States and the San Gabriel Valley unite them politically as Asian Americans?

A critical part of the answer lies in identifying and recognizing what links the distinct and varied forms of discrimination that different groups within the category "Asian American" experience. Recognizing these shared historical and contemporary experiences, long-term and new immigrant residents generate a common culture, a process Joane Nagel (1994) labels "cultural construction." That process contributes to the development of ethnic identities and community formation because, as Nagel explains, "Culture provides the content and meaning of ethnicity; it animates and authenticates ethnic boundaries by providing a history, ideology, symbolic universe, and system of meaning" (p. 162). Discrimination links Asian Americans and through their individual actions (as discussed in the case studies that follow) alerts them to legal and political means to fight discrimination. As part of the process of cultural construction and building a panethnic identity, concepts such as Asian flack and the good immigrant had to be analyzed (and their relationship to such other forms of discrimination as hate crimes and employment discrimination clarified) to reveal the racism that makes all Asian Americans targets of discrimination.

Michael Eng's activities, discussed subsequently, illustrate the process of "collective memory," which is, as George Lipsitz (1988) explains, an understanding of a shared history and critical for the construction of culture. When actively employed, collective memory, in combination with contemporary issues, can be used to generate purpose and goals, bind people together, and create a sense of legitimacy for a movement. Discrimination in the labor market is a major experience that Asian Americans have shared throughout history and an example of a common issue. Before World War II a familiar story among Chinese Americans and Japanese Americans was that of young men who had degrees in engineering but could not find jobs in the mainstream economy. Instead, they worked at tasks that did not require a formal education: helping run the family business and selling fruit from the family's farm at a roadside stand.

Although Asian Americans are now hired in large numbers as engineers, a variation of the old theme is revealed in Yen Fen Tseng's (1994a) interviews with highly trained Chinese immigrant entrepreneurs who have advanced degrees and years of experience with major American firms. Tseng found that the perception of a glass ceiling (lack of promotion opportunities at the higher managerial or executive levels) was a major reason why such individuals decided to leave the U.S. companies and start their own businesses. The U.S. Commission on Civil Rights confirms these findings, stating that U.S.-born and immigrant Asian American engineers "were significantly less likely to be in managerial positions or to be promoted to managerial positions than white engineers with the same measured qualifications" (1992, p. 133). One way in which the Taiwanese government has advanced its high-technology industries is by luring home Taiwanese educated and trained in the United States by emphasizing the marvelous, government-sponsored opportunities in Taiwan compared to the limited chances for advancement in the United States (Watanabe 1989). Although superficially the burgeoning Chinese ethnic economy in the San Gabriel Valley appears to be an unqualified success story, deeper examination reveals the importance of discrimination for its establishment, as is the case for other ethnic economies, including the Cuban enclave in Miami and the Korean enclave in Los Angeles (Light and Bonacich 1988; Portes and Bach 1985).

Thus, restrictive covenants, employment discrimination, hate crimes, the nativism of the slow-growth movement, and racist U.S. government policies regarding immigration and naturalization provide examples of discrimination—expressed in multiple ways and under different circumstances—that transcend differences of ethnicity, nativity, class, or gender. Asian

Americans recognize that despite their varied experiences and backgrounds a shared history of discrimination forms the basis for constructing a group identity. That process of developing a sense of group membership and a basis for political mobilization emerges from the activities, networks, and cultural practices of everyday life and the broader economic and political context of the San Gabriel Valley and the United States.

Political Change in the San Gabriel Valley

Events in Monterey Park provide examples of how major demographic and economic changes in the region created new political possibilities for Asian Americans in the San Gabriel Valley (Saito and Horton 1994). Similar to what took place in the African American civil rights movement, Asian Americans worked to develop resources, networks, and organizations to support their political agenda. They were operating in a political context shaped and altered by the civil rights movement, however, and did not have to contend with the worst forms of discriminatory practices encountered in the earlier era.

After the passage of major legislation such as the Civil Rights Act of 1964 and the Voting Rights Act of 1965, and given an Asian American population that had a proportionally larger professional-managerial class than the African American population of the civil rights era, Asian Americans used their resources to increase participation in grass-roots and electoral politics. They worked for local and regional political representation rather than the widespread social change that was the goal of the African American civil rights movement. Asian Americans worked to implement the commitment to equality written into the new legislation because they understood that legislation declaring racial discrimination illegal meant nothing in the face of the racial privilege and hierarchy deeply embedded in U.S. society—unless it was actively and forcefully employed through political and legal means.

Before 1980 Latinos and Asian Americans were active primarily as individuals in a political structure dominated by whites. A number of highly respected Asian Americans and Latinos were involved in community organizations, and three Asian Americans and one Latino were elected to the city council before 1980.[2] Their electoral campaigns, however, tended to be outgrowths of the predominately white power structure that included the Lions, Kiwanis, and Monterey Park Democratic Club. As a former city council member explained, "The Rotary Club and the Lions Club have always been pretty influential. . . . I think at one point in time . . . everybody on the city council was a member of the Lions Club" (Fong 1990). White men dominated the city council until the election of Leila Donegan, also white, in 1954. The increase of Latino- and Asian American-elected council members in the 1970s followed the growth of those populations in the community.

The Monterey Park Democratic Club's membership included a large number of Jewish Americans. The group was a progressive force in the community and worked on issues such as opening home sales to racial minorities. As Matthew Martinez, a former Monterey Park City Council member and member of Congress, noted in his discussion of the fight against restricted covenants, "All of these people were part of the Democratic Club who were fighting from a strong, heartfelt view of what the Constitution stood for—everybody's equality, everybody's rights. They didn't believe it was right to deny anybody for any reason their right to buy a house where they wanted to buy" (Fong 1990). The club's activism also included supporting Asian American and Latino candidates for local office. Speaking of his election to the city council during the 1970s, George Ige mentioned that he had been "very active" in the Monterey Park Democratic Club. Serving on the city council was seen as a form of community service, an obligation for involved and responsible residents, and one day "they told me it was my turn" [to run for office].

Before the mid-1980s, however, no Asian American political organizations existed in Monterey Park other than local chapters of organizations such as the Japanese American Citizens League, which played a limited role in local politics. Alfred Song (1980, p. 16), an attorney and the first Asian American elected to the city council in 1960, noted that lack of support when he said in 1978, "In all of the years that I have campaigned for elective office, I have never had the help, financial or otherwise, of any organized Oriental group; whatever their origin may be—Korean, Japanese, Chinese, Filipino or any others. . . . in twenty years, I think I could count the individual Asians who have come to my assistance on one hand and still have a couple of fingers left over."

The election of Lily Chen, a Chinese immigrant and established resident, to the city council in 1982 was a turning point because she organized her own campaign and had considerable funding from Asian Americans in Monterey Park and Los Angeles County. That pattern was followed in the election of Judy Chu, a native-born Chinese American, in 1988 and Samuel Kiang, a Chinese immigrant, in 1990. The change signaled a period of political transition—the demise of the white old boy network and the emergence of Latino and Asian American political networks.

Regional Networks: Los Angeles Organizations

The transformation of Asian American politics from individuals dependent on white-dominated organizations to the establishment of an Asian American political base in the San Gabriel Valley was heavily supported by the growing strength of Asian American legal, research, and social service establishments in the greater Los Angeles area. Although Los Angeles has a large number of Asian American political organizations, those groups have not produced coordinated, consistent efforts to support candidates and political issues and are important primarily as sites for members to gain political knowledge and experience and as sources of volunteers and funding. As Judy Chu mentioned in a discussion of the unsuccessful candidacy of Rose Ochi, a Japanese American, for the Los Angeles City Community College Board in 1989, "A problem with the Asian American political scene in the area is that the clubs are not functioning together so no strong network exists to support candidates." Ochi, a staff member of Los Angeles Mayor Tom Bradley, was a Monterey Park resident. Little had changed by 1993, when Mike Woo, a Chinese American and a former member of the Los Angeles City Council, failed in his attempt to become mayor.

Asian American academic, legal, and social service organizations in the greater Los Angeles region are working to build an institutional base that has highly developed networks and resources and fills the void caused in the San Gabriel Valley by the lack of sustained, collaborative efforts among political organizations. Political mobilization fosters relationships among individuals and groups established through the educational, professional, political, and community activities that have created networks covering Southern California and extending across the United States. These groups form the core of a budding Los Angeles political network and capitalize on numerous and diverse Asian American political organizations by drawing on their membership for fund-raising events and community education.

UCLA's Asian American Studies Center is one of the oldest, best-established institutions in the region's—and the nation's—Asian American network. It has generated research and data used by individuals and organizations that have played major roles in the development of Asian American politics in the Los Angeles region and the San Gabriel Valley. Nurturing relationships with community groups, generating policy studies, and building interracial linkages are goals of its educational mission, as acknowledged in the center's brochure: "In response to America the Asian American Studies Center forged a commitment to research and social change.

Emerging from the civil rights struggles of minorities—Blacks, Chicanos and Latinos, Asians, and Native Americans—to define their own history, education, and future, the Center was founded in 1969 as part of the movement for ethnic studies."

At the center, the first national Asian Pacific American public policy research body, was established in 1992. Its objectives are "(1) to establish the Institute as an information and resource clearinghouse, (2) to provide interpretive analyses of U.S. census information related to Asian Pacific Americans, and (3) to articulate policy issues relative to the growing impact of Asian Pacifics in the economic and political arenas" (*LEAP Connections* 1990, p. 1).[3] The center maintains an active publishing program that includes *Amerasia Journal,* the oldest scholarly journal devoted to Asian American studies. It has also conducted and analyzed regional and national exit polls, including those for the 1988 and 1990 Monterey Park City Council elections and the 1996 presidential elections.

The UCLA Asian Pacific American Voter Registration Study (Nakanishi 1986), produced in collaboration with the Southwest Voter Registration Education Project and the Asian Pacific American Legal Center, was the first such large-scale study conducted in Los Angeles County. Mike Eng, an attorney and Monterey Park political activist, and Michael Woo, a member of the Los Angeles City Council who grew up in the San Gabriel Valley, were advisors to the project. It identified Monterey Park as having the county's highest percentage of Asian American registered voters compared to the total number of registered voters. The study also revealed the mixed political party affiliation of Asian Americans by ethnic group, demonstrating the problem they faced in election primaries when voters were restricted to candidates in the voters' political party. That condition was changed by voter approval of Proposition 198 in 1996, allowing balloting for any candidate in primary elections, regardless of political party affiliation.

UCLA's academic reputation has long attracted Asian American students, both from the region and across the country; the 1996 entering class was 36.4 percent Asian American and 32.4 percent white. The institution's Asian American alumni form a strong network, and in the late 1980s they established their own chapter of the greater UCLA alumni association.

The successful campaign of Don Nakanishi, director of the center, to reverse a negative tenure decision involved students, faculty, community activists, and local and state politicians, with support extending across the country.[4] As Glenn Omatsu, a longtime labor activist and employee at the center, wrote about the politicization that occurred during the community effort,

For the first time in their lives, individuals learned how to formulate strategies, organize rallies, speak before large meetings, lobby politicians, testify at public hearings, write articles and leaflets, and build coalitions with other communities.

The three-year campaign for tenure for UCLA Prof. Don Nakanishi represents one such movement for mass empowerment. Don's case mobilized thousands of people nationwide. (1990a, pp. 63–64)

The tenure case strengthened existing networks and created new ones. In the San Gabriel Valley, Janet Lim, an alumna who worked on the staff of Cong. Matthew Martinez, made calls to inquire about the status of the case, and letters of concern were sent by State Senator Joseph Montoya (representative of Monterey Park and a UCLA alumnus) and the West San Gabriel Valley Asian Pacific Democratic Club (with many of its members UCLA alumni).

UCLA has provided a meeting place for Asian Americans and given them a foundation for future civic activities. For example, Stewart Kwoh, director of the Asian Pacific American Legal Center, and Mike Eng attended law school at UCLA in the mid-1970s. Afterward, they opened a poverty-law office in Los Angeles, and each has taught a course entitled "Asian Americans and the Law" at the center since the late 1970s. While in law school, Eng shared an apartment with Fred Hong, born and raised in Hong Kong, who attended Loyola Law School in Los Angeles after finishing his undergraduate degree at the University of California, Berkeley, later practiced immigration law, and lives in Monterey Park. "Fred and I were living together," Eng recalled. "The first time I met Judy [Chu] was when she came over for dinner for a meeting with Fred." When I asked how he had met Hong, given that they had attended different law schools, commenting on the tightly knit group of Asian American activists Eng laughed and replied, "It's a small community."

The Public Policy Institute at UCLA is operated in conjunction with Leadership Education for Asian Pacifics (LEAP), a nonprofit organization established in 1982 "to develop, strengthen, and expand the leadership roles" and to "achieve full participation and equality for Asian Pacific Americans through leadership, empowerment and policy" (Nakanishi and Hokoyama 1996, p. ix). LEAP played a major role in developing the funding and research that lead to the publication of policy books published with the UCLA Asian American Studies Center and organized nationwide conferences to publicize them. Conferences throughout Southern California and a series of workshops to develop leadership and management skills are other LEAP-initiated activities. J. D. Hokoyama, president and executive director of LEAP, lives in Montebello and maintains close ties with the region's leaders.

The Asian Pacific American Legal Center (APALC) of Southern California was founded in 1983 and is located in downtown Los Angeles. It is a nonprofit organization that carries out legal advocacy for Asian Americans and provides free legal assistance to low-income people. Its director and cofounder, Stewart Kwoh, has been featured in a *Los Angeles Times* article highlighting him and the activities of the center, noting that "in 1994, the center's thirty-five-member staff, augmented by hundreds of volunteers, served fifteen thousand people and helped three thousand become naturalized citizens" (Kang 1995, p. 1). The multilingual staff offers legal services in family law, public benefits, tenant-landlord issues, language rights, and immigration. The title of the *Times*'s article, "Building Bridges to Equality," referred to Kwoh's panethnic efforts among Asian Americans and his dedication to linking Asian Americans with African Americans and Latinos. As Xavier Becerra, a Latino member of Congress whose district includes parts of Chinatown, Koreatown, and Boyle Heights, described Kwoh's efforts, "The work he does can be felt here in Washington, D.C. I call Stewart a master bridgebuilder."[5]

APALC established the Asian Pacific American Dispute Resolution Center in 1989. "Designed as an alternative to court proceedings, the Center is the first not-for-profit organization to provide language specific mediation services for the Asian Pacific American community" (Asian Pacific American Legal Center 1991a, p. 3). The center has addressed conflict between African American consumers and Korean American merchants and was involved in mediation among local parents concerning fights between Chinese American and Latino students at San Gabriel High School.

Also part of APALC, the Leadership Development in Interethnic Relations (LDIR) Program has trained individuals in "cultural awareness, dispute resolution and resource building" since 1991. Its focus has been on specific communities, and the San Gabriel Valley is one of its primary sites, along with Gardena and Koreatown. The first brochure that described the program listed two members of the San Gabriel Valley League of United Latin American Citizens, Roland Aranjo and Jose Calderon, as members of the LDIR advisory board. Recognizing the urgent need for greater interracial understanding following the civil unrest in Los Angeles in 1992, the Martin Luther King Dispute Resolution Center/Southern Christian Leadership Conference and the Mexican American Legal Defense and Education Fund added their support.

Recognizing the need for a national legal organization, the APALC joined with the Asian Law Caucus of San Francisco and the Asian American Legal Defense and Education Fund of New York to establish the National Asian Pacific American Legal Consortium in 1991. The organization's mission is to "advance the legal and civil rights of the 8.8 million Asian Pacific Americans through litigation, advocacy, public education and public policy development." Headquartered in Washington, D.C., the consortium focuses on anti-Asian violence, immigration, naturalization, voting rights, language rights, and affirmative action, according to an information and fund-raising letter from the director, Karen Narasaki, in 1996.

The center was also active in Monterey Park in 1988 when Barry Hatch, upset by foreign-language material in the local public library, led an effort to replace the city's library board (which has input regarding the budget and personnel affairs) with an advisory committee. The center provided legal help when a resident group, Friends of the Library, successfully filed suit against the city council, forcing the reinstatement of the board (Calderon 1991; Fong 1994).

The Asian Pacific Policy and Planning Council (A3PCON), founded in 1976, is the largest federation of social service organizations—more than forty—serving Asian Americans in Los Angeles.[6] Social service agencies are heavily dependent on government funding for operating costs, and because their constituency includes large numbers of low-income persons and immigrants who are greatly affected by government actions and policies the agencies are acutely aware of the value of an umbrella agency.[7] Using its vast and diverse network, the council directs efforts to analyze and develop public policy. It also works to focus public attention on critical issues facing Asian Americans.

Service Organizations

National organizations (the Organization of Chinese Americans, Organization of Chinese American Women, and Chinese American Citizens Alliance) and regional groups (the Japanese American Eastside Optimists Club and the Chinese American Association of Southern California) abound in the San Gabriel Valley. They have had little sustained coordinated involvement in the area, however. As one Chinese American mentioned—with only a little hyperbole—at a meeting in Monterey Park, "There are hundreds of Chinese groups in Los Angeles and getting them to agree on anything is impossible." Since the mid-1980s they have become more active, but their endeavors are geared toward one-time efforts such as candidate forums and fund-raising events.

One local political group that has sprung up in the valley is the Chinese American Political Action Committee (C-PAC). A handbook, written in 1990 in English and Chinese and in collaboration with the League of Women Voters, explains the U.S. political process to immigrants and describes the committee as a "nonpartisan organization whose general purpose is to identify, encourage, support and educate Chinese Americans to participate in the full political process." Mike Eng and Lily Chen have been active in C-PAC and have sponsored a major fund-raiser for Sam Kiang's city council campaign in 1990.

As one of the oldest and most active Asian American groups in the San Gabriel Valley, the Japanese American Citizen's League (JACL) represents the kinds of activities carried out by service organizations in the region. The national organization was founded in Seattle in 1930, and membership is restricted to U.S. citizens.[8] The league is an advocacy group for Japanese Americans. Two resolutions adopted at its initial meeting called for the repeal of the 1922 Cable Act that revoked citizenship of American-born women who married immigrants ineligible for citizenship—which at the time meant Asian immigrants—and the right of naturalization for Japanese veterans who served in the U.S. military during World War I. League efforts were rewarded when the Nye-Lea bill was passed in 1935 and nearly five hundred Asian veterans, the majority Japanese, received citizenship. The Cable Act was repealed in 1936. During the 1980s the league was one of the major organizations behind the successful redress and reparations movement. As the largest Asian American presence in the capital, the league often by default speaks for all Asian Americans.

Recognizing the experience and success of the league, Taiwanese Americans called upon it in 1982 to help them establish a similar organization, and the Taiwanese American Citizens League (TACL) was established in 1985. It is headquartered in the San Gabriel Valley, a recognition of the growing presence of Taiwanese in the region. A TACL membership form states, "Just as the Jews and the Japanese formed successful grass-roots and nation-wide organizations, so do the Taiwanese American[s] hope to create a powerful and widely recognized one, namely, the Taiwanese American Citizens League."

The East Los Angeles chapter of the JACL is also in the San Gabriel Valley. Established in the 1970s, it draws membership primarily from East Los Angeles, Monterey Park, Montebello, and Alhambra. Community service activities dominate its agenda; for example, among its major events are an annual dinner to award college scholarships to high school seniors and speech and essay contests for younger students. Although its role in local politics is limited, the league is recognized nationally, and its members are established residents who are active in community events. The group's support for political efforts, such as redistricting in 1991, is actively sought. When Judy Chu ran for Monterey Park City Council for the first time in 1988, her campaign material listed many Japanese American supporters. Many were league members known and respected in the city for their community service.

The UCLA Asian American Studies Center, A3PCON, and the Asian Pacific American Legal Center have worked to establish a strong network among Asian Americans in the Los Angeles region. They have not only supplied political efforts with basic research, legal analysis, technical skills, and organizational efforts but also helped incorporate the membership and resources of the myriad and diverse Asian American groups in the region in such critical issues as redistricting in 1990 and 1991. Political groups such as C-PAC and the JACL are important in efforts to institutionalize a political base in the region. They serve as part of an ever-growing network of organizations that can be called upon to support fund-raising efforts, educate members about politics, and lend their organizational names to support efforts such as redistricting. A challenge for these groups, which are dominated by professionals and claim to represent the entire Asian American community, concerns how to reach out to an extremely complex population that varies in ethnicity, class, nativity, and gender (Espiritu and Ong 1994).

Case Studies

I will describe the process of cultural construction in the development of racial identities, political restructuring, and building a political base using three case studies. These studies illustrate how the demands of local politics created the need for various Asian American ethnic groups to develop networks and organizations at the panethnic level in order to become effective political presences.

Case 1: Grass-Roots Mobilization and Public Hearings

Public hearings are an example of how Asian Americans have mobilized to ensure that their viewpoints are considered in the formation of city policy. Participation has helped establish grass-roots networks to use the political experience and knowledge of established Asian Americans, Asian American political organizations, and the large population of new immigrants. That participation is especially important for residents who are not citizens and thus unable to vote. As residents and taxpayers, new immigrants have a stake in what happens in the community, and public hearings have become an important forum where their views can be expressed and political pressure applied.

City council meetings in Monterey Park are often crowded; residents fill the two hundred seats of the council chambers whenever important or controversial issues are on the agenda. Until the late 1980s these meetings were dominated by older white and Latino residents, and few Chinese immigrants participated. In response to an increasing number of anti-Asian and anti-immigrant sentiments and policies emanating from city hall, however, immigrants and native-born have come together to contest anti-Asian policies. One such instance concerned the public hearings held on the council's impending decision on which language to use on the city's commercial signs. Barry Hatch had spearheaded an effort to eliminate all foreign languages on the advertising—a direct attack against Chinese businesses and part of a broader struggle between immigrants and established residents over the symbolic content of what constitutes "American." His efforts followed his failed 1985 effort to add a measure to the 1986 city ballot that would have made English the city's official language.[9] He was fighting for a strictly Eurocentric definition of America, symbolized by his efforts in the "official English" movement.

For Asian Americans and their supporters in other racial minority communities, Hatch threatened the constitutional right to freedom of speech—removing barriers to political and economic equality and recognizing and respecting the symbols of different languages and cultures. Considering that the businesses using Chinese-language signs primarily served immigrants, the English-only movement also had economic implications. Business signs are major forms of communication and advertisement and contribute to the welcoming ambience of commercial areas.

Hatch lost in his attempt to establish official English, and the old regulations allowing Chinese and English signs remained virtually unchanged. The victory came about through the pressure of two forces. First, the leadership of a coalition of established immigrant leaders, Asian Americans, Latinos, and whites strongly favored civil rights. The mobilization and sheer pressure of protesting Asian Americans and Asian immigrants at public hearings were also influences.

Council member Judy Chu led a strong multiracial coalition during the public hearings. Asian Americans, whether or not they could read the Chinese signs, joined the coalition because they understood the anti-Asian message implicit in English-only campaigns. Liberally inclined non-Asian

Americans also responded to the civil rights issue. Those sentiments helped establish a common interest among native-born and immigrant Asians and between Asian Americans and other racial groups.

Long-term residents of the community and others who had long histories of political activism worked with immigrant leaders to educate the new immigrants about their civil rights, the history of political protest by aggrieved groups in the United States, and the need for political coalitions to effectively address issues generated by local governing bodies. The Chinese American Civil Rights and Education Foundation, based in Monterey Park and organized primarily by Chinese immigrants, organized a forum on November 9, 1988, to discuss the proposed language restrictions. Speakers included Jose Calderon, an immigrant Mexican American and the president of the San Gabriel Valley League of United Latin American Citizens, and Kathy Imahara, a native-born Japanese American attorney from the Asian Pacific American Legal Center of Southern California. Calderon provided a political analysis of the attack on language rights, and Imahara added the legal argument of the constitutional right of free speech.

Thus, immigrant and Asian American organizations in coalition with each other and other racial groups were an important force in defeating sign restrictions. By bringing the issue to the attention of the community and explaining the legal basis for contesting English-only ordinances, Asian Americans were prepared to monitor the ordinance-modification process. That laid the groundwork for the next step—applying pressure on city commissions through the growing number of immigrants who attended public hearings.

Before reaching the city council, issues concerning signs first pass through the design review board and planning commission. Board meetings are held in the city hall's community room, which resembles, and is nearly the size of, a high school classroom. The sparsely furnished room is usually empty except for those who have items before the review board. On the evening the sign ordinance came before the board, in addition to those present who had items on the agenda, a group of eight Asian Americans, native-born as well as immigrant, doubled the usual number of spectators. The group sat quietly, watching and saying nothing. The board discussed the technical aspects of the sign ordinance for several hours, but when it came to the language issue little discussion was needed to keep things the way they were.

The rather routine discussion of the matter that evening belied the behind-the-scenes lobbying that had taken place. Michael Eng, a native-born Chinese American attorney and resident of the community, had telephoned the other Asian Americans, many of whom were immigrants, to notify them that the sign issue would be on the agenda and that they should come and observe the proceedings. Eng had talked to several of the board members beforehand and thought the general feeling to be one of "if it ain't broke, don't fix it." He strongly believed that those in the audience provided a moderating influence on the proceedings and let the board know its discussion and decisions were monitored by the Asian American community. Thus, Eng's organization of community residents and their silent vigil during public hearings were other instances of established Asian Americans educating new immigrants about community politics.

A city hall staff person who was present at the review board meeting discussed the importance of the Asian American residents monitoring the meetings.

> Staff person: I was quite surprised when all the people showed up during the design review board meetings. They didn't say anything, but the pressure was there. They were watching everything that happened. You got the feeling that if something wrong happened, that they would be right on it.
> Saito: Is it possible that the regulations might have been different if they weren't there?
> Staff person: Yes. Maybe stronger changes. Perhaps they might have added direct translation of the signs. But they had to be careful, you can't legislate against one language.
> Saito: Sometimes I wonder how effective citizen participation is on things like that.
> Staff person: It was important.
> Saito: It makes a difference?
> Staff person: Yes, it sure does.

The issue reached the planning commission on January 12, 1989, and the results were similar to those at the review board's meeting. Again, a number of Asian Americans watched the proceedings, and several Chinese Americans spoke in favor of keeping things as they were.

On January 23, 1989, the issue reached the city council. The council chamber was crowded, primarily with whites in their fifties and sixties, Latinos, and a sprinkling of Asian Americans. The usual reporters from the *Los Angeles Times* and the Chinese daily newspapers were also there. A strong coalition of Asian Americans, whites, and Latinos spoke in favor of moderation and constitutional rights and helped push through a compromise ordinance that retained the use of foreign languages.

An Asian American presence at the city council's public hearings is a growing trend in Monterey Park. The experience of speaking in public can be intimidating, however. Cable television monitors focus on speakers, the crowd voices its opinions through applause or jeers, and hostile questions come from council members. One Chinese immigrant who has lived in the city for more than twenty years, regularly attends city meetings, and participates in public hearings, observed, "A lot of Chinese people do not like to get involved, especially in our city hall because someone can embarrass you. . . . Like me, I don't feel it. I just go there and fight back. . . . It really takes some courage. . . . I think more people would come forward even if they have a handicap with the language . . . if they felt comfortable there. But if they go there and maybe get abused by somebody, they say forget it" (Pardo 1990a).

Asian immigrants are learning that participating in public forums is an effective way of ensuring that issues of concern to them are put on the agenda and that their point of view is heard. Understanding the importance of participation, an increasing number of Chinese immigrants appear in the audience and speak during public meetings. During the summer of 1991, for example, Chinese immigrant leaders organized demonstrations to support the use of bilingual dispatchers for the emergency 911 telephone service in Monterey Park. Hundreds attended the city council meeting at which a program of implementation was discussed, outnumbering old-timers in the chamber.

Case 2: Political Organizations: The West San Gabriel Valley Asian Pacific Democratic Club

A major change in the transition from white domination to growing Asian American political power has been the establishment of Asian American political organizations, which embody the institutionalization of networks and the political base needed to create fundamental changes in the political structure of the region. The significance of that change is represented in the contrast between electing someone who happens to be Asian American but is backed by whites and electing someone who is supported by, and accountable to, the Asian American community. As Aldon Morris (1984, p. xii) points out, groups traditionally excluded from mainstream politics must be able to develop political power based on an indigenous foundation. The civil rights movement used the resources, leaders, and networks generated from the community's social, legal, and political organizations, especially African American churches.

Some of the older Asian American organizations in the Monetery Park area include the Eastside Optimist Club and the East Los Angeles chapter of the Japanese American Citizens League. Most members of these groups are Japanese American, and their activities are geared toward community service and social events rather than politics. Membership of some of the traditional business and civic groups such as the Lions and Rotary clubs includes many Chinese immigrants. In some instances, as with the Asian Kiwanis Club, parallel organizations—with ties to the original national or international group—were formed and have a membership that is primarily Chinese. The political clout of traditional organizations such as the Lions Club, once powerful in the election of city council members, has greatly declined. The new demographics of Monterey Park, changing membership of these organizations, and the emphasis on civic, business, and social activities have lessened the political influence of these groups. Since the 1980s, a number of Chinese organizations—the Taiwanese American Citizens League, Chinese American Political Action Committee, and Chinese American Association of Southern California, for example— have become active in local politics.

Asian Americans in California have historically lacked adequate political representation, and they recognized the western San Gabriel Valley's potential as a center for Asian American politics. Community activists established the West San Gabriel Valley Asian Pacific Democratic Club in 1985 to institute the networks, resources, and organization needed to back issues and candidates and work toward political empowerment. One member explained why such a club was needed: "Michael Eng, one of the founding members, was very active in regional politics and was attending many fund-raising dinners. However, he understood that it was very difficult for an individual to make an impact on politicians because of limited resources, and he became interested in forming an organization."

Janet Lim, one of the founding members and president of the club in the late 1980s, explained that the original members had met while working in their respective ethnic communities during the 1960s and 1970s. Two lessons were learned during that early period. First, the idea of "Asian American" was born, meaning that although people may have worked in Los Angeles's separate ethnic communities such as Chinatown or Little Tokyo they recognized the shared political goals of all Asian ethnic groups as they worked to obtain funding for social services and low-cost housing and battled against encroaching development. Second, they learned that each group was too small to lobby effectively for government funding and that a coalition as Asian Americans had to be developed (Kuramoto 1980; Little Tokyo Anti-Eviction Force 1976).

The early idealism and community service of the club's founders was reflected at an executive board meeting held in 1988 at the home of Charles

Yue, the group's vice president. Sitting around a dining room table, the older founding members began talking about the origins of the group, prompted by discussion of the growing membership and diversification of the club. Lim mentioned that most of the first members were teachers and lawyers. At that point Yue, who had taught one of the first college-level ethnic studies classes in the east San Francisco Bay area in the 1960s, began to laugh loudly, and his face turned red as he described the founders as "professional do-gooders." "Activists from the sixties," Janet Lim answered. One of the older members turned to Jeffrey Su, a newer and younger member, and told him that he had "missed out not being around in that era." "People cared then," Lim said, and another person added, "They had ideals."

The founding members were generally in their thirties and forties in the early 1990s. Reflecting the general membership of primarily Chinese and Japanese Americans and long-established residents of the area, the executive board in 1989 consisted of six Chinese and four Japanese Americans. Three of the Chinese Americans were immigrants, and all of the Japanese Americans were native-born. They brought the knowledge, skills, networks, and resources necessary to build an active club. For example, Fred Hong was part of the Pacific Leadership Council, a Los Angeles-based, Asian American, fund-raising and lobbying organization that had raised nearly $1.2 million in 1988 (Espiritu 1992, p. 134) and actively lobbied in Washington, D.C., in support of the 1990 Immigration Act. Other members have held fund-raisers for local politicians, Latinos as well as Asian Americans, in addition to a fund-raiser Mike Eng and Judy Chu organized for the former California State Attorney General John Van De Kamp, a Democrat, in his run for the governorship in 1990. With political and organizing experience, the group has also been helpful in supplying skilled labor for organizing and the day-to-day running of campaigns for local candidates. Because full membership, including voting privileges on club matters, is restricted to registered Democrats, however, few Republicans and non-citizens are active in the club, although anyone may join.

Very much aware of the political potential of the immigrants, club activities include Asian American voter registration drives carried out with the Asian Pacific American Legal Center and Southwest Voter Registration Education Project. Working toward the goal of political empowerment, the Asian Pacific Democratic Club backed Judy Chu in one of her first electoral victories, a seat on the Garvey School Board, which governs elementary schools in San Gabriel, Rosemead, and Monterey Park. The club also met with the area's state senator, assembly person, and member of Congress, all Latinos, to encourage the hiring of Asian Americans and Pacific Islanders to help officials keep abreast of community issues. The group fought against the English-only initiative in Monterey Park and sponsored forums for candidates for the Alhambra School Board, the Monterey Park City Council, and the Los Angeles County Supervisorial District.

Club involvement in local elections was an important step in establishing new organizations to replace groups that had been white-dominated. As one founding member stressed, "If Asian Americans can't focus their political power and get tenure for Don Nakanishi and get Barry Hatch out of office, then I might as well forget it. . . . we have to show results, otherwise what are we doing as a club? As Asian Americans in the political process?"

Non-Asian American grass-roots groups, and elected officials who recognized the growing political force of the immigrant population and want to tap into it, looked to the Asian Pacific Democratic Club. During its early years, the group was continually approached by local political organizations that wanted to hold joint events. The Monterey Park Democratic Club, a liberal group that has a majority of white members, offered assistance when the Asian Pacific Democratic Club wrote its charter, and a strong relationship has endured between the two groups. Joint events are also common with the San Gabriel Valley chapter of the League of United Latin American Citizens.

Recognizing the importance of coalitions in a multiracial community, Mike Eng said during a joint meeting between the league and the Asian Pacific Democratic Club, "During the 1970s we went back to our communities to work on political empowerment. To some degree, we've been successful. Now, we understand the need to go beyond that, to build coalitions, to build our power base. Otherwise, we'll be fighting each other, and we won't be effective."

Case 3: Monterey Park City Council Elections, 1988, 1990, and 1994

Monterey Park council races are generally hotly contested; the city has a long history of community activism even though the council positions are part-time and members receive only nominal payments for their services. Some candidates see a council seat as a step toward higher office because a number of elected officials in the region began their careers there. Two local members of Congress—Matthew Martinez and George Brown—and a former state senator, Alfred Song, had once been council members.

In the 1988 city council election, voters could cast two votes for the two seats up for election. Significantly, in that climate of racial tension and slow growth, Judy Chu received the highest number of votes. Running a campaign that stressed her extensive involvement in community groups and political experience as an elected official on a local school board, she was able to gain widespread support. A professor at a local university, she was viewed as someone who would provide thoughtful, competent, and professional leadership at a critical period marked by heated rhetoric.[10]

Recognizing the need for economic development in a city facing declining tax revenues, Chu established a position between development and no-growth forces and promised in her campaign literature to "reduce traffic congestion and upgrade the quality of development." Realizing that she was cutting off a major source of potential campaign funds from Chinese developers but working to preserve a position of neutrality, Chu "refused to accept developers' money for her campaign" and limited campaign contributions to $200. Unlike the other candidates, who focused primarily on development, she also took a strong position against racial conflict. She emphasized the need for "positive community leadership" and her desire to "improve community relations." "It is time to heal the wounds that have divided our city," she urged. Chu never had to make explicit ethnic or racial appeals to Chinese or other Asian Americans to capitalize on her ancestry. Her name, appearance, and well-known history of community work made that obvious, and such appeals would have alienated many non-Asians.

The second council seat was won by Betty Couch, a member of the slow-growth Residents Association of Monterey Park group who had a long history of involvement in community activities, including membership on the parks and recreation commission. She had added visibility through her family's local business and because her husband was a former member of the council. An important part of her effort involved extensive grass-roots campaigning and meeting voters face to face by precinct-walking and attending community events.

John Horton's (1989, p. 585) analysis of election exit poll data found that race—compared to gender, income, age, party affiliation, or education—was the most significant indicator (at the .01 level) of voting preference in 1988. By substantial margins, whites, Latinos, and Asian Americans voted in the largest numbers for candidates of their own race.[11] Despite tremendous differences within and between each group, a remarkable 89 percent of Chinese Americans and 75 percent of Japanese Americans voted for Chu (table 5). Demonstrating that it was a vote for qualified representation rather than an automatic racial or ethnic vote for a Chinese American candidate, only 22 percent of Chinese Americans and 2 percent of Japanese Americans voted for Victoria Wu. Wu, a Chinese American immigrant, had performed poorly at candidate forums, and it was clear that she did not match Chu in terms of experience in local politics, education, and overall professionalism. Although Wu was the second choice of Chinese Americans voters, her strength was primarily among newer immigrants—whose voting patterns show a stronger emphasis on voting along ethnic lines than native-born Chinese Americans—and a much lower percentage of Chinese Americans voted for her than for Chu (Horton 1995).

Party registration has little effect on voting patterns because of crossover party voting compared to the issues and qualifications of the candidates (Santillan and Subervi-Velez 1991). Although data for party affiliation on an individual level were not available, information was collected for Chinese and Japanese voters as a group (table 5). The nonpartisan council election in 1988 showed that crossover voting is common among

Table 5. Voter Profile by Race and Ethnicity: City Council Election, Monterey Park, April 12, 1988

	Chinese American	Japanese American	Latino	White	Total Number of Votes and Position
Candidates					
Arcuri	2%	2%	8%	11%	622/6th
Balderrama	17	21	63	17	2,129/4th
Briglio	15	19	19	14	1,489/5th
Chu	89	75	35	30	3,594/1st
Couch	12	28	19	45	2,874/2d
Ristic	8	22	15	45	2,486/3d
Wu	22	2	1	1	530/7th
Voter characteristics					
Foreign-born	73	6	15	9	
College degree	71	42	28	41	
Income $50,000+	51	46	31	33	
Party affiliation					
Republican	45	30	16	35	
Democrat	24	60	80	59	
Independent/none	30	10	4	6	
Respondents (N)	397	247	216	266	

Sources: Southwest Voter Research Institute, Monterey Park, Calif., exit poll, April 12, 1988, for the Asian Pacific American Voter Registration Project, cited in Horton (1989) and Fong (1994); Monterey Park municipal election final precinct returns, 1988.

Note: Because voters could cast up to two votes, percentages do not total 100.

Asian Americans. Republicans and those voting as independents or having no parties voted for Chu in large numbers.

Whereas Japanese Americans, most of whom were native-born, saw Chu's U.S. nativity positively, some recent Chinese immigrants criticized her for "not really being Chinese" because she was culturally American. For example, she was not fluent in any of the Chinese languages. Citing her strong educational background and professional career and the need for a Chinese representative, however, Chu was strongly supported by two Chinese-language newspapers that served the Chinese immigrant population and represented a wide range of political views. Clearly, the issue of Chinese American representation in this period of heightened tension surrounding growth and racial conflict transcended intraethnic differences.

Chu won through significant interracial support and had 30 percent of the white vote and 35 percent of the Latino vote. Horton (1989) suggests that although Latinos, long-term residents of the community, supported slow growth they also recognized the city's history of racial discrimination and the fact that the discrimination was linked to controlled growth. In addition, Chu was known among Latinos for her work with their organizations and issues, and some, such as Jose Calderon, were active in her campaign. The 1988 vote for Chu, along with people's comments about discrimination, suggests that Latinos understand the common links between Asian Americans and themselves. Yet the evidence is still weak, and the link is not as explicitly or strongly expressed as it is in the alliance between Asian Americans and Latinos on the issue of redistricting.

The city council election in 1990 followed a similar pattern.[12] In that contest, an exit poll showed that race was the best predictor of candidate choice, as it was in 1988. Samuel Kiang, Fred Balderrama, and Marie Purvis won seats on the council, finishing in that order, and each candidate's highest vote percentage came from their own ethnic groups. Balderrama received 67 percent of the Latino vote, Purvis received 53 percent of the white vote, and Kiang received 90 percent of the Chinese American ballots (table 6).

As the 1988 and 1990 exit polls indicate (tables 5 and 6), Japanese American voters are remarkably similar to white voters, except for higher levels of income, in that most are native-born. In fact, the percentage of immigrants was higher among whites than Japanese Americans, a majority were Democrats, and there were lower levels of education than among Chinese American voters. Japanese American voters in 1990 strongly favored slow growth (called Measure S on the ballot), as did white voters. Unlike the 1988 poll, which contained no questions of opinion, the 1990 poll asked several, and Japanese American attitudes opposing public fund-

Table 6. Voter Profile by Race and Ethnicity: City Council Election, Monterey Park, April 10, 1990

	Chinese American	Japanese American	Latino	White	Total Number of Votes and Position
Candidates					
Balderrama	36%	44%	67%	45%	3,390/2d
Barron	19	37	47	42	2,655/4th
Hatch	10	25	19	37	1,907/6th
Kiang	90	69	30	40	3,880/1st
Purvis	26	34	48	53	2,992/3d
Reichenberger	15	36	21	44	2,473/5th
Voter characteristics					
Foreign-born	74	1	20	6	
College degree	66	43	23	36	
Income $50,000+	54	50	31	35	
Party affiliation					
Republican	47	37	15	35	
Democrat	22	59	80	59	
None	22	1	3	3	
Measure S (slow growth)					
Yes	51	70	65	67	
No	22	15	19	19	
No vote/no response	27	15	16	14	
Bilingual education					
Yes	68	40	57	41	
No	20	45	29	46	
Undecided	7	11	11	12	
Respondents (*N*)	239	131	255	349	

Source: Horton and Tseng (1990).

Note: Because voters could cast up to three votes, percentages do not total 100.

ing of bilingual education were shown to resemble those of whites more than those of Chinese Americans.

Japanese Americans diverged from whites, however, in their vote for political representation and strong support of Chu and Kiang. As one Nisei explained his vote for Chu, "I would prefer a Japanese American, but she's the next best thing." Another discussed his support for Lily Chen, noting that she promised to represent all Asian Americans: "I backed her . . . and I said, all right, if that's what you say you're going to do, and you're going to stick up not only for the Chinese, but for all the Asians, that's including the Filipinos, Samoans, Japanese, whatever." Explaining the importance of race and also the practical concerns of backing a viable candidate, a Nisei said, "She's Asian. Color makes a difference. Because what I face, she faces. You know I don't want to support her just because she's of Asian background. If she was an asshole and can't be elected, there is no use in supporting a person like that."

Political necessity required Japanese Americans and Chinese Americans to pool their resources and support an Asian American candidate. Each group by itself was too small to constitute an effective voting block. In 1989 Chinese Americans were only 23.1 percent of the registered voters in the city, and Japanese Americans were only 12.6 percent. Chinese Americans composed 59.6 percent, and Japanese Americans 32.5 percent, of Asian American voters (Nakanishi 1991). With all Asian American voters (including small but growing numbers of Korean and Vietnamese Americans) combined totaling 38.8 percent of those who were registered, not only was it necessary for Asian groups to join forces but they also needed to support a candidate who would also receive white and Latino votes. Yet support for the Chinese American candidates was high among all Asian Americans because of the need for group representation.

An analysis of campaign contributions for Asian American candidates further illustrates the growing institutionalization of a political base among Asian Americans in Monterey Park. When Alfred Song was elected to the city council in 1960 Asian Americans contributed to his campaign but were not a strong force in it, as he has mentioned. His accounting showed contributions of $1,387 in amounts ranging from $1 to $200, similar to other candidates in that election. Judging from the surnames of the forty-six individuals and organizations donating money, nine (21 percent) were Asian American.[13] In terms of the total amount of money, $217 was from Asian Americans—16 percent.

A contrast is found in the example of Judy Chu. According to her financial statements, her 1988 campaign for city council was unlike Song's. Current regulations require that only contributions of $100 or more need be noted, and 114 individuals and organizations were listed. Again judging from surnames, 102 (89 percent) of the contributors were Asian American. A total of $14,698 was contributed, $13,148 (89 percent) of it from Asian Americans. Those totals, however, are from the listed individual contributors, and Chu's total campaign contributions were substantially higher—$34,233. Judging from attendance at fund-raisers, much of her monetary support from white and Latino sources might be in these figures, although even at these events Asian Americans were in the majority or provided the majority of contributions under $100.[14]

A deracialized campaign strategy is necessary in districts with multiracial electorates to attract all voters (McCormack and Jones 1993; Underwood 1995). Even though candidates in Monterey Park stress issues that have broad-based appeal and do not focus on racially specific issues, that fact does not reveal who supplies campaign resources—the candidates' base of support. Politicians may use a deracialized strategy, but their campaigns may be funded primarily by a particular racial or ethnic group. And, once in office, they must be responsive to the issues and concerns of that group to retain its support. Song, a city council member when Asian Americans were a tiny percentage of the electorate and the general population, had to respond to a very different population than Chu, who held office when Asian Americans were the major funders of her campaign and constituted a significant and growing percentage of the electorate.

In the 1994 city council election, three incumbents—Samuel Kiang, Fred Balderrama, and Marie Purvis—were up for reelection. Balderrama and Purvis won, along with Francisco Alonso, and Kiang lost. Alonso, a resident since 1970 and a former teacher whose parents were immigrants from Spain, was a newcomer to politics and had little experience besides his time on the library's board of trustees. He ran a campaign based on walking precincts and making contact with voters.

First elected in 1990, Kiang appealed to voters because of his work experience as an engineer at the prestigious NASA Jet Propulsion Laboratory and his impressive education credentials. Kiang had master's degrees in business administration and engineering and a law degree from schools in the Los Angeles area. In a city struggling with racial conflict and budget problems, voters saw him as being able to bring his considerable technical and legal expertise to city affairs. A fourteen-year resident of the city, he was relatively unknown during the campaign but managed to establish an image of being a concerned citizen who wanted to serve his community and had participated in a successful effort to remove a state parole office from his neighborhood in 1989.

Significantly, in 1990 voters showed disapproval of Hatch's divisive rhetoric and support of anti-immigrant and English-only issues. He was the lowest vote-getter among all racial and ethnic groups, including whites (table 6).

What proved fatal for Kiang's reelection hopes was a shift in perception among long-established residents regarding his constituency. In 1990 he was seen as an engineer and lawyer who would help all residents by applying his vast training and experience to the complex problems faced by the city, but by 1994 many viewed him as representing primarily the new Chinese immigrants. Contributing to that image were controversies in 1991 over the firing of the city manager, Mark Lewis, and the process of hiring bilingual dispatchers for the emergency telephone system. The city's personnel board had rejected the council's decision to pay bilingual operators more than those who were monolingual. Kiang, stressing the need to hire bilingual operators as quickly as possible in a city with many immigrants, proposed that the council should be granted the power of veto over personnel board decisions. That angered individuals who valued resident input in city affairs.

In a separate matter several months later, the city council voted to fire Lewis, a decision based on issues involving matters of hiring and salary raises and the fact that four of nine department heads had resigned in an eight-month period. Kiang strongly opposed the firing, however, partly because of Lewis's strong record in hiring Chinese. Indeed, Chinese residents carried out several demonstrations in front of city hall to protest the firing of Lewis and the delayed hiring of bilingual operators. During that period Kiang was seen as championing the Chinese. At the same time, Chu's initial support for following city procedures in dealing with the personnel board was misinterpreted as opposition to bilingual operators, and her vote for firing Lewis was seen as evidence of not being a strong advocate of Chinese issues. Working to rebuild support among the Chinese immigrant community, she held a meeting and press conference in July 1991 to highlight the projects she had developed and document her long history with, and strong support of, the Chinese community.

Thus, in the 1994 election, although Kiang made an effort to walk daily and reach all voters as he had before the 1990 contest, his campaign was unsuccessful. As Ronald Wong—a Chinese American political consultant who helped on Kiang's campaign—said, Kiang had worked hard on the council to represent all members of the community. One example of his involvement were his efforts at negotiating a compromise when the Los Angeles Archdiocese planned to replace a white priest who had strong ties to the Latino community with a priest whom Latino parishioners felt was being brought in to develop ties with the Chinese community. Being the majority of the church members, they were upset by the lack of parishioner input into the process. According to Wong, Kiang played an important part in the discussions that followed and strongly supported the Latino church members. Yet the voters overlooked such efforts.

In a city where the majority of voters are not Chinese and where ethnic and racial tensions are still strong, a candidate must have a wide cross-section of support to win an election. Chu stressed that fact after her reelection in 1992: "The strength of a leader is in their ability to represent everybody. This an extremely important issue to people who are not Chinese, especially because of the ethnic feelings here" (Chang 1992, p. J8). Although the Chinese immigrant community was growing rapidly, in terms of voting power it was still unable to elect candidates on its own. Kiang's chances were further damaged by a Chinese- and English-language mailer sent to voters to warn them about the penalties of voter fraud using absentee ballots. The literature was later linked to a development company that wanted to open a gambling club in Monterey Park, something Kiang heavily opposed (Horton 1995).

Conclusion

The political efforts illustrated in the three case studies were marked by a broad range of grass-roots activities that included newly arrived immigrants who volunteered on campaigns or showed support by filling the council chambers during public hearings, permanent residents and citizens who donated money, and voter registration and get-out-the-vote efforts.

Cultural construction and collective memory are part of the process whereby established residents and new immigrants develop an identity using historical and contemporary issues to create a sense of group membership and a basis for political mobilization. Such an identity emerges from the activities, networks, and cultural practices of everyday life and the broader economic and local and national political context. The cultural content of racial and ethnic identities is continually transformed as individual, regional, and national histories are added, reinterpreted, refashioned, and combined with contemporary issues to support and legitimate political movements (Lipsitz 1988). Asian Americans are united by discrimination. Whether through individual projects such as Michael Eng organizing attendance at public hearings or group efforts such as the Chinese American Civil Rights and Education Foundation's forum on language restrictions on commercial signs, both new immigrants and established Asian Americans need to inform themselves about the legal and political means available to fight discrimination.

The peak years of activity for the West San Gabriel Valley Asian Pacific Democratic Club were during the late 1980s and early 1990s. Since then, the group has grown inactive and holds meetings and forums only occasionally. Yet the club provided a site for the political education and training of its members and a base for establishing relationships with other organizations. Such political skills and the community relationships that were established will live beyond the organization's existence. The history of the group illustrates the problems of Asian American political organizations—they come and go. It also illustrates the overall growth of Asian American politics in the region. The group was organized to fill a void: to establish Asian American networks and a political base.

The rise of new political organizations such as the Taiwanese American Citizens League and the Chinese American Political Action Committee that can be linked into local and Los Angeles networks extends the original mission of the Asian Pacific Democratic Club. The establishment of the political consulting, fund-raising, and legislative advocacy firm of Lang, Murakawa, and Wong in the San Gabriel Valley in 1994 (the office moved to downtown Los Angeles in 1997) is also an affirmation of the growing presence and professionalization of Asian American politics in the region.

The support and involvement of Asian American individuals and groups on issues and political campaigns establishes common ground, builds links, and forms bonds of trust, both interethnically and (in the case of whites and Latinos who supported Chu and Kiang) interracially. Kiang's failure to maintain interracial support was a major factor in his defeat in 1994. Assistance from groups from around Los Angeles County—such as the Asian Pacific Legal Center—that can provide expertise and resources for efforts in the San Gabriel Valley and encourage the establishment of networks and organizations is critical for the next stage in politics: combining panethnic politics with interracial alliances in the case of redistricting.

Asian American Political Issues

Reflecting the heterogeneity of Asian Americans, their political activities are affected by their widely divergent histories, ideologies, and experiences. In this chapter, I will examine the relevance of a range of issues for Asian American politics: campaign financing, voting patterns, gender, political partisanship, and class.

The "Yellow Peril" Revisited: Money, Politics, and the Perpetual Outsider

The controversy over campaign contributions from Asian nationals to the Democratic National Committee (DNC) erupted during the 1996 presidential race and received widespread media coverage before and after the election. Considering the importance of Asian capital in the restructuring of the San Gabriel Valley's economy and the fact that major figures discussed in the press, such as John Huang and James Riady, have lived and worked in Los Angeles raises questions about the role Asian capital has played in Valley politics.

On the national scene, clearly there were illegal donations, at minimum money with origins suspicious enough that the Democratic National Committee had returned about $1.5 million by the end of 1996 (Miller 1996). The critical point for Asian Americans, however, is how Republicans and the media focused on donations from Asians and ignored illegal contributions from non-Asians. It was a clear demonstration of the national conversation that constructs and defines the categories of "good immigrant" and "loyal American." Civil rights attorneys Stewart Kwoh and Dale Minami have characterized press coverage as "a mixture of 'yellow peril' and 'yellow journalism'" (Kwoh and Minami 1996, p. 7).

Republicans who used the issue to criticize Democrats and President Bill Clinton acted without fear of reprisal or political costs, understanding that the "foreignness of Asians" is a theme that continues to resonate as it has throughout history, according to an Asian American on the staff of a member of Congress from Los Angeles. In a voice filled with anger and concern, she explained that the current attack was similar to the way she thought Republicans have traditionally manipulated and racialized campaign issues, linking African Americans with crime and welfare and Latinos with illegal immigration. In addition, the categories of "American" and "foreign" create an artificial distinction between domestic and international concerns by ignoring the fact that some individuals live and work in the United States yet maintain familial and business ties throughout the world.

As Asian Americans begin to make major political inroads in the continental United States—as witnessed by the election of the first Asian American governor outside of Hawaii in 1996 (Gary Locke of Washington, a Chinese American) and the growing numbers of organizations and elected officials in the San Gabriel Valley—lumping money donated legally by Asian Americans with money donated illegally by Asian nationals conflates the groups and taints the political progress of Asian Americans.

In a letter sent to major newspapers across the country, Stewart Kwoh and other Asian American leaders discussed coverage of the donations and criticized accounts that negligently failed to distinguish between Asian nationals and Asian Americans. At a news conference, Kwoh declared, "There is an unprecedented attack on Asian Americans in the United States today." The letter stated: "Your [the media's] stories questioning the motives behind campaign contributions made by non-American entities, including Indonesian and South Korean companies, have irresponsibly linked these non-American interests to the political agenda of the Asian Pacific American community. . . . (the stories failed to provide) critical context to the alleged wrongdoings of non-American entities (and) casts suspicion and personal ridicule on individuals who have helped us become a political force" (Kang 1996, p. A11).

Although Asian nationals and companies were the source of contributions in question, Asian Americans became targets of suspicion, as President Clinton observed in a news conference on November 8, 1996: "In the last few weeks, a lot of Asian Americans who have supported our campaign have come up to me and said, 'You know, I'm being made to feel like a criminal. All these people are calling me. I say, "Why are you calling me?" They say, "Because you have an Asian last name"'" (Wu 1996, p. 11). Concerned over political fallout from the media portrayal of the contributions, the National Asian Pacific American Legal Consortium, Asian Pacific American Labor Alliance, Japanese American Citizens League, and Organization of Chinese Americans criticized Clinton's failure to appoint an Asian American to his newly formed cabinet in 1996 and in a press statement on December 20 expressed hope that the controversy over foreign contributions had not entered into the appointment process.

David Lang is co-founder of Lang, Murakawa and Wong, a public affairs, political consulting, fund-raising, and legislative advocacy firm that has raised money for the successful campaigns of Asian American candidates in Southern California as well as Mabel Teng's victorious 1994 campaign for San Francisco supervisor and Gary Locke's gubernatorial race. Lang also worked on Michael Woo's failed mayoral campaign in 1993 that raised about $2.6 million from Asian Americans across the country, more than half of Woo's $5.5 million budget. Lang mentioned that intense media coverage over donations had negatively affected a Los Angeles fund-raising event for Locke. The event was successful, however, and more than two hundred people participated. As he explained, "There were people who were committed to attend the fund-raising banquet for Gary Locke. Before the event, they received phone calls from reporters asking about their status in the U.S., if they had green cards. These were people who wanted to help Asian Americans in politics, but after receiving this sort of harassment, they didn't want unnecessary trouble in their lives and they did not attend." Lang pointed out that Asian Americans need a strong national organization and spokespersons, "a figure like Jesse Jackson" who can command attention and counter media attacks. As Charles Woo, another organizer, said, "Just because of my last name, they (journalists) question which country I'm from and question my patriotism. . . . That's totally uncalled for. . . . For many others, it would be very intimidating" (Iritani 1996, p. A3).

John Huang, at the center of the fund-raising controversy, was born in China, grew up in Taiwan, and came to the United States in 1969. His major San Gabriel Valley connection was a rally and fund-raising dinner that he arranged during Clinton's 1992 campaign. Held in the city of San Gabriel at a large Chinese restaurant in a new shopping mall built with Chinese capital and filled with Chinese businesses, the event raised $250,000. According to the *Los Angeles Times* (1996, p. A1), it was the largest such function for a presidential candidate among Asian Americans in the Los Angeles area. Huang worked in financial institutions, was appointed a deputy assistant secretary in the Department of Commerce in

1994, and became a fund-raiser for the Democratic National Committee in 1995. Concentrating on Asian Americans, he was extremely successful and raised millions of dollars.

Because they were cast as villains in the fund-raising affair and linked with Asia, the work Huang and others had done for Asian Americans was ignored. For example, he, Fred Hong, and Maria Hsia (an immigrant from Taiwan who was named in the January 1, 1989, *Los Angeles Times* as one of the city's major figures because of her fund-raising activities) were co-chairs of the Pacific Leadership Council, which had won the Legal Impact Award from the Asian Pacific American Legal Center of Southern California in 1991. The council was honored for lobbying work on the Immigration Act of 1990, on behalf of which it played "major roles in bolstering the provisions that allow families to reunite under our new immigration law" (Asian Pacific American Legal Center 1991b, p. 5).

Jeffrey Su worked for the council from April 1989 until September 1991, performing administrative work and participating in a lobbying trip to Washington, D.C., on behalf of the act. He and I were co-chairs of the West San Gabriel Valley Asian Pacific Democratic Club, and he told me, "John Huang was a real decent person. He wasn't in it for the personal accolades, he was trying to do work to help the community. The lobbying work we did in Washington was possible in part by the work he did to establish relations with people there."

The council's important work on the immigration bill was acknowledged at one of the West San Gabriel Valley Asian Pacific Democratic Club's meetings. During a break in club business, members gathered to read the July 13, 1989, *Congressional Record* and praise club member Fred Hong for the important work his organization had performed. The *Record* carried a statement by Sen. Alan K. Simpson (R.-Wyo.), who said of the effect of Asian American lobbying on the Kennedy-Simpson immigration bill, "The pressures are tremendous. . . . never before has the Asian community been so galvanized. . . . I am going to give them a grade A."

Ling-Chi Wang has written (1996, p. 7) that the money Huang raised was used to gain political access and influence on foreign issues rather than on matters of concern to Asian Americans: "There is no indication that the big foreign contributors have any interest whatsoever in the concerns and welfare of Asian Americans." Although John Huang was affected by racism toward Asians, Wang argues that he was implicated by the "corrupt system of moneyed politics." Yet Huang's efforts did help Asian Americans, although Wang's analysis of the fund-raising controversy highlights the importance of money in politics. Money and influence were key issues in Monterey Park; the strength of the slow-growth movement in the 1980s and city propositions that called for a moratorium on growth could both encourage developers to back pro-growth candidates.

One question concerns whether money from illegal sources has been funneled into Monterey Park City Council campaigns through legal donors. Although it is impossible to ascertain that information by examining candidates' campaign statements, some residents believed that questionable contributions did occur. Tim Fong (1994, p. 122) mentions that during Lily Chen's (who was seen as pro-growth) failed reelection campaign, "Chen had been the direct target of considerable ugliness during the campaign; under the caption 'Chen's Laundry,' grotesque caricatures of her washing dollar bills against a backdrop of banks with names in Chinese characters had been widely circulated."

The problem is that perfectly legitimate contributions are also scrutinized. Although the Democratic and Republican parties fund congressional candidates around the country, when Asian Americans do the same thing, recognizing the symbolic and material importance of electing Asian American officials, the propriety of such actions is questioned. As Lily Chen said while running for Congress in 1988, "I've been receiving support from New York to San Francisco. You know, I have financial contributions from all over the place, just like March Fong Eu and S. P. Wu and many other Asian American candidates. So I am sure it is going to be used against me. [However] I'm just proud of it. . . . And how would that translate in terms of actual dollars? I still have more dollars from the local area than outside. It will be an issue. I'm sure that my opposition will use that" (Horton 1988).

The money donated in Monterey Park campaigns is minuscule compared to the millions of dollars discussed in the Democratic National Committee affair. What is important is the point Ling-Chi Wang has raised about the power of money to buy access to, and influence with, politicians. Contributions from immigrants who are permanent residents of the United States and from U.S. businesses owned by Asian nationals are legal, and such contributions have entered politics in the San Gabriel Valley. Campaign contributions have escalated in recent years. The question is, How important are such contributions?

Monterey Park City Council races are held separately from state or national elections, and only local matters are on the ballot. Only motivated voters go to the polls, and the elections generally have a small turnout.[1] Direct contact, preferably by the candidate walking precincts or by telephone, has proved to be the most effective way of reaching potential voters. The advantages of incumbency—name recognition and fund-raising—can be offset by grass-roots campaigning. In fact, in order to avoid offending voters, candidates have to be careful to ensure that their campaigns are seen as community efforts and not ones funded by big-spending developers and outside interests. While volunteering at Sam Kiang's 1990 campaign headquarters, for example, I talked with a campaign manager who said they had to be aware of how they used contributions and what image they projected. "They wouldn't want things to backfire, making it look like there were a lot of outside influences involved in Sam's campaign," she said. Looking around the small, sparsely furnished room, she added, "This place is just right, you don't want a place that looks like too much."

In a discussion of the controversy over Asian contributions and the importance of money in Monterey Park elections, Joe Rubin, co-founder of the Residents Association of Monterey Park, a slow-growth group, said, "Give me $12,000, and I'll run a winning campaign—there's only so much you can spend in a small city like Monterey Park." Radio and television advertising, the big-budget items in campaigns covering larger geographic regions, are ineffective in races in smaller communities. Direct mailings are used but can backfire if they give the impression of a slick, moneyed campaign. Therefore, although money for campaigns is definitely useful, it has its limitations. As David Lang explained, "Every candidate needs to raise enough money to run a campaign, but it's more complicated than just raising money. You have to run an effective campaign. You have to target the right voters."

An example of the negative repercussions large contributions can have for candidates not well established in a community is the case of Charles Kim, who raised $96,000 from Korean Americans throughout Southern California for a 1990 city council race in Cerritos, nearly double the combined total of the other twelve candidates (Fuetsch 1990). In a city of 53,240, 45 percent of whom are Asian American, Kim was defeated. Voters viewed him as a carpetbagger because he had moved to the city a year before the election and most of his donations came from outside the city. In contrast, Tony Lam was elected to the city council of the Orange County city of Westminster in 1992. Lam, the first Vietnamese American elected official in the United States, according to *Asian Week*, stresses the importance of going door to door and making contact with voters, "There's nothing better than to talk one-on-one with the voter. People like it that way. They want to see down-to-earth candidates" (Eljera 1996, p. 14).

A survey of Monterey Park campaigns involving Latino and Asian American candidates in the 1980s and 1990s reveals the inconsistent effects of money and incumbency. In 1982 Lily Chen, David Almada, and Rudy Peralta were victorious while raising $29,273, $6,384, and $8,347 respectively. In comparison, the defeated incumbents Harry Couch and Irv Gilman raised $6,383 and $4,123. Conflict over growth issues in a 1986 campaign that had strong racial overtones led to the defeat of the three incumbents despite their substantial fund-raising efforts. Barry Hatch, Chris Houseman, and Patricia Reichenberger—the winning, white, slow-growth candidates—raised $4,253, $11,969, and $2,964 compared to $65,907 for Chen, $26,852 for Almada, and $21,087 for Peralta.

Recognizing the racist and vicious attacks on Lily Chen and valid resident concerns about the influence of developers, Judy Chu refused money from developers and limited contributions. She won easily in 1988, and her contributions outdistanced those of her competitors by a wide margin. She raised $34,973 while the other winner, Betty Couch, raised $6,196. The defeated incumbent, Cam Briglio, raised $26,458, and Fred Balderrama raised $13,057 for his losing effort.

Sam Kiang raised $42,844 for his successful 1990 campaign. With declining city tax revenues an issue, pro-business candidates Fred Balderrama and Marie Purvis were also elected in 1990 and raised $30,230 and $9,654, respectively. They defeated incumbents Barry Hatch and Patricia Reichenberger, who raised $4,735 and $19,454.

The 1992 elections clearly demonstrated the limitations of money, Latino and white voters' fears of growing Asian American power, and the importance of grass-roots campaigning and having a local track record. Bonnie Wai, the candidate who raised the most contributions ($64,238), lost by a wide margin, but Rita Valenzuela won although she had raised one of the lowest amounts ($15,091). She used an extensive door-to-door campaign and capitalized on her extremely strong record of community service, matched only by the other winner, the incumbent Chu.[2] The 1994 election marked the surprise defeat of another incumbent, Kiang, who had received the largest amount of contributions, $55,443, nearly eight times that of Francisco Alonso, who won with $7,025. Incumbents Fred Balderrama and Marie Purvis, who also won, raised $47,130 and $14,802.

The unsung heroes of community politics in places such as the San Gabriel Valley are the volunteers who labor behind the scenes to support issues and candidates (McCarthy and Wolfson 1997; Oliver and Marwell 1992). Although Latinos and Asian Americans are aware of long-standing racist barriers that have hindered their efforts to integrate themselves into society, that knowledge does not translate into do-nothing cynicism.

Instead, they believe the system that has worked to disfranchise can be altered to enfranchise. The hope and beliefs that fueled the civil rights movement of the 1960s continue in Monterey Park's residents' grass-roots activism. As Richard Martinez of the Southwest Voter Registration Education Project has observed, "Organizations like ours have to depend on a feeling on the part of people that there is a higher good in politics, that there is a real important principle at work—the principle of inclusion, the principle of consent of the governed. The volunteers will work and work very hard for an effort that they believe in. All the money in the world cannot buy that kind of heart and soul, those feet and hours and stamina, and a person who believes can defeat odds that under normal circumstances they shouldn't have" (Curran 1991, p. 35).

Judy Chu's most important asset for an electorate that often rejects incumbents is a reputation for integrity, professionalism, and honesty. That reputation is enhanced and sustained by individuals who volunteer time and resources to spread their belief in her throughout the community. The January 17, 1997, reception marking her third campaign for city council was attended by many who had helped Chu win the two previous campaigns. Although the volunteers had to manage full-time jobs and child care, their interest in community affairs and support for Chu motivated them, and they were there to pitch in again. School teachers such as Carol Ono and Linda Tubach were helping with organization and planning, and Bob McClosky, a union worker, handled the effort to assemble hundreds of campaign signs and pound them into lawns.

In addition to direct contributions to campaigns, Monterey Park business interests have sent out political mailers during elections. The effect of doing so is difficult to ascertain, however, because the mailers have paralleled major voter sentiments. In the 1982 city council election (with three seats up for election) several political mailers that endorsed Lily Chen, David Almada, and Rudy Peralta—seen as sympathetic to developer and business interests and who would go on to win the election—were mailed. Although supporters of the two slow-growth incumbents who lost the election—Irv Gilman and Harry Couch—pointed to the mailers as a major factor in the election, the men were vulnerable because of earlier support for a proposal to study gambling as a way of producing city revenue. There were also problems over salary negotiations with police and fire department employees. Chen, Almada, and Peralta were endorsed by the Monterey Park Police Officers Association and, as city manager Lloyd de Llamas explained, "The combination of the Police Department out campaigning for Lily, David, and Rudy, concern with card rooms and crime, plus a message of quality development without racism, is what turned the election" (Fong 1994, p. 93).

Supporters of Sam Kiang's reelection attempt in 1994 placed part of the blame for his loss on a mailer sent out in Chinese and English to warn of the penalties for voter fraud and misuse of mail-in ballots, although Kiang's popularity had already declined and the mailer likely had little effect.

In the 1997 city council race, political mailers exploiting the DNC fund-raising controversy attacked incumbent Judy Chu through renderings of $20 bills, reminiscent of the 1986 tactics used against Lily Chen (chapter 1), and the words, "We've had enough of Judy Chu's financial scandals. It's time for a change" (*Los Angeles Times* 1997a). In response, City Clerk David Barron requested that the California Fair Political Practices Commission investigate the flyers' source. The groups purported to have sent them had not filed campaign reports with the city clerk's office, and the flyers lacked campaign committee identification numbers, both violations of campaign law. As Barron explained, "These were very professional mailers produced at considerable expense and targeted to various parts of the community by groups with names that would draw their sympathies." One local activist thought the flyers had been sent by a company whose efforts to gain the right to erect billboards in Monterey Park were soundly defeated in the 1997 election (Measure B, 86 to 14 percent) by a movement Chu spearheaded. The names of the groups on the flyer were fabricated. The local Republican Party, for example, denied being involved with the mailer sent by the "Republican Club." Chu's response was that "these were fictitious groups with names such as the Southern California Senior Citizens Alliance [the name on the flyer with depictions of $20 bills], the Republican Club of Monterey Park and Monterey Park Latino Assn., which all shared one post office box center." Residents ignored the negative mailers, and Chu was returned to office, as was Rita Valenzuela.

Recognizing the importance of money in politics, Jesse Unruh, former speaker of the California State Assembly, once said that "money is the mother's milk of politics" (Flanagan 1994, p. D1). The undue influence of money in politics is a very real concern, and campaign reform continues to be hotly debated. Yet political reality makes money a necessity. Focusing on illegal donations from Asians while ignoring similar contributions from non-Asians and lumping Asians with Asian Americans plays upon and perpetuates the theme of Asian immigrants and Asian Americans as unwanted and evil outsiders in U.S. society.

The keynote speaker at the 1997 banquet of the Pan Asian Lawyers of San Diego was Fred Korematsu, whose 1942 criminal conviction for challenging the World War II evacuation orders was vacated in a landmark civil rights court case in 1983 (Irons 1989). Robert Brownlie, the group's incoming president and also a Japanese American, was inspired by Korematsu's courage in challenging the orders and his legal team's successful effort and emphasized the importance of Asian American political involvement. Donating money, Brownlie said, is what Americans do in politics, and of course Asian Americans do the same. Attacks that question the legitimacy of the political involvement of Asian immigrants and Asian Americans just as their political influence is increasing demonstrate the continuing importance of efforts such as Korematsu's to challenge legal and social barriers to civil rights and enfranchisement.

Exit Polls: Asian American Voting Patterns

Overall, Asian American, Latino, and African American voters favored Bill Clinton in 1992 and 1996, with whites the only group endorsing George Bush. Latinos and Asian Americans showed significant support for Bush and Ross Perot, however, repeating patterns of crossing party lines in elections and demonstrating the ideological and class heterogeneity of the two groups (Nakanishi 1991; Santillan and Subervi-Velez 1991).[3]

The National Asian Pacific American Legal Consortium (NAPALC) coordinated exit polls of Asian Americans around the United States for the 1996 presidential elections. As part of that effort, the Asian Pacific American Legal Center of Southern California conducted polls in Los Angeles County; the Asian Law Caucus polled in San Francisco and Oakland; and the Asian American Legal Defense and Education Fund canvassed in New York City.

The NAPLAC polls show that Asian Americans favored Clinton by a wider margin than given in the *Los Angeles Times*'s exit poll and contradict the Voter News Service poll—hired by the Associated Press, ABC, CBS, NBC, CNN, and other media to conduct a nationwide exit poll (Yip 1996a)—which shows that Asian Americans favored Bob Dole (table 7).

The use of bilingual poll-takers and questionnaire forms and also a much larger sample differentiated NAPALC's methodology from the other two polls. The *Los Angeles Times*'s poll included nearly 123 Asian Americans in California, and the Voter News Service's poll included nearly 170 Asian Americans, compared to NAPALC's poll of more than nine hundred Asian

Table 7. 1996 Presidential Election

	Percentage Who Voted for		
Race/Ethnicity	Clinton	Dole	Perot
NAPALC Poll:			
Asian Americans(Alhambra, Monterey Park)	66	28	4
Asian Americans (Los Angeles County)	61	32	6
Asian Americans (San Francisco, Oakland)	83	9	n.a.
Asian Americans (New York)	71	21	2
Los Angeles Times Poll: California			
Overall	52	38	7
African American	87	6	5
Asian American	53	40	4
Latino	75	18	6
White	42	46	8
Voter News Services Poll: United States			
Overall	49	41	8
African American	84	12	4
Asian American	41	49	9
Latino	70	22	6
White	44	46	8

Sources: Asian American Legal Defense and Education Fund (1996); Asian Law Caucus (1996); Feng and Tang (1997); *Los Angeles Times* exit poll (1996); Voter News Service, *Wall Street Journal* (1996).

Americans in Los Angeles, more than five hundred in San Francisco and Oakland, and more than 3,200 in New York City. The *Los Angeles Times* (which used Spanish-language questionnaires) and Voter News Service polls did not use Asian-language forms or poll-takers.

The NAPALC polls could be criticized methodologically for focusing on four cities rather than sampling the entire country, raising questions about geographical bias. They are likely to offer an accurate picture of the Asian American vote, however, because most Asian Americans live in urban areas, the polls were taken in the major Asian American communities outside of Hawaii (where most Asian Americans are Democrats), poll sites were selected to include a range of Asian American ethnic groups, and the sample size was large. As Larry Shinagawa, principal investigator of the San Francisco poll, commented, "You're going to get more highly educated, mostly native-born, and very English-proficient Asian Americans. The majority of our community is the opposite of that. The majority are foreign-born, bilingual, with limited English skills, and recent arrivals. How can anybody make any statement about the Asian population without having bilingual speakers or forms?" (Yip 1996b, p. 8). "I think we tapped into the true feelings of Asian Americans," Don Nakanishi said (Yip 1996b, p. 8).

Strong support for affirmative action, growing political participation, and the importance of bilingual voting materials were key findings. It was evident that Asian Americans supported affirmative action and had voted strongly against Proposition 209—which was to eliminate affirmative action policies in government and public schools—a confirmation of the predictions of community leaders (table 8). Karen Narasaki, director of NAPALC, commented, "Given the conversations we had with community members throughout the country, we knew there was strong support for affirmative action. Now we have proof that we were right" (Yip 1996b, p. 8).

Supporters of Proposition 209 used Asian Americans as an example of a group that would be discriminated against by affirmative action, and when Asian American organizations such as the Japanese American Citizens League and the NAPALC spoke in favor of affirmative action they were criticized for not reflecting the sentiments of their communities. As Art Takei of the Asian Pacific American Labor Alliance said, "The first thing this is going to do is raise eyebrows and destroy some of the myths that we tend to be conservative and mainstream" (Ha 1996, p. 1). A seventy-one-year-old voter stated as he left the Geen Mun Neighborhood Center, a senior service facility in San Francisco's Chinatown, "I'm Chinese. . . . I voted against Proposition 209 because it is unfair to Chinese. I have more than ten grandchildren and I care about their future, so I voted against 209" (Yip 1996b, p. 8).

African Americans and Latinos also strongly voted against Proposition 209, but it passed because of the strength of white voters in the state (table

Table 8. 1996 California Proposition 209: Anti-Affirmative Action

Race/Ethnicity	Percentage Who Voted	
	Yes	No
NAPALC Poll:		
Asian Americans (Alhambra, Monterey Park)	24.6	75.4
Asian Americans (Los Angeles County)	24	76
Asian Americans (San Francisco, Oakland)	16	84
Los Angeles Times Poll: California		
African American	26	74
Asian American	39	61
Latino	24	76
White	63	37
Los Angeles County	45	55
Overall	54	46

Sources: Asian Law Caucus (1996); Feng and Tang (1997); *Los Angeles Times* exit poll (1996).
Note: NAPALC poll results rounded.

8). The Supreme Court rejected a challenge to the proposition on November 3, 1997, and state and local government agencies began the complex task of interpreting and implementing the resolution (Savage 1997).

Breaking down the Los Angeles region data by ethnic subgroups shows that the highest margin of Chinese Americans voted for Clinton, whereas Vietnamese Americans favored Bob Dole (table 9). Of the Asian Americans polled, 35.7 percent were Democrats, 40.2 percent were Republicans, and 24.1 percent listed no party or "other," continuing the pattern of an electorate divided by political affiliation but united by voting patterns.

In contrast to their support for Dole, Los Angeles–area Vietnamese Americans strongly opposed Proposition 209 and were second only to Korean Americans in their vote against the measure (table 9). In discussions of the vote, Linda Trinh Vo, who studies Asian American politics in Southern California, attributes that apparent contradiction to the distinction Vietnamese American voters make between general ideological themes that guide federal policy and translate into a Republican vote (anticommunism) and local issues that affect their lives in an immediate way (affirmative action). Edward Park suggests that the strong vote against Proposition 209 was the result of extensive campaigning in the Korean American community that included distribution of thousands of information guides and also media coverage.

The 1992 civil unrest was another major factor influencing the vote. Korean Americans believed that city officials abandoned the community, exemplifying the racism shaping government policies and actions. Park (1997) cites a prominent journalist, K. W. Lee, who stated that the event was to the Korean American community what the World War II internment was to Japanese Americans.

Asian American voters are believed to have turned out in record numbers in 1996, according to Don Nakanishi, who observed that "people are be-

Table 9. 1996 NAPALC Polls: Los Angeles Asian Americans—Presidential Election and Proposition 209

Ethnicity	Percentage Who Voted for			Percentage Who Voted	
	Clinton	Dole	Perot	Yes	No
Chinese	65.9	30.2	1.7	27.7	72.3
Filipino	52.2	43.3	3.0	29.0	71.0
Japanese	55.8	28.2	11.6	27.5	72.5
Korean	59.0	30.7	5.7	15.5	84.5
Vietnamese	44.3	49.9	1.2	21.0	79.0

Source: Feng and Tang (1997).

ginning to realize the enormous potential that Asian Pacific Americans have, whether as candidates, contributors, and as voters. This has been a benchmark election by which we have taken things to another level" (Yip 1996b, p. 8). Important factors in the turnout included voter registration and outreach drives by Asian American community organizations, Proposition 209, and the importance of proposed anti-immigrant legislation such as the cancellation of Supplemental Security Income for approximately one million elderly and disabled documented immigrants (of all groups) in the United States and 220,000 in California (McDonnell 1997). "My guess is that a lot of Asian Americans feel threatened because of the anti-immigrant sentiment" commented Larry Shinagawa (Yip 1996b, p. 8). "The study [exit polls] refutes much of the charges of voter apathy among Asian Pacific Americans, and shows that Asian Pacific Americans vote decisively on issues that affect them personally," he said (Asian Law Caucus 1996).

Congressional cutbacks on aid to immigrants, attacks on affirmative action, and the legacy of Proposition 187 (which would have denied services to undocumented immigrants) also sparked a high turnout among Latinos for the November 1996 elections and contributed to unexpected victories. Loretta Sanchez, a Democrat, defeated Robert Dornan, a Republican twelve-term incumbent, for an Orange County congressional seat, for example, and in December 1997 Cruz Bustamante from the agricultural community of Fresno was the first Latino to be elected speaker of the California Assembly. The Southwest Voter Registration Education Project found that 70 percent of registered Latino voters had balloted in the November elections, compared to the statewide average of 65.5 percent (Newton and Gold 1997).

The region's changing demographics were apparent in the historic shift in voting that occurred in the 1997 Los Angeles mayoral race, when for the first time in the city's contemporary history more Latinos voted than African Americans. According to a *Los Angeles Times* poll (1997b), 15 percent of the voters were Latino, 13 percent were African American, 4 percent were Asian American, and 65 were white. "The so-called 'sleeping giant' is finally awake," proclaimed *Los Angeles Times* columnist Frank del Olmo (1997, p. M5).

Thirty-three percent of the Asian Americans polled by NAPALC in Los Angeles were first-time voters, one indication of the growing number of immigrants who become politically active naturalized citizens. As Nakanishi said, "An indicator like this—one-third were first-time voters—shows that this is an election that mattered to Asian Americans. And it even mattered here in L.A. where there was no Asian American running for office" (Yip 1996b, p. 8). Discussing the events with a reporter, Nakanishi has also said that the year had marked a critical turning point for Asian Americans: "I think this election will be remembered as a major political milestone for the API population because of the extremely high turnout of voters, the inordinate and negative media and partisan attention paid to Asian and Asian American campaign contributions, and the election of Gary Locke as governor of Washington, a state which does not have a large API community."

More than half of the Asian Americans surveyed in the NAPALC polls used forms in an Asian language, a demonstration of the critical need to enforce provisions of the Voting Rights Act that require bilingual election material for groups meeting minimum population requirements. "We had people who spoke Chinese, Korean, Tagalog, Vietnamese," Nakanishi commented, "and 53 percent of the people who answered the survey used the questionnaire in languages other than English. This is consistent with what the Asian American electorate looks like in terms of linguistic preferences and gives additional credence to why we need bilingual voter materials and bilingual interpreters" (Yip 1996b, p. 8). Karen Narasaki added, "[Bilingual assistance] makes a difference. We see that in the numbers. This is a policy that we need to defend to make sure that Asian Pacific Americans have a voice in the polls" (Yip 1996b, p. 8).

According to a *Los Angeles Times* exit poll taken in 1994, Asian Americans had voted 53 to 47 percent against Proposition 187. The actual vote was likely larger, considering the number of immigrants among the Asian American population and the methodological problems of sample size and language associated with exit polls. African Americans—although few in California are immigrants—understood the discriminatory provisions of Proposition 187 and also voted 53 to 47 percent against it. The Latino vote was 77 to 23 percent against. Showing the continued dominance of white voters—who voted 63 to 37 percent in favor—the proposition carried, 59 to 41 percent. The implementation of Proposition 187 has been delayed in federal court while its constitutionality is determined.

The title of the *AsianWeek* article that compared the 1996 results of the NAPALC and the Voter News Service polls, "Dueling Data" (Yip 1996a), points out the importance of establishing organizations that can collect data using methods appropriate for the Asian American population. Sample size and language issues are key to gathering data that accurately reflect basic voting trends such as the vote for presidential candidates, and more detailed breakdowns on various ethnic groups within the panethnic category.

Political Campaigns and Representation

Studies of racial and ethnic electoral politics often rely on empirical indicators such as the number of elected officials and the demographic composition of political districts to estimate the political representation, participation, and influence of racial and ethnic groups. In the case of Monterey Park, with its long history of electing ethnic officials, such indicators would miss the transformative impact on politics resulting from the development of Asian American networks and organizations that have transformed raw numbers into a political force.

The number of elected ethnic politicians is at best only a preliminary measurement of political representation. First, it says nothing about a politician's knowledge about, or responsiveness to, racial issues. Population figures and the racial or ethnic identity of politicians reveal little about the political beliefs of elected officials and the political realities of their districts. For example, S. I. Hayakawa, a naturalized citizen from Canada and the former U.S. senator representing California, was a Republican. Yet even though he was Japanese American and represented a state that had a large Asian American population, he cared little about specifically Asian American issues. In fact, Hayakawa opposed redress and reparations for Japanese Americans incarcerated during World War II and supported the official-English movement. When asked his advice for Asian Americans in politics, he responded, "Well, first forget that they are Asian-Americans. . . . One reason for some of the problems we are facing today stems from ethnic politics" (Jo 1980, pp. 161–62).

A deracialized campaign strategy is necessary in districts that have multiracial electorates to attract voters from all racial groups.[4] Ethnic candidates and elected officials in districts that have small racial minority populations have to be careful about the issues they advocate or they will weaken their bases of support. Supporting racial issues too strongly, for example, might alienate white constituents. Samuel Kiang's pro-Chinese positions in the controversies surrounding Monterey Park's city manager and bilingual telephone operators, even though a majority of the city's population was Asian American, contributed to his failure to win reelection. And during a fund-raising event geared toward Asian Americans in Los Angeles, Robert Matsui—a Japanese American member of Congress from a California district centered around Sacramento and containing few Asian Americans—noted that his endorsement of redress and reparations had cost him some long-time supporters. "I had friends call me, people who had known me for twenty years, call the office and say, tell Bob not to send me an invitation to the next fund raiser because this shows that he has his own agenda and he doesn't represent me. We [Asian Americans in Congress] could have not pushed it and let it die, but we knew that it was too damn important. It transcended our own reelection."[5] During the campaign for the redress and reparations bill in the 1980s Matsui was an established representative (he was first elected to Congress in 1978 after serving on the Sacramento City Council), and he continued to win reelection in the 1990s. For others, however, especially first-time Asian American candidates, the ability to set an agenda is restricted by the political and demographic characteristics of their districts.

The lack of an Asian American population base and the political constraints it imposes are shown by the examples of contemporary Asian American candidates. For example, at a Chinese Historical Society Banquet held in Monterey Park in 1990, a Chinese American man spoke about his experiences in a losing battle for a city council position. He had run in Orange County, an area dominated by white Republican voters. "No one will vote for someone who runs on a platform saying that it is time to elect a minority," he explained. "That person will be viewed as a crybaby. Instead, it's necessary to stick with the [non-racial] issues of the community. Mike Woo, winning a [Los Angeles] city council seat in a white area where Asians are a minority is my role model, not Judy Chu who won where Asians were in the majority."

Asian American candidates who have labored in predominantly white areas are astounded by the differences in campaign styles and organizational support created by large Asian American populations. Mark Takano, a native-born, Japanese American, Harvard-educated, middle-school teacher, stressed his educational background and occupation during a successful campaign for a seat on the Riverside Community College Board. The district is east of the San Gabriel Valley, and approximately 2 percent of the voters there are Asian American. He was interviewed while attending a fund-raiser for Sophie Wong, a successful candidate for the Alhambra School Board in 1990. Takano expressed his amazement at the number of people there, mentioning that he couldn't believe that there was such a big function [about four hundred] for a local school board race. Looking at the number of people, he shook his head and said, "The economic strength here is amazing. The politics are a lot different here." He added that he was surprised that a person [Wong] with an accent could run. He was impressed with the strongly expressed feeling of support for Asian American politics, in contrast to his district, noting that an Asian American man he sat by that evening said that he didn't care if the candidate was a Republican or Democrat, he supported Asian Americans.

The second point about political representation is that population percentages and the number of elected representatives reveal nothing about the responsiveness to Asian American concerns of elected officials who are not Asian Americans. In areas where Asian Americans are a significant part of the electorate, are organized, and can pressure and reward politicians who are responsive to their needs, this is an exercise of power not measured by counting Asian American politicians. For example, Art Torres was a state senator who ran unsuccessfully in 1991 for a seat on the Los Angeles County Board of Supervisors in a district carved out of the San Gabriel Valley. In recognition of his long history of support for Asian American issues in the state legislature Torres was backed by most Asian American community leaders and elected officials in the region. Supporting his efforts, they held a fund-raiser for him in a Chinese restaurant in Monterey Park that was attended by more than two hundred. After the event, one of the organizers reported that a member of Torres's staff had told him that the event had been one of the best of the campaign in terms of money raised and attendance.

Because Monterey Park has a large Asian American population and is a regional entertainment and business center, the city has become a highly visible gauge of the social and economic status of California's Asian Americans. Local demographics, the importance of the city to Asian Americans in the region, and the lack of Asian representation have all made Monterey Park a focal point for those in the Los Angeles area who donate money, volunteer time, and provide political and technical expertise to support Asian American candidates and issues. Considering that the region contains the largest number of Asians and Pacific Islanders in the United States, such interest translates into economic and political clout.

The shifting source of campaign funds for former California Secretary of State March Fong Eu and the logistics of her final campaign clearly demonstrated the impact of new Chinese immigrants. An estimated 25 percent of Eu's campaign money came from Asian Americans when she began her political career during the mid-1950s. By the mid-1980s, 75 percent of her support came from Asian Americans, most of it from Chinese Americans (Tachibana 1986). Recognizing the material and symbolic importance of Monterey Park to the state's Asian American community, Eu located her fund-raising office and election night victory party there in 1990. The office's telephone number ended with 8888; the word *eight* in Cantonese sounds like "prosperity, wealth."

Elections in Monterey Park show that individuals can become involved politically before they are naturalized citizens. With limited budgets usually the rule, campaigns need many hours of volunteer labor and many forms of donated services. Providing facilities for telephone banks and office work, for example, is one way in which business people often participate.

Crossing Gender Boundaries in Community and Society

Considering the way that men dominated Monterey Park's City Council until the 1980s, the conditions that favor their selection are critical factors that shape participation in elected offices.[6] Just as an expanded conceptual framework that goes beyond electoral politics is needed to examine the range and complexity of racial and ethnic politics (Nakanishi 1991), focusing only on elected officials misses the range of political work performed by women. In the San Gabriel Valley, Asian American women and Latinas are involved at all levels. They are members of city commissions and ad hoc city and neighborhood groups, they speak at public hearings, they manage and volunteer on campaigns, and they run for elected office.

The women often become involved in politics by pursuing concerns that originate from "traditional" women's roles such as family responsibilities; they then couple the private concerns of home with the public realm of politics, in contrast to the traditional view of politics that portrays the issues as separate and unconnected (Pardo 1990a, 1995). Women may begin political careers by using roles and conventions that appear to be limiting, but these are employed to create political opportunities.

Another aspect of women's activism concerns the gendered categorization of appointed and elected positions in community politics. Work that involves such traditional women's duties as family care and cultural production—for example, school and library boards and arts and culture commissions—is open to women, whereas resource formation and allocation and control of major policy are viewed as being male purviews. In the San Gabriel Valley, however, women have used elected and appointed positions connected with traditional work as training grounds for elected offices—e.g., city council and state assembly positions—that have been dominated by men.

The women have entered politics through traditional routes, erasing and refiguring gender borders in the process of crossing boundaries by increasing access to higher elected offices. Gender and race are intertwined as women pursue issues linked with family safety (e.g., environmental racism) and children (e.g., bilingual education), changing traditional roles of

Asian American women and Latinas and addressing the discrimination racial minorities experience (Kaplan 1982; Pardo 1990a; Sacks 1988; Zavella 1987). Women as well as men are not simply individuals whose particular attributes or characteristics shape their political choices and effectiveness. Instead, they are part of a community setting in which race, class, and gender are linked to social patterns of relationships that influence interests and strategic possibilities (Pardo 1990a).

The education of children is traditionally understood to be the responsibility of women, and the involvement of women on school boards is partly an extension of that belief, as illustrated at the first annual San Gabriel Valley League of United Latin American Citizens Scholarship and Community Service Award dinner in 1990. Honored for achievements as elected officials, Antoinette Fabela and Virginia Gutierrez were members of the Garvey School Board, and Dora Padilla was a member of the Alhambra School Board. When she accepted her award, Gutierrez explained that her commitment to education had begun when she learned that her son had a learning disability and she became involved at his school to make sure he received the kind of instruction he needed. Running for the school board extended that concern to all children who had special learning needs.

Similarly, one of the first Asian American women elected to public office in the region and one of the longest in office, Eleanor Chow, a Korean American born in 1921, was a member of the Montebello Board of Education from 1971 to 1994.[7] Her experience shows how concern for children and discriminatory policies that affect racial and ethnic groups can motivate involvement in electoral politics. "There was a lot of prejudice in the town," she recalled. "At my intermediate school, I couldn't swim in the eighth grade because they didn't allow non-Anglos in the pool. The main thing that motivated me to politics was to make sure all children would have an equal chance" (Chu 1989, pp. 414–15).

Because school board elections are generally not as competitive as city council or state office elections (i.e., those for state assembly and senate) and require fewer resources, board elections are seen as a feasible first step for women wishing to enter politics. They offer an opportunity to gain experience and credibility before moving on to higher office. After Leila Donegan's election, more than two decades passed before the next woman, Louise Davis, was elected to the city council in 1976. In contrast, city records show that Myrtle C. Northrup in 1912 was the first woman elected to the Alhambra School Board, and women were elected on a regular basis in the years that followed. Similarly, although records are incomplete, women were elected to the Garvey School Board at least as far back as

1928, when Edna R. Hawthorne became a member. Of the five Asian American women serving as elected officials in the west San Gabriel Valley in 1991, all were either on school boards or their first elected office was a school board position.[8]

Hilda Solis, a Latina, was elected to two terms on the Rio Hondo Community College Board of Trustees before being elected to the state assembly in 1992 and state senate in 1994. Diane Martinez, also a Latina, was on the Garvey School Board before her election to the state assembly in 1992. In 1995 there were three women on the five-member Alhambra Board of Education, the school board responsible for the greatest number of students in the Monterey Park–Alhambra region. Dora Padilla, a Latina, had served since 1978–79; Phyllis Rutherford, who was white, since 1984–85; and Sophie Wong since the 1990–91 term.

Judy Chu's political career demonstrates the progression that women often follow from school boards to more competitive positions whereas men in the region often skip the earlier steps. Her first elected position was to the Garvey School Board in 1985, and she was then elected to Monterey Park's city council in 1988 and reelected in 1992 and 1997. She ran for the state assembly in 1994, losing in the Democratic primary to the incumbent, Diane Martinez. Running for a school board position in 1985 fit Chu's personal and professional interests as an educator. Compared to some men—Sam Kiang, for example—who successfully ran for city council positions as their first attempt at elected office, Chu was more experienced in community affairs and better known in the city. Had she been male and uninterested in educational issues she could have skipped the first step of running for a school board position.

The difficulties women experience when running for higher elected offices are typified by the career of Gloria Molina, who was elected in 1991 as one of only five Los Angles County supervisors and is one of the most powerful elected politicians in the region. In 1982, when Molina wanted to run for an open assembly seat in East Los Angeles, she received enthusiastic support from Latinas because of her long history of political work. Yet Latino elected officials and other male political activists told her it was not yet her turn and ran a man against her (Tobar 1993). Molina won, but not without having to fight the Latino political establishment. Race thus affects the gender discrimination women face in politics from society at large and translates through the culture of their ethnic communities (Chow 1987; Garcia, A. 1989; Glenn 1985).

Like Chu, other Asian American women in the San Gabriel Valley ran for school board positions after establishing professional careers and strong records of community involvement. Sophie Wong, from Hong Kong, was a prominent local realtor. The literature for her successful 1990 campaign for the Alhambra School Board lists numerous board and organizational memberships, including the presidency of the Monterey Park Chamber of Commerce in 1988 and 1989 and membership on the advisory boards for California State University Los Angeles, East Los Angeles College, and the California Board of Medical Quality Assurance. Showing the strength of her community and business contacts, she was endorsed by the four mayors of the cities covered by the Alhambra School District.

Judy Chu and Sophie Wong were the first Asian American school board members for their respective districts, so their victories were path-breaking for Asian Americans in general.[9] As the only Asian American to be elected as California's secretary of state, March Fong Eu was the highest elected Asian American in a state office. The beginning of her political career—a school board position—resembled the political paths of Chu and Wong. Eu, born in 1922 in California, received a B.S. degree in dental hygiene. She then worked with the Oakland city schools, developing curriculum to help teach dental care. Next, she earned a Ph.D. in education from Stanford University in 1956 and began teaching at the University of California School of Dental Hygiene and became president of the state and national hygienist associations. Her experience in the Oakland schools and in professional associations led to election to the Alameda County School Board in 1956. She then represented the Oakland area for four terms in the state assembly. Eu was elected California's secretary of state in 1974, an office she held until 1994 when she became U.S. ambassador to Micronesia. Interviewed in the mid-1980s, she said, "I want to be remembered as an Asian and as a woman who achieved high political office during a difficult time in California history. I want to be a role model for women and Asians to emulate" (Block 1986, p. 549).

Eu's progression exemplifies how women understand and maneuver through the gendered world of politics. Because their political involvement is not as readily accepted by society as men's, concern for the safety of children often combines with the educational process to create a socially acceptable route into political involvement for women. As with Eleanor Chow, Antoinette Fabela, and March Fong Eu, school-related activities can lead to elected office, creating not only possibilities for women but also, as in the case of Asian Americans, for an entire community through precedent-setting political victories.

Yet some women pursue other avenues for election. Using personal wealth or capitalizing on political opportunities or family reputations, some have entered elected posts at other levels. Lily Chen, born in the People's Republic of China, immigrated from Taiwan—where her father was a member of the legislature—to the United States in 1958. She earned a master's degree in social work from the University of Washington and is an administrator in the Los Angeles County Department of Children's Services (Arax 1985). She recognized the vacuum created by a lack of Asian American representation in Monterey Park and was elected to the council in 1982 after her first attempt and defeat in 1981 in a special election. Her candidacy, however, parallels those of other women in terms of an interest in children and school issues. As Chen explained her motivation for running for the council:

> I've been a long-time resident of this city. I remember when I wanted to run for the city council of Monterey Park, the immediate reason was because I was active with our local PTA and we always had been doing bake sales. Trying to build an auditorium. And so I said to myself, my gosh there must be better ways to build an auditorium than having bake sales. Sure enough, after I was elected, that was one of the first things I did was to apply for state funding. So it's very gratifying to see the young children enjoying what I was able to do. (Horton 1988, n.p.)

"That was my proudest moment as mayor. It seemed to make everything worthwhile," Chen proclaimed when the council obtained a $1.7 million state grant to build the auditorium (Arax 1985).

Just as "women's issues" extend from the immediate household to the school and into the political arena, the definition of motherhood and attendant concerns also broadens to include women who are not mothers and mixes with race when discrimination enters community issues. A childless Latina who lived in East Los Angeles supported the successful efforts of a grass-roots community group, Mothers of East Los Angeles, to block the construction of a prison in their neighborhood, for example. She explained, "When you are fighting for a better life for children and 'doing' for them, isn't that what mothers do? So we're all mothers. You don't have to have children to be a 'mother'" (Pardo 1990b, p. 4).

The very use of the word *mother* in the name of the group capitalizes on society's understanding of the role of women as family protectors and legitimizes their political activism. Similarly Diane Ho, the president of the Los Angeles chapter of the Organization of Chinese American Women, stressed that although she had no children she was interested in school issues in the San Gabriel Valley because political pressure must be applied at many levels if concerns of Asian Americans and others are to be addressed. "One thing that I really believe," she said, "politics isn't just restricted to government functions and people, politics is everywhere."

Another route into community service and politics is through city commission positions, and in Monterey Park, with its high levels of activism, such appointments are highly sought after. Although juggling the responsibilities of work and family are common to both men and women who wish to serve on a commission, women must often deal with the sentiment that politics is not in their domain (Chow 1987; Garcia, A. 1989; Keohane 1981). Concern over economic survival and adaptation adds another burden for immigrants.

The experience of a woman from Taiwan who works full time and is active in Monterey Park and state politics illustrates how women must consider the concerns of family and friends. She said that although her husband strongly supported her activities, some family members and friends did not: "New immigrants have to survive first. They consider survival more important than anything else. Just like my in-laws. They don't understand what I am doing with activities and politics. Some of my friends don't understand either. They criticize me. They say, your activities are like a drug (addiction). You just can't get rid of it. They say don't get involved. You sacrifice too much. They just think it is fate for a woman to stay at home and help your kids, period" (Fong 1990, p. 10).

She felt compelled to enter politics, however, because of the strong anti-immigrant feelings in the United States. The sentiment was made clear when her landlord told her that "we have enough new blood; we don't need anymore" and a neighbor said, "You people don't give of yourself to this country, but you share our social benefits" (Fong 1990, p. 5). Another negative view of immigrants was expressed when her father visited from Taiwan. During a dinner she had arranged with a couple whom she greatly respected, the woman asked her father what he liked and disliked about the United States. When he replied that he was concerned about the crime, the woman said, "Asian people bring crime into this country. Look at those refugees!" (Fong 1990, p. 5).

Dismayed by such beliefs, the woman had chosen to become involved with politics and accepted a position on the Monterey Park Human Relations Commission. A resident of the United States since 1983, she earned a master's degree in business and employs her knowledge to mediate between two cultures: "I am recognized as an effective bridge builder between people of different backgrounds. I think I am good at helping Pacific Rim people better understand the American way of life and vice versa" (Fong 1990, p. 14).

The Monterey Park City Council appoints residents to the eleven city commissions, and the 1988 list shows that seventy-six members—forty women and thirty-six men—serve on city commissions and boards (table 10). These figures are misleading, however, because membership on specific commissions reveals clear gender and racial patterns. For example, the three commissions that exercise power on decisions affecting significant aspects of city operations (the design review board, planning commission, and personnel board) include fifteen resident members, eleven men and four women. Men dominate the commissions and show the continued power of established white residents in the community. The four women on the three commissions were white; the four Asian Americans and two Latinos were men.

In contrast, the three commissions connected with the concerns or areas seen as the traditional domains of women (art and culture, community relations, and library board) have twenty-eight members—twenty-two women and six men. Female representation by ethnic groups was roughly equal—eight Asian Americans, six Latinas, and eight whites. The number of whites was once again much larger relative to their percentage of the city population, however. Although the commissions carry out work that is important to the welfare of the community and, as in the case of the li-

Table 10. 1988 and 1993 City Commissions and Boards: Gender, Race, and Ethnicity

	1988		1993	
	Women	Men	Women	Men
All Boards and Commissions				
Asian American	10	10	8	14
Latino	8	5	6	6
White	22	21	22	24
	40	36	36	44
Design Review, Planning, and Personnel				
Asian American	0	4	0	6
Latino	0	2	0	1
White	4	5	5	5
	4	11	5	12
Art and Culture, Community Relations, Library				
Asian American	8	3	7	2
Latino	6	1	2	2
White	8	2	9	7
	22	6	18	11

Sources: Lists of commissions and boards, Monterey Park, 1988, 1993.

brary, involves considerable amounts of money, their overall political and economic impact is less than the three commissions dominated by men.

Appointments are for four years, and in 1993, allowing for a change in personnel, the gender and racial patterns remained relatively stable. Men and white women dominated the three commissions with more power. Yet women have been able to use their service on commissions to gain experience, contacts, and visibility. The work is not only a valuable service to the community but also a springboard to elected office, as demonstrated by the example of former commission member Rita Valenzuela, who was elected to the Monterey Park City Council in 1992.

Similar to many of the Latinos and Japanese Americans in Monterey Park, Rita Valenzuela was born and raised in nearby Boyle Heights in East Los Angeles. Since moving to Monterey Park in the 1960s, she has had a long history of community activism, including nearly six years on the arts and culture commission, fifteen years teaching children in her church on weekends, volunteering with the scouts when her children were growing up, and working with the seventy-fifth anniversary committee of Monterey Park. Her volunteer work illustrates the links among family responsibilities, gender roles, and political action and shows how private concerns translate into public work (Ackelsberg 1984; Kaplan 1982; Zinn 1975).

Valenzuela had not thought about office until a group of friends convinced her to do so, but once she made the decision, Valenzuela was intensely committed to the task, went out into the community, and "walked every single day" to talk to voters. In the 1992 election to fill two seats, incumbent Judy Chu received 26.7 percent of the votes, Valenzuela received 21.1 percent, and Bonnie Wai finished a distant third with 13.7 percent. Valenzuela had become the first Mexican American woman to hold the position. She became mayor of the city in 1995, a position that rotates among the council members.

Valenzuela was on a modest budget based on small contributions and spent about $10,900; Wai, according to the candidates' campaign statements, spent about $56,500. Using literature in English and Chinese that she had written on a friend's home computer, Valenzuela contacted whites, Latinos, and Asian Americans as she campaigned with Louise Davis, a former member of the council who was running for reelection as treasurer. She believed that she was able to reach voters on "quality of life issues," based on her conviction that they were concerned about the kind of city they would "leave to their children."

In a community marked by rapid demographic and economic change, Valenzuela's thirty-year history as a resident and volunteer was a strong factor among voters, most of whom were also long-term residents and concerned about quality-of-life issues in the face of rapid urbanization. Although some might not have recognized her on sight, they would later connect her with an event, saying, "Oh, you're Rita Valenzuela, I know you from Cinco de Mayo, or so-and-so committee."

Judy Chu, the keynote speaker at an event sponsored by the Los Angeles chapter of the Organization of Chinese American Women in 1992, finished a slide show and talk entitled "Asian American Women: After Ten Years, Where Are We Now?" by discussing the genuine progress Asian American women have made in establishing "role models, breaking barriers, and changing perceptions that society has of us." Diane Ho closed the evening by underscoring the group's reason for being and the continued need to "seek methods to have our needs [as Asian American women] known and met."

Asian American women and Latinas are thus involved in politics at all levels, and their success as candidates and work on city commissions, along with many other activities, have been critical in constructing Asian American and Latino political bases in the San Gabriel Valley. These women are involved in activities that accomplish much of the political work at the community level, and their efforts have dismantled barriers to elected office by building a new political culture that recognizes and rewards their efforts. The success of women in politics is also breaking down the stereotypes of Asian Americans in general as being "unwinable" candidates or uninterested in politics. Most women remain accountable for their households and family duties; what has changed is their families' recognition that "family boundaries" and concerns extend into the community and support for the political activity because "the women are carrying the flag for the family" (Pardo 1990a, p. 343).

Immigrant Characteristics and Political Activity

Nina Glick Schiller's (1992, 1994) work on immigrants and the concept of transnationalism challenges traditional views of immigrant adaptation and identity formation. Rather than being uprooted and disconnected from their countries of origin, immigrants may have multiple connections with different places in the world, and their identities may be based on experiences and histories from those locations. The characterization of immigrants as sojourners, viewing their situation in the United States as temporary, ignores transnationals who may have strong political and economic ties to both their places of settlement and countries of origin. As a result, immigrants may be active in local politics and have political interests that cross national boundaries, with special concern for events in their countries of origin and also with U.S. foreign policy.[10]

For immigrants interested in facilitating and protecting capital accumulation, citizenship can have a strictly utilitarian purpose. In the U.S. Immigration Act of 1990, for example, Congress included provisions for a visa for persons who invest $1 million in any enterprise that creates at least ten jobs (Louie and Ong 1995; Ong 1993). Immigrants understand that involvement in politics is important because of government policies that directly affect their interests. They concern themselves not only with abstract court battles over symbolic civil rights issues that have little affect in everyday life—such as de facto housing segregation—but also with concrete matters such as regulations affecting their businesses and immigration policies that determine whether people will be able to reunite their families in the United States. Asian immigrants, who often have a high degree of entrepreneurship, are directly affected by local, state, and federal regulations and local social movements such as slow growth. Because many entrepreneurs are highly educated professionals from industrialized urban areas in Asia, their educational backgrounds, professional experience, and familiarity with urban bureaucracies facilitate adjustment to life in the United States and becoming involved in politics (Kim 1981).

Naturalization and voting are critical steps toward political involvement (Pachon 1991). Alejandro Portes and Ruben Rumbaut (1990) have compared the naturalization patterns of immigrants from North and South America, Asia, and Europe and have found that Asian immigrants generally become citizens at the fastest rate. Naturalization rates vary widely within and among groups and are affected by levels of education, location of country of origin, and reasons for immigration. Education is tied to English ability, awareness of the benefits of citizenship, and ability to negotiate the maze associated with the naturalization process. The latter two factors are connected to the "reversibility of migration." Because of distance and costs, it is easier, for example, to return to Mexico than it is to Taiwan, and refugees may not have the option of returning to their countries of origin (Portes and Rumbaut 1990, p. 124). Filipinos have the highest rate of naturalization—a result of the political and cultural ties between the United States and the Philippines (table 11). The Japanese have the lowest, most likely due to Japanese corporations in the United States and affiliated personnel who are in the country temporarily (Ong and Nakanishi 1996).

Fifty-three percent of eligible Asian Americans register to vote, compared to 61 percent of African Americans, 53 percent of Latinos, and 69 percent

Table 11. 1990 Naturalization Rates of Asian Immigrants

Ethnicity	Years in the United States		
	6–10	11–15	16–20
Asian Indians	26%	53%	68%
Chinese	34	67	80
Filipinos	45	73	83
Japanese	7	18	35
Koreans	27	62	82
SE Asians	32	62	n.a.

Source: Ong and Nakanishi (1996).

of whites. Asian Americans have the highest rate of voter turnout (76 percent), compared to 63 percent for African Americans, 64 percent for Latinos, and 73 percent for whites (Ong and Nakanishi 1996). The difference is possibly due to the characteristics related to their registration in the first place—levels of education, economic level, and time in the United States—and the positive correlation of those characteristics with electoral activity.

Political Partisanship

Registering as a Democrat or Republican expresses key beliefs about the proper role of government in the business affairs and personal lives of U.S. residents and how that government should conduct its foreign policy. Partisanship reflects a process of political resocialization as immigrants incorporate their homeland experiences with experiences in the United States when considering the implications of party affiliation and the ideology and goals of each party (Nakanishi 1991).

The highest percentage of Asian Americans in Los Angeles County in 1984 registered with the Democratic Party (table 12). Of that cohort, Filipinos and Samoans had the highest registration rates, while Vietnamese and Chinese had the lowest (Nakanishi 1986). Among Chinese Americans in Monterey Park in 1984, however, 43.1 percent of registered voters favored the Democrats, 30.8 percent identified themselves as Republicans, and 26 percent were of no or "other" party. In 1989 only 34.9 percent of Chinese Americans were registered with the Democratic Party, 37.1 percent were Republicans, and 28 percent were of no or "other" party. Japanese American voter registration remained fairly stable: 55.3 percent Democrat, 32.4 percent Republican, and 12.3 percent with no or "other" party in 1984, and 51.9 percent Democrat, 33.9 percent Republican, and 14.1 with no or "other" party in 1989 (Nakanishi 1991).

Table 12. Party Affiliation of Asians and Pacific Islanders, 1984 Los Angeles County

	Democrat	Republican	No Party/ Other Party
Asian Indian	59.1%	23.6%	17.4%
Chinese	41.9	36.4	21.7
Filipino	63.3	22.8	13.8
Japanese	54.9	32.3	12.8
Korean	48.5	29.4	22.1
Samoan	61.0	25.0	14.5
Vietnamese	40.0	35.9	24.0

Source: Nakanishi (1986).

The fact that many new Asian immigrants register as Republicans or no party/independent once they become naturalized U.S. citizens contrasts to Mexican Americans and African Americans, who register predominantly as Democrats. Exit polls (Horton 1995; Shinagawa 1995) suggest, however, that as immigrants spend more time in the United States registration rates with the Democratic Party tend to increase; they also increase in succeeding generations. That is likely the result of the Democratics' more liberal stance on immigration, language, and educational issues and the party's record of representing the interests of racial minorities.

Evidence in Monterey Park suggests that Chinese immigrants and native-born Asian Americans find the Republican Party attractive because of their dislike of communism; emphasis on such traditional values as a strong work ethic, family, and education; and approval of the concepts of limited social welfare and government regulation of business (Cain, Kiewiet, and Uhlaner 1988). A number of Cuban Americans are also Republicans, in part because of their strong anti-communist stance because of the Castro takeover in 1959 and also because of income levels that are higher than those of other Latinos (Portes 1984; Portes and Mozo 1985). These points were reflected in a discussion with Sophie Wong, who lives in Monterey Park:

I'm a Republican because their philosophy matches mine. I came here as an immigrant. My family was poor. We stressed education and hard work. The elderly, people who are disabled and can't work, they should get help from the government. If a person is disabled but his mind is okay, then he should be given the opportunity to work from his wheelchair. I don't believe in giving money to people who are capable of working. I believe in providing people the opportunity to work. I've worked hard. I've wanted to help my family, my brothers and sisters. Sometimes Republicans think I'm too liberal with social services. The Republican Party believes in providing opportunity. A small businessman wants to start a business, I'll help him get a loan. I believe, when it comes to business, that people should have opportunities, [be] helped with the tools to start with, given help to grow, to be productive and contribute to society. Taught how to be independent. I believe in helping people get started, I don't mind helping and giving money [to] people who want to help themselves grow and to build, and then they can help others. I think we agree, Democrats and Republicans, in the basic principle of the betterment of society. The two-party system is wonderful, [the] check and balance of our government. As Asians, we should be active in both parties so that they can relate to us in the middle. Too conservative or too liberal is bad.

The importance of self-help, the work ethic, and opposing aid to people considered able-bodied were echoed in a discussion with Eleanor Chow about the Republican Party and social welfare. She recognized the need for public assistance because her own family had benefited from it, but she objected to those who were overly dependent on it.

I think that people earn respectability by doing something to get a pay check. Some people really need it, I agree with that, but not generation after generation, not the people who believe that if they have more kids they get more money. My father was a migrant farm worker, a grape picker, so I understand that life. My father died, and there were seven kids in the family. We had help, but not forever. I believe that the next generation should pay back. I'm against the abuses of the welfare system and food stamps. Time to put a halt to the abuses. I believe in social services, but I disagree with some of the abuses of services.

The belief that the free market rather than the government should regulate business was a common theme among Chinese immigrant entrepreneurs. As a businessman in his fifties whose family had moved back and forth between the United States and China told me:

The Republicans have similar beliefs to Chinese. Both groups believe in limited government and [that] volunteerism should be stressed. The government should help those who need help, but able-bodied people shouldn't receive government help. My grandfather left his village in China and sneaked into the United States. If you can imagine, a poor, timid man from the country, went all the way to the United States. I know of another Chinese man who literally swam across a river to enter the United States. [Laughed.] He really was one of the original wetbacks. My father was also born in China and went to the United States. The free market should guide business not governments. The Democrats are leaning more toward protectionist legislation. Business people involved in banking, real estate, development, they are interested in as little government interference as possible. Especially since they are operating between different countries.

A Chinese immigrant complained about being forced to sell a tract of land to the Alhambra Redevelopment Agency—which has the power to take over and buy property in commercial areas of the city that are part of city plans for redevelopment and economic revitalization—at what he felt was a price below fair market value. His experience was insignificant compared to what had happened to a white business acquaintance, however:

> He committed suicide. The Redevelopment Agency was taking over one of his stores. He was really upset by it. I heard him speak about it one night at a city council meeting. He couldn't understand how they could do that. It has been in the family for such a long time. He said that his grandfather and his father owned the building. They have been good citizens in the community. And because his family had lived here so long and they were active in the community, he knew the people on the council. He hung himself in his store.

An employee of Alhambra's Redevelopment Agency explained to me, however, that although the family had first resisted redevelopment plans to purchase their store, the problems had been worked out and the family supported the city. What is significant is that the Chinese immigrant entrepreneur attributed the event to unreasonable involvement of local government in private business matters.

Although the Republican Party may be favored among entrepreneurs for its free-market policies, neither major party has made a strong, consistent effort to recruit Latinos or Asian Americans, either in California or nationally, and neither has been particularly responsive to the issues and concerns of either group. As Bruce Cain (1991, pp. 10–11) notes, although Republicans have tried to lessen the predominantly "white" image of their party, Democrats worried that "their party had become too closely identified with special racial and ethnic interests" and needed to regain white voters.

The Democratic Party cannot take the support of such groups for granted or conflate the unique interests of various constituencies. After Phil Angelides, then the California State Democratic chair, met with the San Francisco Chinese American Democratic Club on July 2, 1991, Roland Quan, the past president of the organization, expressed dissatisfaction with Angelides's and the party's apparent lack of interest in Asian American issues.

> He [Angelides] gave the generic pitch to Democratic loyalists. After the meeting, I asked him for his reaction concerning the perception of the Chinese American community that the Democrats don't see the Chinese Americans as part of their primary constituency. His reply was he didn't reply. "What Angelides was

trying to say is, 'Ask not what the party can do for you, ask what you can do for the party.' That's not good enough for the '90s. People don't do things based on a promise anymore. The Democrats have to address issues that are important to the Chinese American community. They just can't get involved in personalities and various non-issue type things." (Lau 1991)

In addition to philosophy and values, what prominent individuals or political parties actually do plays a role in a person's decision. For example, Eleanor Chow explained why she changed her registration from Democrat to Republican:

> I think a strong point of the Republicans is that years ago there were restricted areas, even here in Montebello, where Asian Americans could not live. After the Second World War, we were not allowed to live in certain areas. Sammy Lee [a Korean American who won an Olympic medal in diving], we are of the same generation, worked actively to have those restrictions lifted. Eisenhower worked to have those restrictions lifted across the nation. I changed my party to vote for him. I had respect for him, I wanted to support him.

Both parties have also been extremely weak in supporting Asian American and Latino candidates. Judy Chu (1989) has pointed out that although many Asian Americans hold appointed positions and staff positions for elected officials, the parties mentor and support few as electoral candidates.

In 1993 Dolores Huerta, vice president of the United Farm Workers and executive board member of the Fund for the Feminist Majority, spoke at a conference on women of color in electoral politics at the University of California, San Diego. Her topic concerned the attempts of the California Democratic Party to undermine a major statewide effort to elect women of color. Three Latinas had run for office in newly drawn Latino areas, but rather than support them the party had run a group of white, male candidates. As Huerta explained, "The Democratic Party leadership response to our efforts was negative: They showed us their true colors. . . . They [the Democratic Party] decided to run in those same districts, not Latinos or Latino men, but Portuguese men who had Latino-sounding surnames" (1995, p. 83).

Eleanor Chow recalled her unsuccessful campaign for the state senate in the early 1980s:

> You can say that I received little support ten years ago, but there was a handful of people who really helped. Bill Campbell, the minority leader in the state senate really helped with the fund-raiser. But in the last few years, Republicans have finally had to admit that there are big changes happening. Republicans now see that Asians are a vital part of the political process. Asians will play an impor-

tant role in politics. We have the money. We are the second largest group [in terms of racial minorities], there are now more Asians than blacks in California.

The split in party affiliation among Asian Americans creates a different issue in primary elections in which voters can only participate in elections involving their party. In the San Gabriel Valley, with Asian Americans divided among Republicans, Democrats, and independent or no party, that reduces the amount of votes a candidate supported by Asian Americans can receive. Lily Chen, a former mayor of Monterey Park who ran against the incumbent Matthew Martinez in the Democratic primary for U.S. Congress, attempted to persuade Republican and no-party Chinese to become registered Democrats so they could vote for her in the primary, which in this heavily Democratic district usually decides the election. Her tactic failed because only a few Chinese did change their registration (Nakanishi 1991). As a result, division of new immigrants among Republican, Democrat, and no party weakened the electoral power of Asian Americans. That, however, has changed since the March 1996 election in California and approval of Proposition 198, the "open primary" ballot measure that allows voters to cast their ballots for any candidate, regardless of political affiliation. Although that change can potentially benefit Asian Americans by allowing them to cross party lines and vote as a more effective bloc, the impact in demographically and politically complex areas such as the San Gabriel Valley remains to be seen.

City Council Elections: Class, Race, and Ethnicity

Development, the slow-growth movement, and electoral politics in Monterey Park illustrate how class and racial interests generate political issues and how class and race are given meaning, woven into, and used to shape events. People have multiple identities and interests based on a number of characteristics such as class, nativity, political partisanship, race, and ethnicity. When people cast ballots, voting is an expression of that mix of interests and a temporary shifting and ranking of priorities. In the 1988 city council election, for example, the issue of growth and the interests of Chinese developers had to be considered in relation to the need for Asian American political representation in an atmosphere of heightened tension and overt racism.

An overlap of racial and class lines has frequently occurred in conflict in the United States. Latino farm workers who wanted to unionize, Japanese American farm owners who opposed their efforts in California during the early 1970s (Fugita and O'Brien 1977; Wollenberg 1972), and the conflict between Korean shopkeepers and their African American clientele in New York, Los Angeles, and Philadelphia during the 1980s and 1990s are examples of conflict based primarily on class but heavily influenced by race.

Because racial and ethnic lines in Monterey Park roughly followed class lines in the conflict over development, accusations that the slow-growth movement, largely led by white residents, was motivated by racism and nativism were countered by movement leaders who charged developers with using race to divert attention from shoddy, poorly planned projects (Fong 1994; Horton 1995). While the case of redevelopment and Atlantic Square demonstrated the existence of genuine concerns among long-term residents about the effects of rapid development, it also uncovered how such issues were racialized when "European" was classified as "American" and "Asian" as "foreign" in terms of restaurants and architecture.

Within the Asian American community, the struggle over growth involved Chinese immigrant developers and entrepreneurs who favored a free-market approach to urban development. In opposition were Chinese and Japanese American native-born professionals who supported city planning controlled by residents, city staff, and council members.

Judy Chu supported slow growth in her successful 1988 city council campaign, potentially alienating Chinese developers. Per capita tax revenues in Monterey Park, however, were among the lowest of cities in the San Gabriel Valley, and "leakage" of retail sales tax dollars to neighboring communities was an important consideration in the debate. Although Chu would not accept money from developers, she recognized the need for development to increase tax revenues, as her campaign literature stated, for "quality shopping centers and businesses that will help generate sales tax revenue."

Before the election, many of Chu's campaign volunteers were liberal Asian American professionals, individuals who had been politicized during the 1960s and 1970s and had pioneered social programs in ethnic communities such as Little Tokyo and Chinatown in Los Angeles. Yet she also received organizational support from Asian American developers and business people, many of whom were strong Republicans, who attended a fund-raising event held at a local restaurant.

In the 1988 election the Asian American community put aside its differences over development to work for group representation (table 5). It was a demonstration of the fact that individuals and groups cannot be labeled simply as pro- or anti-business and assumed to have political interests that automatically follow. Categories such as class and ethnicity have little analytical value in themselves as abstract classifications of groups. Instead, the conditions that create different interests and conflicts between groups, whether within the same ethnic group or among ethnic groups, need to be examined (Bonacich 1972, 1976, 1980; Thompson 1979).

Interpreting the results of the election and untangling class issues that flowed from business and political interests was difficult. It was possible that Chinese business people may have viewed Chu as an improvement over candidates who were clearly anti-business and anti-Asian and seen her race simply as a bonus. Entrepreneurs believed their interests would at least receive a fair hearing from Chu, whom they viewed as well-educated, articulate, and hard working. Developers who owned city buildings may have benefited from restrictions that followed the election because the value of existing commercial space would increase if shortages developed.

Interviews and ethnographic involvement in political campaigns reveal a common thread among the various groups, however. Anti-Asian hate crimes, English-only ordinances, slow-growth initiatives perceived by Asian Americans as anti-Chinese, attacks against immigrants by city council members, and treatment of Asian Americans as outsiders were issues that transcended class interests and united voters along ethnic and racial lines.

Thus anti-Asian activities and an almost total lack of Asian Americans on local school boards and city councils generated a strong need among Asian Americans for representation in local politics and resulted in strong support for Chu. Recent anti-Asian activities were not viewed as isolated events that would disappear with time but were understood as part of a larger history of local and national discriminatory activities. Asian Americans clearly understood that they needed to unite politically to address and protect their political, economic, and social interests.

A different issue concerns the class character of Asian American politics. Those involved in forming political organizations and networks are primarily professional and business people. Because they set the agenda, it is their interpretation of Asian American interests that is addressed— concern with slow growth instead of affordable housing, for example, or a focus on traffic and parking instead of mass transit. People who are politically active represent only a tiny percentage of the total Asian American population, yet they are the ones shaping future issues.

Because these people are professionals and business people, they have access to funding, technical skills, and legal and political knowledge that allow them to become involved in areas such as political campaigns and redistricting that require resources. Such access also shapes the form their politics take—a mainstream, within-the-system approach as opposed to a politics of protest that asks for radical change.

Although it is clear that at certain times ethnic interests can supersede class interests, Yen Espiritu and Paul Ong (1994) point out the need for broadening the class backgrounds of those who are part of Asian American organizations currently dominated by middle-class professionals. The legitimacy and survival of these organizations require a representation of interests and goals that matches the diversity of the Asian American community. Yet Asian American leaders have demonstrated deep commitment to grappling with issues of their diverse community, as shown by the history of contemporary activists. Some, for example, who are attorneys and teachers have developed social service programs to serve the needs of low-income and immigrant residents of urban centers. And organizations such as LEAP—which coordinated studies (Ong) that graphically demonstrate the extreme levels of poverty among Asian Americans and are used by social service agencies to pursue funding to address poverty-related issues—and the Asian Pacific American Legal Center are also proof of serious middle-class commitment.

During the 1980s in Monterey Park, Asian Americans were working toward basic goals that most could support, such as electing representatives supportive of Asian American issues. As those basic goals are met, however, and the issues become more sharply defined, differences according to factors such as class and nationality will become more important. That was the case in the controversy over the firing of Mark Lewis, the city manager, and the implementation of a plan for hiring bilingual operators for the city's emergency line.

5 On Common Ground: From Agricultural Struggles to Urban Politics among Latinos and Asian Americans

Cooperative efforts between Latinos and Asian Americans in the multiracial coalitions backing Judy Chu's city council campaigns emerged not only in response to distinctly new historical circumstances and conditions but also reflected a long tradition of shared struggle against racialized hierarchies and privileges. The "politics of prejudice" (Daniels 1974) channeled Asian Americans and Latinos into similar occupational, residential, and political spaces and created common interests and concerns for similarly racialized workers, consumers, and citizens. The experiences of both groups forced them to confront the contradictions between promises of universal inclusion in the United States and the nation's actual practices of racialized exclusion.

Memories of racialization and the struggles mounted against it created affinities among groups that might otherwise have seen themselves as antagonistic competitors for scarce resources. That heritage of shared struggle provided a key resource for contemporary community activists in constructing coalitions across racial lines in labor organizing and political mobilizations alike. For example, in the major Japanese American newspaper published in Los Angeles, *Rafu Shimpo*, Ryan Yokota (1994, p. 3) described some of the historical alliances among early-twentieth-century agricultural workers and used them to provide a context and foundation for ongoing labor organizing efforts in the city's Little Tokyo. In reference to unionization attempts among Latino and Asian employees at the New Otani Hotel—which is owned by a Japanese company that has long resisted the efforts of its employees to unionize in the United States and Japan (Bernstein 1996)—Yokota wrote:

Through the 150 years of shared experience here in America, the connections
between the Asian Pacific Islander and the Chicana/o, Latina/o communities have
been close and fruitful.

From the sugar beet fields of Oxnard in 1903 to the grape strikes of Delano
in 1965, our people have stood together in solidarity through history, defining
the great moments of the past through inter-ethnic coalition.

For many of the first Asian immigrants in California, a cycle of recruit-
ment as a source of cheap labor was followed by laws banning immigration—especially targeting male laborers. The cycle created waves of Asians
who came to work in gold fields, build railroads, work in mines, labor in
agriculture, and open small businesses.[1] Of course, Mexicans had inhabited California long before the state was annexed by the United States
through conquest and the 1848 Treaty of Guadalupe Hidalgo, but their
numbers in the labor force were relatively small. That changed during the
early 1900s when the Mexican population increased dramatically in the
United States because of the completion of railroads linking the two nations, a revolution in Mexico, and U.S. labor recruiters who sought replace-
ments for the diminishing supply of Asians (Almaguer 1994; Barrera 1979).

Throughout their history in the United States, Latinos and Asian Americans desired to work, raise families, and, in some cases, become Americans, but those efforts were thwarted by extreme forms of discrimination
that limited occupational choices, where they could live, whom they could
marry, and the quality and location of the schools their children could
attend. As a result, the politicization of Latinos and Asian Americans came
as those groups waged a battle for economic, political, and social equality. For them, racial identities were not merely symbolic and celebrated by
ethnic food and holidays (Gans 1979; Waters 1990), but had material
consequences. That self-conscious awareness of the historical and contemporary importance of race created the potential for recognizing and establishing links between Asian Americans and Latinos. Both groups had in
common the fact that they were racialized minorities.

Shifting racial and class positions along with particular historical and
regional conditions constantly altered the contexts for relationships.
Conflict rather than cooperation frequently characterized minority relationships. For example, disidentification with the targets of the worst forms
of white racism and xenophobia occurred when Japanese immigrants attempted to distance themselves from the Chinese after the passage of the
Exclusion Act of 1882. Similarly, Chinese Americans sought to distinguish
themselves from Japanese Americans when the latter were incarcerated
during World War II (Daniels 1988; Ichioka 1988).

The pattern also occurred among organizations geared toward integration; for example, the Japanese American Citizens League (JACL) and the League of United Latin American Citizens (LULAC) restricted membership to U.S. citizens (Gutierrez 1995). In Monterey Park in the 1970s and 1980s a similar reaction occurred among established Japanese and Chinese Americans toward the new Chinese immigrants, who came under attack by racist and nativist residents. Latinos likewise sought to align themselves with whites in the early period of conflict.

Such disidentification between Japanese and Chinese, and between citizens and non-citizens, originated from actions supporting white racial privilege rather than from direct conflict among minority groups. Changing contexts and class relationships in agricultural and urban experiences also created distinct sites of conflict between Latinos and Asian Americans. Latino farm workers in California went on strike in the 1930s against Japanese American berry farmers, for example, and the United Farm Workers (UFW) attempted to organize Mexican workers on Japanese American farms in the 1970s. The class positions of workers and employers were rooted, as was the immediate crisis, in the dispute over wages and working conditions rather than a common position as racialized minorities. Similarly, the class-defined relationship of store owner and customer structures interactions between Korean shopkeepers and their Latino and African American clientele. Embraced by African and Korean American leaders in churches and civil rights organizations, an understanding and relationship built on the common position of the two groups as subordinate minorities in a racial hierarchy that has whites at its top have proven elusive among the majority of community residents (Chang 1993; Park, E. J. W. 1996; Park, K. 1995, 1996). The harsh realities of everyday life disrupt attempts to develop solidarity based on notions of commonality far removed from the more pressing concerns of inhabitants of low-income communities who contend with disappearing employment opportunities, an educational system in crisis, and inadequate housing and store keepers who struggle to adapt to a new country and fight off bankruptcy.

Cooperative efforts among Asian Americans and Latinos developed primarily when similar racial and class positions developed, creating obvious shared circumstances and interests. From poor labor conditions and low wages in the agricultural sector to political disfranchisement in urban barrios and suburban enclaves, Asian Americans and Latinos established common ground based on shared goals and keen understanding of their subordinate positions in U.S. society.

Yokota (1994) highlighted examples of Latino and Asian American cooperation by relating the history of the Japanese-Mexican Labor Association and the creation of the UFW. By emphasizing those events and ignoring such examples of disunity as Mexican workers organizing against Japanese American farmers in the 1930s and 1970s, Yokota's selective use of history demonstrates how collective memory strategically uses elements from the past to support and legitimate current efforts. As Raphael Sonenshein (1993) has affirmed, however, in a study of the Jewish and African American alliance that elected Tom Bradley as Los Angeles mayor in 1973, a common liberal political ideology and an understanding of their position as disfranchised groups did not ensure cooperation between Jews and African Americans. Shared interests, in this case the goals of ending exclusion from city hall and gaining power and the development of long-term working relationships proved to be the critical factor.

That Latinos, Chinese immigrants, and established Asian Americans would move from intense and bitter conflict to political alliances in the San Gabriel Valley—echoing their history of cooperation and confrontation in agriculture— demonstrates that racial and ethnic relationships are highly fluid and influenced by local circumstances, national policies, and individual and group histories and perceptions. San Gabriel Valley Latinos and Asian Americans, middle-class professionals or entrepreneurs who have high rates of home ownership and live in a community with good schools, did not have to struggle for everyday survival; nor did they need to challenge conditions that produced the 1992 civil unrest in areas of Los Angeles decimated by deindustrialization and disinvestment. Instead, they could draw on community resources and skills to establish networks and political organizations to address issues such as hate crimes, English-only initiatives, and anti-immigrant policies. Members of organizations such as LULAC or the West San Gabriel Asian Pacific Democratic Club were able to focus specifically on the needs of their own racial and ethnic communities. Later, such organizations would provide the institutional base for the formation of alliances and joint political action.

Working the Ground: Laborers and Farmers

Yokota's call for the support of Latino and Asian American union efforts in the 1990s draws upon a long history of labor alliances. The timing of immigrant flows and limited occupational choices created an overlap in California between Asian—primarily Japanese and Filipino—and Mexican workers. Asians and Latinos have been the major source of the seasonal labor force throughout the history of agriculture in the state (Chan

1986), with its often physically grueling work and harsh living conditions. As they helped harvest the same fields, Asians and Mexicans overcame barriers caused by language and differential treatment by whites and joined forces to press for higher wages and better working conditions.[2]

The first major cooperative effort between Japanese and Mexican farm workers occurred in Oxnard's sugar beet industry. The two groups, the majority of workers who harvested the crop, formed the Japanese-Mexican Labor Association and went on strike in 1903. Their numbers soon grew to include more than 90 percent of the beet workers in the area.[3] Their concerns centered on diminishing wages and the high commission fees of the labor contractor—the Western Agricultural Contracting Company—that controlled their employment.

Labor unions in the West did not recruit Asian workers during this period and had a long history of promoting anti-immigrant, anti-Asian sentiment as a way of increasing membership and support among white workers (Daniels 1974; Saxton 1971). When the group applied for admission to the American Federation of Labor (AFL), it agreed on the condition that Japanese farm workers be excluded. The Mexican members refused the AFL's offer and expressed solidarity with their Japanese co-workers: "We would be false to them and to ourselves and to the cause of unionism if we accepted privileges for ourselves which are not accorded to them. We are going to stand by men who stood by us in the long, hard fight which ended in a victory over the enemy. . . . We will refuse any other kind of charter, except one which will wipe out race prejudices and recognize our fellow workers as being as good as ourselves" (Almaguer 1994, p. 202). The Mexican workers also understood that even when unions proposed membership to racial minorities the offers were based on efforts to increase membership and dues and neglected specific work problems such as discrimination in hiring and promotion.

The Japanese-Mexican Labor Association was the first agricultural union formed by racial minorities in California. Both immigrant and U.S.-born members overcame major cultural differences in their efforts to establish a basis for collective action and develop tactics. As an example of their remarkable adaptability and seriousness of purpose, meetings were held in three languages: Spanish, Japanese, and English. The workers' efforts paid off. Wages increased, and they won the right to negotiate contracts directly with growers.

A half-century later Asian Americans and Mexican Americans again recognized common interests that transcended racial lines and formed the UFW in 1966, echoing the experience of the Japanese-Mexican Labor

Association. Filipinos joined with Mexicans to create the UFW in one of the most productive agricultural regions in the world, the San Joaquin Valley of central California. Although Cesar Chavez has become synonymous with the UFW and the organization is seen as primarily Latino, that image ignores the union's biracial origins and the pivotal role that Philip Vera Cruz and other Filipinos played in the strike and negotiations that led to the founding of the UFW.

Vera Cruz—who was born in the Philippines in 1904 and died in 1994—came to the United States in 1926 and did a variety of things, including farm labor in California, restaurant and box factory work in Washington, and toil in the cannery industry in Alaska. He became a part of the large Filipino labor force in the western United States and Hawaii, which had a history of such labor activism as strikes in the cane fields of Hawaii during the 1920s (Scharlin and Villanueva 1992).

On September 8, 1965, Vera Cruz and other Filipino members of the Agricultural Workers Organizing Committee (AWOC), AFL-CIO, met in the Filipino Hall in Delano and voted to go on strike and reject grape growers' demands to accept reduced wages in Coachella. As he described the events and significance of the day, "It was like an incendiary bomb, exploding out the strike message to the workers in the vineyards, telling them to have sit-ins in the labor camps, and set up picket lines at every grower's ranch. . . . The strikes before that one would last only two or three days. But this one, started solely by Filipinos, took five years. It was the strike that eventually made the UFW, the farmworkers movement, and Cesar Chavez famous worldwide and it lasted until 1970 when we finally won our workers' contracts with the growers" (Scharlin and Villanueva 1992, p. 30).

Eight days later, on September 16, Cesar Chavez and the National Farm Workers Association (NFWA) joined the strike. Chavez, who was born in 1927 in Arizona and died at the age of sixty-six in 1993, worked as an organizer for the Community Service Organization in California until 1962, when he moved to Delano to begin organizing Mexican farm workers and establish the NFWA.

AWOC and the NFWA joined forces a year after the strike began to become the United Farm Workers Organizing Committee, the predecessor to the UFW. As Vera Cruz explained, the merger was part of an attempt to counter Teamsters Union efforts to sign contracts that AWOC felt did little to benefit workers. Vera Cruz became a member of the UFW board and second vice president, with Dolores Huerta and Cesar Chavez above him. The highest-ranking Filipino in the organization, he left in 1977, tired and discouraged with what he felt was the union's neglect of Filipino worker issues.

Vera Cruz's break with the UFW underscores the difficulty of meeting the needs of diverse constituencies, even when class interests overlap. Asian Americans moved from being farm laborers to farm managers or owners. That growing class differentiation created new economic relationships between Latinos and Asian Americans, specifically as employer and employee, and also created new sites of potential discord. Not only did labor-grower conflicts result in splits between Latinos and Asian Americans but those disputes also divided the Asian American community along varying ideological and class lines.

Drawing on their pre-immigration backgrounds in agriculture and entering farming niches left behind by Chinese who moved on to more profitable enterprises in produce wholesaling and distribution, Japanese immigrants established farms in Los Angeles County. Developing crops that required intensive labor, they grew fruit and flowers and produced 75 percent of the vegetables consumed in Los Angeles in 1916 (Mason and McKinstry 1969). With the shift from being laborers to being growers, a series of labor struggles developed between Japanese farmers and Mexican workers as restrictive immigration laws cut off Asian laborers and Mexicans filled the need for low-cost labor.

In the San Gabriel Valley, where Japanese farmers controlled berry production, the two groups clashed in the El Monte berry strike in 1933. Cuts in wages exacerbated by the depression and appalling living conditions in migrant labor camps prompted Mexican workers to go on strike in the middle of the harvesting season. With widespread labor struggles throughout the state that year, white farmers and business owners were concerned about their economic interests and joined the battle on the side of the Japanese farm owners, enlisting the help of the Los Angeles and El Monte chambers of commerce, Los Angeles police, county sheriffs, and white strikebreakers. The strike ended with marginal gains for the workers. Strikes in 1936 and 1937, however, won greater wage increases and union recognition when class differences between Asian workers and farmers created new alignments as newly established Japanese and Filipino labor organizations joined forces with Mexican workers (Modell 1977; Wollenberg 1972).

Four decades later, major struggles reappeared in the 1970s when the United Farm Workers Union attempted to organize Mexican workers on farms owned by Japanese Americans. As Stephen Fugita and David O'Brien (1978, 1991) explain, the farmers believed that the UFW, with its predominantly Mexican American membership, was targeting them and in response formed the Nisei Farmers League (NFL) in 1971. The league claimed that fourteen of the seventeen farms picketed by the UFW in 1971 were owned by Japanese Americans. The UFW had targeted the farms for economic rather than racial reasons, however. They provided vulnerable targets for organizing; they were much smaller than the average farm in California and heavily dependent on migrant labor because they grew crops unsuitable for mechanization.

Both the UFW and the NFL used ethnic appeals to gain community support. The UFW linked its efforts to the larger Chicano, or Mexican American, struggle to gain civil rights. Japanese American students, as part of the Asian American movement and efforts to link the struggles of "third world people," emphasized economic interests and political ideology. They identified with the fight for better wages among workers of all races and supported the efforts of the UFW (Fugita and O'Brien 1978).

Harry Kubo, the head of the NFL, linked his U.S. concentration camp experience with the need for Japanese Americans to close ranks and resist unfair labor practices: "1942. WWII. Tule Lake Japanese American detention camp. My family lost everything. I was twenty years old and I gave up my personal rights without a fight. Never again" (Fugita and O'Brien 1978, p. 150). The NFL's appeals to other Japanese Americans for support against the UFW met with mixed results, however, and the community fractured along economic and ideological lines. When asked for their endorsement, the national JACL declined to become involved in what was seen as an economic rather than racial or civil rights issue. The UFW received the support of the Chicago JACL chapter (which focused on the labor-employer relationships), whereas the Central California District Council of JACL (with its close ties to farmers) supported the NFL. The issue was partially settled in favor of the NFL by the 1976 defeat of Proposition 14, which would have increased funding for the state's 1975 Agricultural Labor Relations Act, assisting UFW efforts (Fugita and O'Brien 1978).

Workers in Oxnard named their group the Japanese-Mexican Labor Association, and Japanese American farmers called themselves the Nisei Farmers League. By using racial and ethnic labels combined with their occupational categories they emphasized that their struggles were based on the intersection of race and economic interests rooted in U.S. history. Asian and Latino workers were acutely aware of the efforts of white labor organizations and businesses alike to racialize labor and restrict the occupational opportunities of non-whites. Harry Kubo's reference to his family's incarceration in Tule Lake was not merely an emotional plea for ethnic solidarity; it was an evocation of the history of discrimination that has hampered Japanese American entrepreneurial efforts. Nisei farmers had to cope with tactics such as the Alien Land Laws white farmers used to restrict competition. The UFW did not target Nisei farms because they were owned by Japanese Americans but because Nisei farmers faced discriminatory restrictions that forced them to operate under conditions that made them vulnerable to union efforts. They were small in size, unable to cope with sustained losses, and focused on crops that depended on migrant labor and were unsuitable for mechanization.

Even though Mexican American laborers and Nisei farmers both suffered from discrimination, the vastly different economic positions and forms of racism they faced made alliances unlikely. Meanwhile, in urban neighborhoods, critical interrogation of their position as racialized minorities and the recognition of shared interests established a basis for alliances.

Urban Politics

Moving into urban areas and encountering restrictive covenants, discriminatory lending practices by financial institutions, and racial steering practices by real estate brokers, Mexican and Japanese Americans inhabited the same segregated neighborhoods, literally finding common ground once again. They also established a shared political space as they united to combat residential and economic segregation and politicians who ignored them.

Using one of the region's early coalitions in electoral politics, Edward Roybal, a Mexican American, won a Los Angeles city council seat in 1949. He built a grass-roots alliance composed of Latinos, African Americans, Asian Americans, and whites to become the first Latino council member in the twentieth century.[4] Roybal grew up in Boyle Heights (an area from which many current Latino and Japanese American residents of the San Gabriel Valley migrated), his major base of support. Multiracial (Russian Jews, Mexicans, Japanese, and Italians were among the many immigrant groups that settled there) and with low-income and working-class residents, Boyle Heights was poorly served by the city.

Roybal campaigned with a small budget—$5,500—compared to the $15,000 average of other candidates of the era (Griffith 1949). He overcame the limits of his budget, however, with an extensive grass-roots campaign staffed by dedicated volunteers who talked to voters over the telephone and walked precincts six nights a week. The members of the Community Service Organization, which Roybal helped create following his first and failed attempt to win the council seat in 1947, contributed to his efforts. Before his election to the council Roybal had been a social worker for the California Tuberculosis Association. Concerned about conditions in low-income communities—such as poor housing, roads, and health care—he had used the organization to engage residents politically and back improved neighborhood services. The organization grew rapidly and became an important political force (Gutierrez 1995; Underwood 1992). Looking back on its founding, Roybal explained, "We realized that Americans of Mexican ancestry would achieve representation in public office only with voter education and organization" (Griffith 1949, p. 64).

Roybal campaigned on practical issues such as discrimination in housing, and he supported a fair employment practices commission ordinance, a civilian police review board, and improved community services. Although his platform focused on issues and services rather than race, his support for fair housing policies and labor market practices clearly targeted racial discrimination. Shortly after World War II, Roybal, a veteran, had experienced these issues firsthand. As a personnel officer for a fruit and produce company, he had been instructed not to hire African Americans, Jews, and Mexicans. He had also been refused a GI housing loan because of his race (Griffith 1948; Horwitt 1989). When African Americans asked why they should vote for him, he replied, "Our skin is brown—our battle is the same. Our victory cannot but be a victory for you, too" (Griffith 1948, p. 66).

Roybal's record on racial issues and ethnic identity were clear to those familiar with his history of community activism (as were Judy Chu's during her campaigns in Monterey Park). Little Tokyo, directly west of Boyle Heights across the Los Angeles River, sat squarely in Roybal's council district, directly involving him in Japanese American interests, and Japanese Americans campaigned for him. In contrast, the district skirted the eastern and southern edges of downtown's Chinatown and attracted less attention from the Chinese American community.

Wilbur Sato, a longtime resident of Los Angeles, was among Roybal's Japanese American supporters. When I asked him if it was important that Roybal was Latino, he replied, "Yes, oh yes. That meant that there would be a minority voice. At that time, everybody [elected officials] was white, in East Los Angeles, around the Coliseum [near the University of Southern California]."

Sato, born in Pasadena, was living on Terminal Island in Los Angeles harbor when Japanese Americans were given a forty-eight-hour notice to evacuate after the United States entered World War II. He moved with his family to a friend's home in Boyle Heights, where they stayed briefly until they were sent to Manzanar concentration camp. Sato was interested in issues such as housing discrimination, which Roybal supported. While a student at UCLA he had worked on Roybal's campaign: "We put together an informal committee of Japanese Americans. . . . We were just getting our feet wet [in politics]. We worked on publicity for the campaign. We went through phone books, looking for Japanese names, typed labels for our mailings."

George Yoshinaga, a journalist, was another Japanese American who supported Roybal. Born in Redwood City in Northern California, Yoshinaga moved into a boardinghouse near Little Tokyo after his release from Heart Mountain concentration camp. As a reporter and editor for Japanese American newspapers, he concentrated on the day-to-day life of those resettling in Los Angeles after the war. He also followed politics and had attended many campaign functions. When asked why he supported Roybal, Yoshinaga stressed the need for representation: "We didn't have any Nisei council members, or people in congress. Backing a Hispanic, I figured he'd have the same approach, we're on the same playing field." When I asked what sorts of issues Japanese Americans and Latinos shared, he answered, "We didn't have any status. As a newspaper man, I had a little clout in the Japanese American community, but none outside. We shared that. We were facing the same kind of problems."

Yet Yoshinaga was quick to point out the many differences that existed between Latinos and Japanese Americans: "Just like today, we are facing the same kind of problems, but we have our own individual problems, too." Political alliances are critical for political influence, but equally important he believed that national identities should be preserved rather than submerged in panethnic groupings, "As Asian Pacific Islanders, we have more clout, but we lose our identity as Japanese Americans and I oppose that."

Roybal's multiracial efforts demonstrated the effectiveness of alliances, and the Community Service Organization's successful efforts to mobilize residents showed the importance of established groups for grass-roots electoral politics. His victories and strategy resonate in the San Gabriel Valley, where people developed local networks and organizations as well as established regional links with Latino and Asian American associations.

Creating the Foundation: Latino Organizations

The importance of organizations for political empowerment, such as the Community Service Organization's role in Edward Roybal's electoral success in Los Angeles, is underscored by Aldon Morris (1984) in his study of the U.S. civil rights movement. Morris points out that groups that face institutionalized discrimination and exclusion from mainstream politics must develop their own organizations to generate the resources, networks, and leadership necessary to participate effectively in electoral politics and influence government policy formation and resource distribution. Morris documents the importance of black churches for grass-roots mobilization and fund-raising and the importance of church support for the National Association for the Advancement of Colored People's legal actions in the South. As counterparts to the organizational capacity of black churches and the legal strategy of the NAACP, Latinos in the San Gabriel Valley used LULAC, the Mexican American Legal Defense and Educational Fund (MALDEF), and the Southwestern Voter Registration Education Project (SVREP). The Asian Pacific American Legal Center (APALC) and the UCLA Asian American Studies Center played similar roles for Asian Americans in the region.

The League of United Latin American Citizens

Mexican American servicemen who returned to their communities after World War I created organizations to protect and advance their interests in the face of intense discrimination. LULAC, founded in 1929 in Texas, became one of the first Mexican American civil rights organizations.[5]

In a society marked by housing, occupational, and educational segregation, LULAC worked to remove barriers obstructing the economic, political, and social integration of Mexican Americans. As David Gutierrez (1995) notes, however, limiting membership to citizens, stressing integration into U.S. society, and demonstrating to whites that Mexican Americans are loyal citizens marked a fundamental change from earlier Mexican American organizations that involved citizens and noncitizens alike. Considering the large number of Mexican immigrants in Texas who were not citizens, defining the organization's constituency in such an exclusionary manner was an extremely difficult and controversial decision. It meant cutting off a significant part of the population—indeed, creating a divide among members of the same family. Gutierrez observes that a pragmatic, cautious assessment of political conditions formed the basis for the decision. In contrast, charges were made that LULAC's founders were motivated by the self-promoting wishes of its primarily middle-class professionals and small business owners.

"Operation Wetback" prodded LULAC to rethink its policies. Beginning in 1954, the Immigration and Naturalization Service and the Border Patrol rounded up and expelled undocumented Mexican immigrants. The Immigration and Nationality Act of 1952 (the McCarran-Walter Act) expanded the grounds for the deportation of non-citizen immigrants and was widely condemned by Latino organizations because of its many discriminatory provisions.[6] More than three million people were expelled (some deported more than once) in the mid-1950s, primarily in California and Texas (Grebler, Moore, and Guzman 1970, p. 521). The expulsions included longtime residents as well as citizens, such as the U.S.-born children of undocumented immigrants. Families and communities throughout the Southwest were disrupted. This egregious violation of human rights "became one of the most traumatic recent experiences of the Mexican Americans in their contacts with government authority. No Mexican-American community in the Southwest remained untouched" (Grebler, Moore, and Guzman 1970, p. 522), creating a racialized experience that resonated with the wartime U.S. concentration camp experience of Japanese Americans. Such milestones became deeply fixed in the collective memories of each group. The active importation of Mexican laborers through the bracero program of the 1940s through 1960s, in conjunction with forced expulsion through Operation Wetback, demonstrated the government's categorization of Mexican immigrants as disposable laborers rather than as valuable residents.

Critical issues affecting Latinos, such as the abuses of Operation Wetback and the McCarran-Walter Act, prompted LULAC members to reevaluate their organization's limited focus on the rights of U.S. citizens. They eventually recognized the connection between the struggle for civil rights for Mexican Americans and immigrant rights. The change in attitude was clearly expressed in the 1977 First National Chicano/Latino Conference on Immigration and Public Policy, where LULAC joined with other Latino organizations such as MALDEF, the Center for Autonomous Social Action, and the G.I. Forum to object to anti-immigrant reforms proposed by the Carter administration (Gutierrez 1995).

Ideologically moderate since its founding, LULAC stressed involvement in politics, including voter registration drives and fighting segregation in schools and public facilities. Its battle against segregation, including *Mendez et al. v. Westminster School District,* which outlawed segregated classrooms in California in 1946, contributed to the legal foundation that eventually led to *Brown v. Board of Education* in 1954.

State-sponsored discrimination that deprived racial minorities of privileges while protecting those of whites—such as laws that prevented Asian immigrants from becoming naturalized citizens, and segregated schools and housing—provided one of the key areas of racialization that minorities fought through the courts. And while pursuing their own goals minority groups have helped others. The struggle for African American political empowerment and the passage of the Voting Rights Act of 1965, for example, greatly benefited both Latinos and Asian Americans. Combating discrimination and white privilege through the courts is a compelling reason to pool resources and skills, and minority groups have acted collectively, cognizant of shared interests and goals.

The Mexican American Legal Defense and Educational Fund

MALDEF was established in 1968 to use advocacy and litigation for social change in education, employment, and politics based on the model established by the NAACP and its independent Legal Defense Fund. Pete Tijerina, a LULAC member, was among those who recognized the need for such a group. The effort was assisted by the NAACP Legal Defense Fund's staff—such as attorney Vilma Martinez, who later became president and chair of the board of directors of MALDEF (Vigil 1990). Originally based in San Antonio, MALDEF's national office is now in Los Angeles.

Some of MALDEF's major cases involving politics include victories against at-large elections in the Supreme Court case *White v. Register* (1973), involving the Texas House of Representatives, and the Ninth Circuit Court of Appeals decision *Gomez v. City of Watsonville* (1988), involving city council elections. Victories against gerrymandered districts include *United States and Carrillo v. Los Angeles* and *Garza v. the County of Los Angeles* in the 1980s. As a result of the *Garza* case, which charged that Latinos had been consistently divided into separate Los Angeles County supervisorial districts, fragmenting their population and diluting their political power in direct violation of the 1965 Voting Rights Act, a district was created that would consolidate them in the San Gabriel Valley. That led to the election of the first Latino to the board of supervisors in this century—Gloria Molina. Antonia Hernandez, MALDEF's president and general counsel, noted the importance of the *Garza* case for all disfranchised groups.

> The Hispanic community in Los Angeles displayed a new sense of political empowerment this past March as they gathered in the Board of Supervisors meeting chambers to watch, and applaud enthusiastically, the swearing in of Gloria Molina, the newest member of the Board. . . . We went up against one of the most powerful governing bodies in the country. We engaged in one of the longest and most expensive voting rights cases in the history of the U.S. . . . Throughout this process we also are working cooperatively with the African American and Asian communities which also seek to increase their political influence. (MALDEF 1990–91, p. 2)

MALDEF has explicitly acknowledged the issues Latinos share with Asian Americans and African Americans and the organization has a strong track record of collaborative efforts with those communities. MALDEF criticized the Immigration Reform and Control Act of 1986 for its employer sanctions against the hiring of undocumented workers. Antonia Hernandez noted that the act's anti-immigrant bias would single out Latinos and Asian Americans: "MALDEF remains concerned over the potential for discrimination against those who look 'undocumented, too ethnic or foreign'" (MALDEF 1987, p. 2). In *Gregorio T. v Wilson* the U.S. District Court ruled in November 1995 that those portions of California's Proposition 187 (passed by voters in 1994) denying primary and secondary education based on immigration status and requiring proof of immigration status before enrolling students were unconstitutional. The Asian Pacific American Legal Center had joined with the American Civil Liberties Union and MALDEF to file the lawsuit on the "grounds that it violates the federal government's sole authority to enact immigration law" (Asian Pacific American Legal Center 1995, p. 1).

Language discrimination is another concern shared by Asian Americans and Latinos. As Hernandez explains the political implications, "Language-based discrimination also has a critical nexus to political access. We will continue our efforts to thwart the enactment of proposals that would eliminate multilingual ballots and voting assistance. Such proposals deny non-English speaking Americans their right to participate fully in our democratic process" (MALDEF 1995–96, p. 1). *Lau v. Nichols* (1973), the Supreme Court decision that San Francisco public schools were required to provide special instruction for Chinese-speaking students (Wollenberg 1978), became the benchmark for bilingual education programs and was used by MALDEF and other groups to advocate for similar programs for Spanish-speaking students (Avila 1984).

The Southwest Voter Registration Education Project

The Southwest Voter Registration Education Project was founded in San Antonio, Texas, in 1974, by Willie Velasquez, a longtime activist. With strong networks in the Midwest and Southwest, voter registration and electing Latino officials have been the main goals of the organization. The project played a major role in the increase of Latino registered voters in the Southwest, a number that grew from 488,000 in 1976 to more than a million in 1985 (Acuna 1988). As Juan Gomez-Quinones (1990, p. 166) describes the project, "It is the clearest example of the belief in voter registration and voting as the priority, and one in which numbers are the measure." The organization's California office is in Montebello.

In preparation for the 1996 presidential elections, the project launched Accountability '96, a program created to "register one hundred thousand Latino votes, initiate fifty thousand Latinos into the citizenship process, GOTV [get out the vote of] three hundred thousand Latino voters as well as educate millions of Latino voters with original survey research and media products" (SVREP 1995). The program used an established, grass-roots network estimated to include twenty-five thousand community leaders and elected officials. According to project figures, the number of Latino registered voters reached 6,610,000 in 1996, an increase of 28.7 percent over the 1992 figure of 5,136,000, and five million Latinos voted in the presidential election, primarily for Bill Clinton (SVREP 1997, p. 1).

Understanding the importance of redistricting and election procedures, the project has also worked with MALDEF to bring suits challenging gerrymandered districts and at-large election schemes that dilute Latino political power. In 1986 the project established the Southwest Voter Research Institute to carry out its extensive efforts involving telephone surveys, exit polls, studies of Latino voting patterns, and research aimed at increasing political participation.

The individual efforts of LULAC, MALDEF, and the project have been impressive. The organizations have developed a critical perspective on race relations, articulated the workings of white privilege and racial discrimination, and begun dismantling racial privilege in the courts. Research provided by the project and MALDEF, voting rights cases won by MALDEF, and voter registration and mobilization by LULAC and the project have greatly advanced the political voice of the community. The groups have also energetically pursued interracial alliances; for example, they have built strong working relationships with the NAACP and the Asian Pacific American Legal Center in Los Angeles.

Building Ties: Los Angeles Organizations

The history of working together shared by the major Latino and Asian American groups in Los Angeles and the San Gabriel Valley is fostered by an ideology that stresses increased political power across racial and class lines, a pragmatic assessment of the need for alliances, an understanding of whiteness based on lived experiences and professional knowledge, and a history of personal and working relationships.

The leaders of the organizations knew firsthand about being unwanted outsiders. Antonia Hernandez, born in Mexico, entered the United States at the age of eight in 1956. When her family crossed the border at El Paso, she remembers, "My father pointed to a sign that said, 'No Dogs—No Mexicans.' He told us, 'Don't ever forget being proud of who you are. You're just as good as anyone—if you work hard enough'" (Naylor 1991, p. 59).

Asian Americans also understand about being outsiders. Stewart Kwoh often tells of the time a white waitress in a North Carolina restaurant asked where his family was from: "My great-grandfather mined in New Mexico, my grandfather was a tailor in Oakland and my mother was born in Stockton. To this, the waitress asked, 'So how do you like your new country?'" (Kang 1995, p. A1).

A contributing incident that turned Don Nakanishi's interests away from medicine and toward Asian American studies occurred during his freshman year at Yale University in 1967. On the anniversary of the bombing of Pearl Harbor, Nakanishi was studying in his dormitory room when a group of students entered, pelted him with water balloons, and shouted, "Bomb Pearl Harbor! Bomb Pearl Harbor!" Discussing the event and the way Asian Americans are connected to their countries of origin in ways that European Americans are not, Nakanishi stated, "It made me wonder why I was being identified with an event I had nothing to do with, one that involved Japan, and why my fate was wrapped up in U.S.-Japan relations" (Kang 1993, p. A1).

Asian Americans, African Americans, and Latinos live and work in the same spaces in many regions of Los Angeles. What is called "Koreatown" because of its commercial enterprises is primarily inhabited by Latinos, and the 1992 civil unrest—in which many Korean-owned businesses were ransacked and burned by Latinos—graphically revealed the deep tensions that exist between the two groups (Ong and Hee 1993). Similar to the rapid demographic shifts in the San Gabriel Valley, large areas of Los Angeles once considered black neighborhoods are now primarily Latino (Oliver and Johnson 1984; Park 1995).

Recognizing the strong tensions that have resulted in outbreaks of conflict, the need for understanding how both communities view change, and the importance of working together, Antonia Hernandez commented:

> South-Central Los Angeles has gone from African American to Latino in just the last ten years. If I were in their shoes, I would also feel threatened—so from the Latino community there is a certain understanding. Sharing power is not easy. . . . It's so difficult to share, and so the transfer of power, even under the best of circumstances, is a difficult prospect. So to minimize tension, first we have to get both communities to realize what's going on, how quickly our communi-

ties have changed. And secondly, we have to look at the long haul. We are go-ing to have to work in coalitions—it's in everybody's self-interest. There is go-ing to be no majority as we now know it. So the question is: How do we work together to serve everybody's interests? (Proffitt 1992, p. M3)

Even as Latinos gain political power and their numbers greatly exceed Asian Americans and African Americans in California, Hernandez recog-nizes the importance of cooperative efforts among all groups. Sharing political concerns as well as neighborhoods, Latinos, Asian Americans, and African Americans have gone beyond multicultural rhetoric and joined to protest and fight such discriminatory policies as Proposition 187.

> Our strength cannot lie in numbers alone. The demographic forecasts that name Latinos the dominant minority of the twenty-first century are not enough to ensure that we will replace current defeats with future victories. We must be strategic and thoughtful. We must build strong coalitions. . . . On November 9th [1994], the day after the election, MALDEF took two very important actions. We filed lawsuits against Proposition 187, and we joined other community lead-ers in a press conference. At the press conference, I was struck by something very positive. As I stood on the platform with other community leaders, it became apparent that a strong coalition had been created. It is not a Latino coalition; it is not a minority coalition; it is a civil rights coalition. (Hernandez 1995, p. 8)

In 1990, when MALDEF, APALC, and the SVREP were preparing for redistricting in California, the strong professional and personal relation-ships that had been built up through the years among Latinos and Asian Americans laid the foundation for a coalition. Antonia Hernandez—who received her bachelor's and law degrees from UCLA had known Stewart Kwoh while they attended law school. Because Hernandez lived in Pasa-dena, about fifteen minutes north of Monterey Park, she was also famil-iar with the San Gabriel Valley. During one of the first redistricting meet-ings between Asian Americans and Latinos in 1991 she had impressed Asian Americans with her detailed knowledge of voter registration and citizenship patterns among the diverse Asian American ethnic groups.

Hernandez also stressed MALDEF's commitment to redistricting and working with Asian Americans: "We have the in-house machinery to do the maps. We are prepared to go to court. MALDEF has its goals, and we want to consider the interests of Asian Americans and African Americans." She was clear about the problems of cooperation and aware that the task of establishing a working agenda within a heterogeneous Latin communi-ty was difficult and added yet another layer of complexity through the for-mation of multiracial coalitions. As she said, "Redistricting can get nasty.

We have to communicate. We know that the Asian community is like the Latino community. Not one perspective, but many shades of perspectives."

Richard Martinez and members of the Southwest Voter Research Institute of San Antonio had also participated in a number of projects with APALC and the Asian Americans in the San Gabriel Valley: the 1986 UCLA Asian American voter registration study, APALC's 1988 voter registration drive, and the 1988 Monterey Park City Council exit poll, which involved APALC and the UCLA Asian American Studies Center.

At an Asian American redistricting meeting in 1990 Stewart Kwoh stressed the importance of MALDEF: "Latinos had MALDEF, which is a national organization, and Southwest Voters, and people like Leo Estrada [a UCLA professor] who was crunching out the numbers and providing the groups with the information they needed. Asian Pacific Americans need to build up these kinds of institutions. . . . We're lucky to be working with them [MALDEF]. . . . We [APALC] have joint projects with them. . . . They are good groups to work with, they will listen to us." Kwoh also employed personal contacts and discussed the Voting Rights Act and its implications for Latinos and Asian Americans with Richard Fajardo, an attorney at MALDEF who worked on redistricting, and Joaquin Avila, one of the preeminent voting rights attorneys in the United States, who had worked with MALDEF in a number of its landmark victories in the Southwest.

Clearly, Asian American and Latino legal and political organizations— staffed with experienced, talented, and highly skilled personnel—had a strong history of joint efforts and provided an important resource base for the Los Angeles region. The groups would be a crucial ally of the rapidly growing Latino and Asian American population in the San Gabriel Valley as they waged political and legal struggles over language issues, economic development, and voting rights.

Building Ties: The San Gabriel Valley

Native-born, middle-class professionals, some tracing their roots to the land-owning elite of the 1800s (the "Californios"), Mexican Americans in Monterey Park were ambivalent about the cultural content and political significance of their ethnic identity when Chinese immigrants began moving into the region (Calderon 1991). A similar case concerned the native-born Nisei and Chinese Americans whose ethnicity, in terms of transplanted culture, was either rapidly diminishing or had disappeared altogether. Although identifying as Hispanic, one Mexican American expressed uncertainty about what such an identity meant: "Hispanic? It's just a nice category. It doesn't mean anything to me. It is a way to classify yourself. . . . I eat Mexican food but I don't speak the language. But, retain my culture—retain what culture? My parents consider themselves Californios" (Calderon 1991, p. 72).

Becoming established in suburban Monterey Park during the 1960s and 1970s meant joining the city's white-dominated political and social organizations and thinking about themselves in individual terms rather than as Mexican Americans. Yet as with Asian Americans, events in the community racialized residents' experiences and community politics, compelling Mexican Americans to recognize the salience of race in their everyday lives and become "reluctant" ethnics. Fearing the translation of population into political power and an economic threat to his livelihood, one Mexican American developer believed that the growing number of Chinese immigrants initially prompted Latinos to align themselves with whites because both were established groups whose interests were being threatened: "It is my feeling that Orientals have made Latinos and Anglos closer to each other. If there had to be a choice in choosing sides in this community, who would you team up with? Latinos and Anglos would team up with each other. The city is being taken over. The real power is going to be the 'Orientals'" (Calderon 1991, p. 89).

The increasingly hateful rhetoric and discriminatory policies aimed at the new Chinese immigrants, emanating from residents and city hall alike, drew Latinos into the debate as participants and targets. The growing number of Asian immigrants and their increasing influence over public space, local politics, and the economy exposed the traditional white power structure and brought the defense of privilege directly into public view. Although it ostensibly targeted Chinese, for example, the failed English-only initiative in Monterey Park also alarmed Mexican Americans because it attacked their experiences. As one city commissioner related, "Ever since I can remember we had Mexican signs which advertised tamales . . . and they were in Spanish and no one ever objected. . . . Now all of a sudden, you know, they're touchy because the sign is in Chinese or Japanese" (Calderon 1991, p. 123). Another Mexican American placed foreign-language signs squarely in the context of American history, noting, "I've been a little disappointed because I think the gradual change is what's happened in our country, whether it would have been Russian or Jewish bakeries, they all start only with big signs . . . and originally when they come here it is the only language that they can express themselves in and they can't very well put up an English sign if they can't read English or they don't feel that comfortable [with English]" (Calderon 1991, p. 122).

Although English-only proponents argued that signs in a foreign language divided residents, in their speeches and actions they made no real attempts to include immigrants in society and actively defined Americans as being white and not Asian. As a Mexican American member of the city's staff declared, "I noticed the way he [Hatch] talked about Americanism . . . I mean, in the paper the other day, he referred to the Asians as 'Judy Chu's people.' You know, 'her people.' We are the real 'white Americans.' He wraps himself in the American flag and real Americans are blonde, blue-eyed types" (Calderon 1991, p. 123).

In fact, Asian immigrants had attempted to conform earlier in the century. After witnessing the passage of the Chinese Exclusion Act in 1882, and aware of white sentiment that Japanese were "unassimilable aliens" as well as the growing support for Japanese exclusion, Japanese immigrants attempted to comply to American standards of behavior. As Yuji Ichioka (1988) documents, they tried to adapt by avoiding Japanese wording on business signs, wearing American clothing, and eating American food. The fundamental issue was race not outward appearances and behavior, however. The Gentlemen's Agreement of 1907–8, for example, banned Japanese immigrant laborers, and Japanese Americans were incarcerated during World War II. Operation Wetback was a similar reminder for Mexican Americans of the government's rejection of their efforts to integrate.

Latinos soon recognized that much of the sentiment against development was rooted in concerns over race and immigration rather than language and increasing building density. Linking the Residents Association of Monterey Park's no-growth position to anti-Asian sentiments, one Mexican American public official stated, "They wanted to stop all the development because they felt that if they could stop the development, they could stop the Asians" (Calderon 1991, p. 110). A Mexican American woman, a community resident and activist for twenty years, explained why Latinos who supported the slow-growth movement were ignoring the defense of white racial privilege, locally and throughout U.S. history:

> People who would vote for the gringos are saying, "Down with development, down with the Chinese, down with these people who are coming in and changing our community." I can see how a lot of Mexican Americans or Chicanos would respond to that kind of an argument. It is based on a lack of knowledge of what it is that makes up the U.S. You know, which has basically been a white supremacist society. . . . A lot of our concerns are based on ignorance if we think

that the Chinese are our enemies. Most of the appeal in most of the literature is anti-development. Development means Chinese. (Pardo, unpublished fieldnotes 1988)

The importance of multiracial efforts and the understanding that an attack on Asian immigrants was also an attack on Latinos coalesced in the efforts of Asian Americans, Latinos, and whites who created the Coalition for Harmony in Monterey Park (CHAMP) to rescind Resolution 9004, passed by the city council in 1986. CHAMP members petitioned the council to rescind the resolution because they opposed its declaration that English was the official language of the city and its anti-immigrant provisions. The effort proved successful and revealed residents' misconceptions about the English-only movement, such as the belief that it provided funding for bilingual programs. Many who had supported it changed their minds when they learned its intent. Jose Calderon, a professor at nearby Pitzer College, gathered signatures for the petition outside a supermarket and later observed:

> Standing outside of Albertson's [now a Ralph's] grocery store, in Atlantic Square Mall, I was surprised to find how many Latinos were confused about the resolution and Proposition 63. Many thought that "English as the Official Language" was all about financial support for teaching their children English, for bilingual education, for English as a Second Language, and for literacy programs. I found some Spanish-speaking Mexican immigrants supporting the resolution and initiative because they wanted their children to learn English. . . . When I explained to them that the English Only movement was really attempting to the very opposite, they signed the petition. (1991, p. 125)

Proposition 63 passed statewide in 1986 by a wide margin: 73 percent to 27 percent (*Los Angeles Times* 1986, p. 1). Although it also passed in Monterey Park, it did so by a much smaller percentage (56 percent were in favor), a difference Calderon attributes to education efforts exposing the intent of English-only activities in the city (Horton and Calderon 1992).

The transition from thinking of oneself as an individual to being a member of a racialized group, and to considering the political consequences attached to such an identity, was embodied in the efforts of the Latinos who joined CHAMP's efforts to rescind Resolution 9004. Although the resolution was aimed at the new Chinese immigrants, Latinos understood that its racist and anti-immigrant provisions did not stop with Asians; they attacked the history and culture of Latinos, too. As with *Lau v. Nichols,* the two groups were linked by language issues. CHAMP's multiracial efforts continued with the development of Latino political organizations in the San Gabriel Valley and alliances among Asian Americans, Latinos, and whites.

The San Gabriel Valley Hispanic Roundtable and LULAC

The Hispanic Roundtable of Monterey Park was founded in 1986. With the election of Latinos its primary goal, the group met regularly for several years before it eventually disbanded (Calderon 1991). In contrast to Latinos, who early in their lives thought of themselves simply as Americans and were later compelled to recognize their racial identities, members of the Roundtable had long histories of political activism as Chicanos or Mexican Americans.

The group's members experienced the dilemma and ambivalence felt by Latinos in Monterey Park who sought a better life and empowerment but instead were faced with a growing Asian American population. They had moved to the city from low-income, working-class East Los Angeles (which includes Boyle Heights) and saw the San Gabriel Valley as a move up to a middle-class area that had excellent public schools and a newer, larger housing stock. With a growing Latino population and social and geographical connection to East Los Angeles, the valley was seen as a place where Latinos could establish a strong political presence. One Latina explained, "I felt that Monterey Park was like ELA East. You see, I thought of Monterey Park as becoming a Latino community and one where eventually it would be a good base for us to elect councilmen and congressmen" (Pardo, unpublished fieldnotes 1988).

When she moved to Monterey Park in the mid-1960s she could not have foreseen the dramatic changes that would turn the city into the regional center of a rapidly expanding Chinese immigrant residential and commercial community. The defeat of two Latino incumbent council members in 1986, David Almada and Rudy Peralta, and the election of two new white council members created a council composed of four whites and one Filipino American. Clearly, a Latino voice in politics required an institutional base, and supporters of Almada created the Hispanic Roundtable. As a founding member explained:

> I was working on the campaign, and on the night of his defeat, I saw all the people that were behind him in Monterey Park. There was a core group of people who were interested in supporting Latinos. We shouldn't lose the motivation and the energy that I saw there that Almada was able to mobilize. It is to gain control of our destinies, so to speak. To have representation so that the needs of the Hispanic community are taken into consideration, when the power brokers are wheeling and dealing so that the city council has the kind of representation that a Roundtable can make accountable. (Pardo, unpublished fieldnotes 1988)

With the election of council members Fred Balderamma in 1990 and Rita Valenzuela in 1992, and with the state assembly and senate members, members of Congress, and Los Angeles County supervisor serving Monterey Park all Latino in 1996, Latinos could realize their goal of living in a large, powerful political community.

Just as returning Mexican American veterans of World War I recognized the need for an organization that would advance their interests and created LULAC in 1929, a number of Latinos, among them Jose Calderon and Abel Amaya, director of the USC Chicano Studies Center, expressed interest in establishing a Latino political organization in the San Gabriel Valley. A local chapter of the league had been organized in the 1950s, gone inactive in the 1970s, and was reestablished in 1986 (Calderon, unpublished fieldnotes 1988, 1991). Tony Nevarez, a dean at a nearby community college, and Delia Nevarez, a local teacher and formerly LULAC's national woman of the year, provided historical viewpoints as past members of the earlier chapter and offered to help reestablish the group. Because of its politically moderate platform, LULAC could appeal to the primarily middle-class Latinos active in the San Gabriel Valley. As part of the largest Latino organization in the United States the group gained immediate political clout.

Before LULAC was established its members were already active in a number of community organizations and events. The league provided an institutional platform from which members could express political and cultural interests as Latinos and also strengthen the interracial relationships they had worked to develop, in contrast to the nationalistic goals of the Hispanic Roundtable. They helped organize, for example, Monterey Park's annual Cinco De Mayo celebration and used it as a vehicle to celebrate their Mexican heritage, a demonstration of the league's change in position from early avoidance of such ethnic events to a later recognition that keeping their cultural heritage alive and fighting for immigrant rights were integral parts of citizenship.

The event also provided a chance to build bridges with other community groups, regardless of their races or political beliefs. Chinese lion dancers as well as mariachi groups would participate in the celebration. A local Chinese American resident, Peter Chen, had first brought the suggestion of a lion dance to Calderon in 1989. The planning committee enthusiastically embraced the idea, especially when they learned that local Chinese American business people would cover the cost of the performance. "This will be a unique event at a Cinco de Mayo," Calderon reflected. "I don't know if it has happened anywhere else before—where the dance and culture of another ethnic group, in particular Chinese, is presented as part of a celebration that is primarily devoted to expressing the beauty of the Mexican culture" (Calderon, unpublished fieldnotes 1989).

Cinco de Mayo became an opportunity for all residents to mingle in a festive and informal setting. People often carefully maintain social distance at public events, however, even though they inhabit the same space and exchange polite greetings and smiles. An event at the end of the evening changed that, however. The Alienz (a rock band named satirically in reference to the term *illegal aliens*) had just finished playing a set of hard-driving Latin rock. Jose, microphone in hand, suggested that everyone should join hands and form a circle, representing that we are a family, as the theme for the afternoon, "Somos Una Familia" [We are one family] suggested. I thought to myself, a nice but corny idea, no one will do this. So, I was surprised to see people—children as well as adults—getting up and joining hands. I got caught up in the spirit and I said to Mary Pardo, "Get up, let's do this." I asked Joaquin—one of Jose's sons—who was sitting a few feet away, to join us. After a few minutes, everybody in the audience was joined together in a huge circle in front of the stage, stretched along the grass and through the bleachers. Jose explained that the song, "De Colores," talks about people of all different types coming together and that while we were singing, we should look at the people next to us, and if we or they need help in the coming year we should think of them. I was astonished to see several members of the band—I thought that they would be too "cool" to participate in the neighborhood event—enthusiastically join Jose on stage with their guitars, singing and playing. I began moving with the music, and as I looked around I noticed that the whole circle was moving back and forth, different sections moving in different ways. It was a nice moment, the lights from the stage reaching out into the night, casting a glow over the circle of people hemmed in by darkness. The people, mainly Latinos but also with a conspicuous scattering of Asian Americans and whites, sang and swayed as the evening's events began to wind down.

Although a politically moderate group that was founded in the 1920s to champion the rights of Mexican Americans, the San Gabriel Valley LULAC chapter transformed their organization to meet local community needs and support a progressive program that included a strong multicultural component. Recognizing that cultural celebrations have little impact on the political and social inequalities that exist in a community, for example, LULAC also supported candidates and built links with other organizations in the region, especially Asian American groups. Although the league's bylaws prohibit chapters from endorsing candidates, local members did so individually. Many were part of Judy Chu's core group of volunteers in her first city council campaign in 1988.

Chu's campaigns reflected the strong grass-roots multiracial efforts of Edward Roybal's Los Angeles City Council campaigns but adapted them to the changing conditions of contemporary politics and growing economic strength of the Chinese American community through her exceptional fund-raising efforts. Facilitating grass-roots involvement in structural change, Chu established a multiracial "kitchen cabinet" of community activists who met monthly at her home after her election. As Calderon explains, "What stands out is the importance of leadership in taking multiethnic unity from a level of cultural and social interaction to one that involves all ethnic groups in the process of creating structural change. . . . The Judy Chu 'kitchen cabinet' best exemplified the ingredients of empowering multiethnic unity. It combined participatory democracy at the grassroots neighborhood arena with policy-making at the city council governance level" (1991, pp. 247–48).

Based on their similar political interests and close ties built on a history of working together on political issues and interaction during social occasions, LULAC and the West San Gabriel Asian Pacific Democratic Club have worked aggressively and thoughtfully to build and maintain their relationship. Maintaining close, informal ties, members of each group telephone each other to extend invitations to respective annual banquets. There have also been a number of joint events, including a candidates' forum for the Monterey Park City Council election in 1990, a forum on redistricting in 1991, and a forum on immigration in 1993. Yet another indication of Latino–Asian American cooperation was a forum that the Chinese American Civil Rights and Education Foundation held in 1988 on proposed language restrictions on business signs. The foundation, a local San Gabriel Valley group, included speakers from LULAC and the Asian Pacific American Legal Center of Southern California.

The Multi-Cultural Community Association and the Alhambra School District

Racial violence in local high schools, growing conflict among parents along racial lines as they struggled to resolve student issues, and the unresponsiveness of the Alhambra School Board prompted concerned residents to reconcile differences and join to force the school board to act. The local LULAC chapter and the Chinese American Parents and Teachers Association of Southern California (Chinese American PTA), based in the San Gabriel Valley and founded in 1979, established the Multi-Cultural Community Association to end the fragmentation of parents' efforts along racial lines and persuade the board to implement policies to alleviate racial conflict.

In the mid-1980s a fight involving Asian Americans, Latinos, and whites resulted in a non-fatal stabbing of a Chinese student. Two more fights involving Latinos, whites, and Asian Americans were reported in 1991 (Calderon 1995). When parents expressed concerns before the school board, some white members of the board dismissed the fights with explanations of "youthful hormones" and "boys will be boys."

The members of the Chinese American PTA did not agree with that explanation and in a letter to the board stated that "racial conflicts led to the stabbing of a Chinese student at Alhambra High School" and "two Chinese students were victims of an unprovoked beating by a group of Latino students on campus" in 1991 at San Gabriel High School (CAPTASC 1991). After the 1991 fight, 225 Asian American students also wrote and signed a letter—written in Chinese and translated by the Chinese PTA—to the board of education. In it, they described some of the forms of harassment they faced at San Gabriel High School, which, according to the Alhambra School District (1990), was 42 percent Asian American and 44 percent Latino:

> On our campus, the Chinese American students are often insulted by Hispanic students. Some of the things that they do to us Asian students are: use foul language against us, verbal assaults, nasty gestures, bump into us on purpose, hit us with their backpacks, step on our feet, pull the girls' hair, take french fries and popcorn from us in the lunch room, spit on us, etc. We try to take all these abuses in stride, and tolerate them. We complained about these incidents and sometimes told our parents. But the more we put up with them, the more some of the Hispanic students do things to us. If we continue to not stand up and protest against it, we are afraid that we will be beaten as these other two Chinese were. We want to officially bring this up and hope to get attention from our school district. This petition urges our school district to take a firm stand to solve the problems of campus violence and racial conflict. (CAPTASC 1991)

The history of the Chinese American PTA was explained during a discussion that involved white, Latino, and Asian American residents who had gathered around the issue of school violence during the coalition-building process. Why, a Latina asked, had a specifically Chinese PTA been created? Why had parents not joined the local PTAs? Ironically, she was an active member of LULAC, and her experience with politics should have made her aware of the way traditional organizations interpreted and handled racial issues. A member of the Chinese PTA explained that the organization had been created because existing PTAs did not meet the unique needs of Chinese immigrant parents, many of whom did not speak English and were unfamiliar with even the most basic practices of U.S. schools:

> Our members are mostly not English-speaking. They knew nothing about the United States' school system, what report cards meant, what universities to go to. We originally began as a network with bilingual people helping Chinese speakers. Then it became bigger, lobbying the school districts and politicians. And I also belong to the local PTA, but they mainly do fund-raising. They are so entrenched and have traditional views. They refuse to have translators at their meetings and are not pro-bilingual in terms of school curriculum.

It is confusing and intimidating for a monolingual, Chinese-speaking person to attend a meeting where English is the only language used. The refusal to use translators during meetings of the school-based PTAs demonstrated an unwillingness to recognize the concerns of new immigrants and created a need for an organization that could deal with critical issues related to education and involve parents in matters of safety and well-being. Asian American parent groups have also been created in other Southern California communities that have large Asian immigrant populations; there is a Chinese group in Arcadia, Korean and Chinese groups in Cerritos, and a Korean group in Fullerton (Seo 1996).

At the same time the Chinese PTA was lobbying the Alhambra School Board, members of LULAC were also attending board meetings and requesting that the district address conflict in the schools. Tension between Asian American and Latino parents was exacerbated by the board's reluctance to deal with conflict on campuses and the attempts of some board members to shift responsibility from the schools to the parents, pitting Latinos against Asian Americans.

Calderon, one of the founders of the multiracial coalition that emerged from the struggle, viewed (1995) the initially antagonistic relationship between Latinos and Asian Americans as being due to the misconceptions of each group. Latinos wrongly assumed that the Chinese PTA could use the large amounts of capital controlled by Asian American entrepreneurs to give themselves much greater access to local politicians and attorneys. Although the Latino middle-class population was sizable, it was composed primarily of salaried professionals who believed they did not have access to the same level of resources controlled by Asian Americans. Asian Americans, however, incorrectly believed that Latinos had greater political influence on members of the school board because most local politicians were Latino.

Calderon, representing LULAC, and Marina Tse, an immigrant and president of the Chinese PTA, worked with a number of other individuals to try to overcome the "narrow nationalist" aims of each group and combine the two to form one organization (Calderon 1995). Rather than be combatants on opposite sides of a racial issue, Calderon and Tse stressed that parents should be united by the larger goal of seeking quality education in a school system where complex problems based on economic and demographic restructuring, class differences, cultural misunderstanding, and race were grossly oversimplified as racial conflict.[7]

Calderon had a long history of coalition-building, demonstrated by LULAC's numerous meetings with the West San Gabriel Valley Asian Pacific Democratic Club and his involvement in multiracial politics in Monterey Park. His credibility among Latinos, Asian Americans, and whites was a critical part of the process as members of different organizations worked to consider the quality of education and conflict management. MALDEF and the Asian Pacific American Legal Center also contributed legal aid for students involved in the fights and mediation to help settle disputes among parents. These individuals and organizations worked over a number of months and formed the Multi-Ethnic Task Force (later called the Multi-Cultural Community Association). They were successful in changing the school district's policy of handling conflict after the fact through containment and punishment to instituting prevention programs that addressed the roots of the conflict.[8]

Conclusion

Mexican Americans and Asian Americans occupy subordinate positions in the U.S. racial hierarchy, but their situations through history have had distinctly different consequences with varying levels of access to rights and privileges routinely granted to whites. Early Asian immigrants were denied the right of naturalization, whereas Mexicans could become citizens. When the Japanese-Mexican Labor Association applied for membership in the American Federation of Labor, Mexicans were offered the opportunity to join but not Japanese. And in the redevelopment of Monterey Park, the concept of "Mexican" was linked to the history of the region and deemed acceptable (although "whitened" to Mediterranean), whereas "Asian" was considered foreign and excluded.

In response to the anti-Asian movement that followed the entrance of the new Chinese immigrants in the San Gabriel Valley, the first inclination of Latinos was to align themselves with whites. The pronounced xenophobia and racism expressed in the slow-growth movement and local politics, however, quickly caused Latinos to realize that they were racialized differently than Asian Americans and did not enjoy equal status with whites. Although both groups recognized their different histories and racialized positions in the United States, they were also cognizant of a common position in a racial hierarchy supporting whiteness.

Excluded from the centers of economic, political, and social power, Latinos and Asian Americans understood that their ethnic and racial identities and communities represented resources that corresponded with their concerns and base of power. Forming organizations and mobilizing politically based on such identities used a sense of community and history through cultural construction and collective memory.

Like members of the Japanese-Mexican Labor Association at the turn of the century, community activists of the San Gabriel Valley now recognize shared interests and racial positions. Latinos and Asian Americans in LULAC, the Asian Pacific Democratic Club, and the Multi-Cultural Association based alliances on common ground as racialized minorities struggling to improve political and economic conditions. In contrast, conflicts between Mexican workers and Japanese American farmers during the 1930s and 1970s were echoed in contemporary conflicts among Korean shopkeepers and Latino and African American residents, a demonstration of the extreme difficulties involved when groups have no clear interests that transcend immediate sources of conflict.

Arthur Schlesinger (1991) has argued that to focus on race and ethnicity shifts the emphasis from integration and national identity to segregation and divisiveness. He criticizes the development of ethnic or race-specific organizations because he views such groups as establishing boundaries and creating barriers. Schlesinger's unspoken—and inaccurate—assumption is that Americans have united and have all been given equal access to the political system. That ignores the fact that political rights have been circumscribed by race, class, and gender since the founding of the United States, when the right to vote was restricted to white men of property. Throughout the history of the United States race has been used by whites—a category that has also shifted through time—for legitimizing and creating difference and social, economic, and political exclusion. Latinos, African Americans, and Asian Americans in Los Angeles and the

San Gabriel Valley, however, have used race to mobilize in an effort to integrate their communities into American society.

Asked whether Latinos have not assimilated, Antonia Hernandez replied, "Hogwash. You know, it's ignorance and xenophobia at its best. For immigrants like the Italians and the Germans, the flow came, and stopped. Those people had to assimilate, and they did. With Latinos, people just keep coming, and coming, so the perception is that we are not assimilating. But I am a first-generation immigrant, and if you don't call me mainstream and assimilated, I don't know what you can call me" (Proffitt 1992, p. M3). In fact, Hernandez's efforts to use judicial and political means to advance the rights of Latinos and other racial minorities clearly demonstrates her goal of structural integration and refutes Schlesinger's separatist arguments. To do nothing supports the forms of apartheid that exist in the United States (Massey and Denton 1993).

The individual life stories of Japanese Americans and Mexican Americans in Monterey Park exemplify the experiences of organizations such as JACL and LULAC and the histories of Asian and Latin American immigrants. Such individuals and organizations have worked to integrate themselves or their members into U.S. society. Their goal was acceptance as good neighbors and citizens and ultimately as Americans. The work to accomplish that goal, however, was continually obstructed by racial barriers imposed by whites.

As part of the effort to be good citizens, one of the most controversial decisions JACL's leaders ever made was to support the executive order to incarcerate Japanese Americans during World War II. That decision was compounded by a denouncement of Japanese Americans who protested the government for drafting incarcerated members of their community for military service. The latter issue continues to reverberate within the Japanese American community, and at the request of JACL members a series of forums was held in chapters across the western states during the late 1980s to discuss the wartime issues.[9] These events culminated in a ceremony conducted by JACL's Pacific Southwest District Council in 1995 to apologize to draft resisters (Mizobe 1995); the national league, however, has resisted proposals to apologize formally for its activities involving resisters.

In order to avoid the effects of white racism, people have attempted throughout U.S. history to disassociate themselves from others of their own ethnic and racial groups and also from other populations. The actions of JACL and LULAC to restrict membership to citizens were in part a response to anti-immigrant legislation and a focused effort to further the interests of their group as defined by citizenship status. Similarly, in the 1970s the UFW's opposition to growers' use of undocumented workers to undermine strikes and impede efforts to unionize farm workers led to the organization's strong stance against undocumented immigrants and support for deportation plans (Gutierrez 1995). The efforts of the Japanese to distance themselves from Chinese after the Chinese Exclusion Act (and Chinese Americans to distinguish themselves from Japanese Americans during the World War II incarceration) were later echoed in attempts of Japanese and Chinese Americans in Monterey Park to distinguish themselves from the Chinese immigrants who were the targets of racist and anti-immigrant rhetoric.

LULAC and JACL remained politically moderate organizations, and removing barriers to integrating U.S. society continued as their primary goal. What changed was their understanding that cooperation with the U.S. government—such as in the case of JACL and the concentration camps—was not recognized. Similarly, the UFW shifted its strong stance against undocumented immigrants and its support for deportation. Concentration camps for Asian Americans and Operation Wetback for Mexican Americans clearly demonstrated the extreme forms of discriminatory actions that the U.S. government was capable of executing well into the twentieth century.

The groups were operating with limited resources in an environment where the extreme forms of discrimination they were trying to dismantle were backed by the power of the state. Their options for reform were limited. Mario T. Garcia has responded to critics of LULAC's early activities by rejecting the interpretation of these actions as "'accommodationist' (in the worst sense)" (1989, pp. 17, 19). He argues instead that the era served as a foundation for the politics of the Chicano movement of the 1960s: "It [the era] possesses a character of its own, a richness of political struggle, and a deep search for identity."

The campaign for equality and justice continues, and the alliances formed by Latinos and Asian Americans in the 1903 Oxnard sugar beet worker strike and the United Farm Workers Union have not been forgotten. They are recalled in the current attempt to unionize workers at the New Otani Hotel. The labor conflict pits Japanese Americans against Japanese nationals, highlighting the importance of experiences in the United States for the development of labor and political alliances rather than emotional and imaginary ties based on common ancestry (Yancey et al. 1976).

Coming full circle, John J. Sweeney, president of the AFL-CIO (the AFL denied the membership application of the Japanese and Mexican workers in Oxnard in 1903) has supported the efforts of New Otani employees to unionize, and he led a group of nearly two thousand through downtown Los Angeles to demonstrate at the hotel on February 19, 1997 (McDonnell and Silverstein 1997).[10]

Connecting the 1903 Oxnard strike, the UFW, and the efforts at the New Otani Hotel, Ryan Yokota (1994, p. 3) has observed, "Our communities have steadfastly stood together in the battles of the past, and possess the ability to collectively better our situation for the present." The reference to "our communities" is a recognition of the complex relationship between class and race. The conditions that led to the Alien Land Laws and the importation of Latin Americans and Asians as cheap sources of labor persist, echoed in the poor quality of services available in low-income Latino and Asian American urban communities, continued labor struggles, and efforts to gain political power in the suburbs of the San Gabriel Valley.

6 The Case of Redistricting:
The Growing Organizational Scale
of Politics and Interracial Alliances

Redistricting and reapportionment throughout U.S. history have reflected the importance of race. White politicians—representing predominantly white constituencies—have manipulated political boundaries to create districts that reflect their interests. The 1965 Voting Rights Act recognizes the importance of political concerns that emerge from race and attempts to provide a legal remedy for the historical political disfranchisement of racial minority groups (Davidson 1992).

The process of redistricting in the San Gabriel Valley illustrates how government policies—in this case, the Voting Rights Act—influence the development of racial and ethnic identities. The federal government provides a legal framework that establishes a foundation for the enfranchisement of members of racial or ethnic minority groups, but the interpretation and application of that framework are affected by conditions at the state and local levels. The tremendous amount of resources required to participate in the redistricting process and related court cases drive the growing organizational scale of politics and encourage panethnic and interracial alliances (Saito 1993b). Supreme Court interpretations of the act also promote panethnic grouping by imposing requirements concerning population size and political cohesiveness.

After each decennial census, political districts are reconfigured to reflect changes in population. Redistricting is critical for the political interests of racial groups because it creates local, state (assembly and senate), and federal (congressional) districts from which officials are elected. Historically, politicians have divided geographic concentrations of racial groups into many districts, diluting their political influence. Redistricting was a key issue for Asian Americans, who have experienced extreme fragmentation under previous plans. There was no Asian American in the 120-member state legislature between 1980 and 1992 (Eljera 1997).[1]

The fact that the law provides a basis for collective action means nothing unless groups act on it and establish a case. Recognizing the need to institute organizations that could participate in such a technical, political, and bureaucratic process, Latinos and Asian Americans each formed statewide and regional groups to advocate the interests of their respective communities to the California State Legislature, which is in charge of the redistricting and reapportionment process. The Coalition of Asian Pacific Americans for Fair Reapportionment (CAPAFR) was formed in 1990 from more than 150 organizations representing, as the group's statement of goals and objectives says, "Community members from social service agencies, academia, leaders, political organizations, private and public institutions." For operational purposes, the statewide coalition was divided into Northern and Southern California divisions.

Legal, social service, and educational institutions rather than political groups took the lead in mobilizing Asian Americans in the redistricting process. CAPAFR was established at a conference entitled "The Other Side of (the) Census: Reapportionment and Political Empowerment" held on March 3, 1990, at the Asian Pacific American Legal Center.[2] Four organizations launched the group: the Asian Pacific American Legal Center, UCLA Asian American Studies Center, Asian Pacific Policy and Planning Council, and Alliance of Asian Pacific Labor.[3] It would be one of the largest, most sustained Asian American political efforts in the history of the region.

The basis for any Voting Rights Act claim starts with raw numbers, population, and the fact that California's Asian American population more than doubled between 1980 and 1990. Demographic change in the San Gabriel Valley was particularly dramatic. In Monterey Park the Asian American population increased by 90.6 percent, bringing it to 57.5 percent of the city's population. Similarly, in the nearby cities of Alhambra, Rosemead, and San Gabriel, the Asian American population increased from 289 to 372 percent, forming between 32 to 38 percent of the population in those cities (U.S. Bureau of the Census 1990c). In the four cities between 1980 and 1990 a dramatic rise occurred among the Asian American population, with a corresponding drop in the white population; the Latino presence was also significant (table 13).

The Asian Pacific American American Legal Center was essential throughout the process for the legal and organizational assistance it provided, as were members of the Asian Law Caucus in San Francisco. Both

Table 13. Racial and Ethnic Composition, Alhambra, Monterey Park, Rosemead, and San Gabriel: 1980, 1990

	African American	Asian American	Latino	Native American	White	Total Population
	Number and Percentage of City's Population					
Alhambra						
1980	670	8,227	23,855	222	31,441	64,615
	1.0	12.7	36.9	0.3	48.7	
1990	1,643	31,313	28,706	351	19,924	82,106
	2.0	38.1	35.0	0.4	24.3	
Monterey Park						
1980	658	18,890	20,541	213	13,866	54,338
	1.2	34.8	37.8	0.4	25.5	
1990	389	34,898	18,002	198	7,129	60,738
	0.6	57.5	29.6	0.3	11.7	
Rosemead						
1980	80	3,927	24,082	266	14,089	42,604
	0.2	9.2	56.5	0.6	33.1	
1990	320	17,725	25,035	250	8,197	51,638
	0.6	34.3	48.5	0.5	15.9	
San Gabriel						
1980	200	2,659	11,181	275	15,726	30,072
	0.7	8.8	37.2	0.9	52.3	
1990	394	12,044	13,134	199	11,294	37,120
	1.1	32.4	35.4	0.5	30.4	
Four-city totals						
1980	1,608	33,703	79,659	976	5,122	191,629
	0.8	17.6	41.6	0.5	39.2	
1990	2,746	95,980	84,877	998	46,544	231,602
	1.2	41.4	36.6	0.4	20.1	

Sources: U.S. Bureau of the Census (1983, table 59; 1990c).

interpreted the voting rights law, initially enacted to address the circumstances faced by African Americans in the South, to cover the situation of Asian Americans in California.[4]

The act of challenging political procedures that disfranchise racial groups is supported by legal precedent and federal laws. The Voting Rights Act of 1965 and the 1982 amendment to its section 2 prohibit practices that result in minority vote dilution, for example, through redistricting plans that fragment ethnic communities (Davidson, ed. 1984). In *Thornburgh v. Gingles* (1986) the Supreme Court established three criteria to determine whether a population is covered under the Voting Rights Act and whether a violation has occurred. One was that a racial group must constitute a majority in a district, a possibility for Latinos and African Americans in many areas throughout the United States but an impossibility for Asian Americans outside of Hawaii in 1990. Therefore, the applicability of the act for Asian Americans was in question.[5]

Attorneys arguing on behalf of Asian Americans cited *Garza v. County of Los Angeles* (1990), in which it was ruled that Latinos had been consistently divided into separate Los Angeles County supervisorial districts. As a result of the *Garza* decision the districts were redrawn to end the fragmentation of the Latino population. In testimony submitted to hearings of the California Assembly, Robin Toma, Stewart Kwoh, and William Tamayo argued that in the *Garza* case the "*Gingles* requirements do not strictly apply where it is shown that the governmental body engaged in intentional discrimination at the time the districts were drawn" (Toma, Kwoh, and Tamayo 1991, p. 5). They also noted (p. 6) that when the Court ruled that discrimination had occurred, 1981, Latinos "could not have constituted a citizen voting age majority in any conceivable district." Therefore, even though Asian Americans may not represent 50 percent of a district, as in the *Garza* case, fragmentation of their communities and the dilution of their political power violates the Voting Rights Act.

Numbers remained important, however. Asian Americans argued that although they may not have been able to create districts where they would be a majority, by consolidating concentrations they could create districts that would allow them to exert considerable influence, especially considering the population growth expected during the ten years district lines would remain in place. The creation of influence districts, according to their interpretation, should be covered by the Voting Rights Act.

The Southern California division of the statewide coalition targeted three areas in Los Angeles County that had large and rapidly growing Asian American and Pacific Islander populations: Central Los Angeles, the South Bay area, and the San Gabriel Valley. Regional coalitions were organized, and the San Gabriel Valley Asian Pacific Americans for Fair Reapportionment was formed in 1990. Reflecting the demographic mix of the area, most of the group was Chinese, with some Japanese Americans. As a nonpartisan organization and reflecting the population, Republicans and Democrats were active. Stewart Kwoh, executive director of the Asian Pacific Legal Center and one of the key organizers of state and regional redistricting efforts, emphasized that the group's founding was a historic occasion. It was the first time that Asian Americans had entered the redistricting and reapportionment process as active participants from the start of the proceedings.[6]

The major goals of the Asian American organizations included reversing the existing fragmentation of communities into separate political districts, educating people about the politics of redistricting and reapportionment, and establishing links among ethnic groups in the Asian American community as well as contacts with Latinos and African Americans. Judy Chu, a city council member and the former mayor of Monterey Park, spoke on behalf of the San Gabriel Valley coalition. "Our votes are fractionalized," she testified before the Senate Committee on Reapportionment on March 9, 1991. "The cities [in the west San Gabriel Valley] . . . are divided into two supervisorial districts, three assembly districts, three senatorial districts, and three congressional districts. It is no wonder that Asians in California are virtually unrepresented anywhere beyond the local level."

Gingles further reinforced the need for Asian Americans to establish panethnic ties by requiring that groups demonstrate that they are "politically cohesive," that is, that they vote along racial lines (Davidson 1992, p. 41). In oral and written testimonies submitted to the state assembly and senate committees on redistricting the Asian American coalition outlined the issues that followed racial lines and argued that there was indeed an Asian American community. A key piece of evidence for that being the case were the exit poll results from Monterey Park's 1988 and 1990 city council elections, which showed the strength of collective voting among Asian Americans. That pattern was explained by a wide range of factors in the region and state: anti-Asian activities such as hate crimes and English-only movements, employment discrimination, lack of social service funding to agencies equipped to handle the unique needs of Asians and Pacific Islanders, immigration policy, discriminatory admission policies at California state universities, and racist political rhetoric linking immigration to social problems. Judy Chu also stressed those issues in her testimony:

> Without concentrated districts, the ability for Asian Americans to express their concerns about issues will be diluted. For instance, Monterey Park faced an anti-immigrant movement in the mid to late 1980s. There were attempts to restrict languages other than English from being spoken in public, from being written on city materials that went to the public, and from being on commercial signs. There were attempts to prevent foreign-language books from being in our library. While these efforts have been defeated in Monterey Park, some of the issues are still being pushed in other parts of the San Gabriel Valley where there is not organized opposition. . . . Asians need advocates for programs that will help Asian immigrant children and adults learn the English language and make the transition to American society successfully. Unfortunately, those programs are sparse or have long waiting lists.

Another member of the coalition, in testimony submitted to the assembly committee on June 28, 1991, cited employment discrimination in Alhambra: "In 1990, the United States Justice Department sued the city of Alhambra and its Fire and Police Departments with charges of employment discrimination against minorities. The U.S. Justice Department does not sue a city unless there is strong evidence of discrimination in hiring and employment procedures and an egregious disparity between the ethnic makeup of the department and surrounding region."[7]

Divisions along ethnic lines also existed, the most notable being the case of Filipino Americans. One of the largest Asian American groups in the Los Angeles region, they believed their numbers were used to legitimize the panethnic label of Asian American organizations yet they did not receive services or recognition commensurate with the size of their population (Espiritu 1992). Several Filipino Americans emphasized the problem and expressed reservations about joining an Asian American effort. They met at a redistricting conference organized by the Rose Institute in Claremont, California, on June 22 and 23, 1990. One who attended said:

> I didn't give myself the name Asian Pacific American. There is a festering problem that remains, that is, the intricate relationship between politics and funds that flow to the social service agencies. We, as representatives of Pilipino groups, are here as the result of an "anger" of not receiving our fair share of funds.
>
> Another man began to speak. He did not speak loudly, but his voice trembled occasionally, as if he was holding back great emotion. He said, "Even now, there are stonewalling attempts in the funding patterns to the social service agencies. APPCON [now A3PCON] has never formally acknowledged our concerns. We are planning to separate on the issue of reapportionment so that we can meet as equals with the groups that we decide to, with Asian Pacific Americans, with Latinos. When we first joined Asian Pacific Americans, our numbers were smaller. Now, twenty years later, things have not changed in the way we are dealt with in the group. We want to deal as equal partners rather than as subordinates."
>
> When he finished speaking and sat down, Filipinos in the crowd clapped loudly.

Although major Los Angeles Filipino organizations did not participate in CAPAFR, some organizations, such as Search to Involve Pilipino Americans, a social service agency, did take part because they recognized that the coalition was the only organized voice for Asian Americans in redistricting.

The major fund-raising event of the Southern California coalition was organized by the San Gabriel Valley group and took place in Monterey Park on April 6, 1991, at a large Chinese restaurant. Nearly four hundred attended, including local Asian American politicians and March Fong Eu, then the secretary of state of California. Working to establish links with

Latino officials, State Senator Art Torres, long an advocate of Asian American interests, was the evening's keynote speaker. Xavier Becerra, the assembly person for the Monterey Park area, also spoke. In addition to fundraising, the event was intended to draw together diverse groups within the coalition, educate the community about redistricting and reapportionment, and demonstrate community support and interest to members of the state legislature.

The fund-raiser illustrated several characteristics about the San Gabriel Valley coalition. First, new immigrants were a vital part of it. Although many organizers were native-born or established immigrants, a significant number of them and the others present were new immigrants, and the sound of Chinese languages filled the air during the reception preceding the dinner. Second, money is critical for political activities, and Asian Americans acknowledge that the new immigrants are extremely effective fund-raisers. Third, ethnic identities have multiple levels generated by varied, often contradictory issues and goals that are expressed simultaneously. Many attended the fund-raiser as members of ethnic-specific political or social organizations. Yet the groups are able to come together as Asian Americans when faced with important issues such as redistricting that require groups to unite to combine economic and political resources and identify common concerns. The groups also reflect diverse nativity. Members of some organizations are primarily native-born (e.g., the Japanese American Citizens League), whereas members of others are both immigrants and native-born (the Taiwanese American Citizens League and the Chinese American Association of Southern California).

Asian Americans involved in politics clearly understand the framework under which they must work because of resource requirements and the legal implications of the Voting Rights Act. Cognizant of the harmful effects of racism and racial lumping—such as hate crimes—and also aware of the changing political context and the opportunity to lower barriers to political participation, they know the importance of combining their populations and acting in concert. In doing so, they are able to employ government-imposed categories and federal policies to take advantage of such court rulings and the Voting Rights Act. As one Asian American elected official stated at an early meeting to discuss the redistricting process: "Asian Pacific Americans is a political term. We have gone from [in the eyes of society at large] gook, chink, jap, flip, to Oriental to Asian to Asian Pacific American and Filipino, and Pacific Islander. These are political constructions."

Building a Coalition: Asian Americans in the San Gabriel Valley

Mike Eng and Judy Chu played central roles throughout the process of coalition-building and planned and organized the meetings, which they held in their home. As the Asian American holding the highest elected office in the region (she was a Monterey Park City Council person and mayor), Chu had a great deal of visibility and credibility. To the American public—especially immigrants—redistricting is an obscure political process. Although a few Asian Americans grumbled about Chu's participation, arguing that it seemed too self-serving because she was a potential candidate for districts that would result from redistricting, no one else in the area had the political reputation to bring people together. Chu and Eng contributed hundreds of hours to the redistricting effort, studying the issues, organizing meetings, and attending public hearings. Jeffrey Su, Steven Ling, and Ronald Wong of the West San Gabriel Valley Asian Pacific Democratic Club were also active throughout the process.

Don Nakanishi was likewise a key figure early in the process in the San Gabriel Valley. Well-known among Asian Americans and a respected educator, his involvement gave credibility to the project. Nakanishi attended the early meetings and explained some of the general principles of redistricting. He and Paul Ong, a UCLA professor in urban planning, established a working group at the UCLA Asian American Studies Center to provide analysis of demographic and political data throughout the redistricting process; Tania Azores (a Filipina American) and Philip Okamoto were the primary research associates. Stewart Kwoh also attended meetings in the San Gabriel Valley to explain the legal aspects of the Voting Rights Act. Along with Allison Tom and Mindy Hui, the Legal Center played a key role in the day-to-day operations and strategic planning of the Asian American organizations and meetings with the Latino organizations.

During early discussions about the legal and logistical aspects of redistricting the leaders made it clear that the process would require a great deal of work. As Kwoh stated:

> There will be hearings, meetings with legislators, staff. The staff can fool you so fast, you won't even know what's happening. We need to set goals for this area. We have to be clear about what districts we want. Personally, I think it's a mistake to split up, we should try to concentrate our population. Don [Nakanishi] and Paul [Ong] can help draw lines [for districts]. The [Asian Pacific Legal] Center can give legal help. We have to anticipate our strength in the future. Lay

the basis for a future victory. Emphasizing what I have said, time is short. Like it or not, some of you may be asked to testify. We can look like a bunch of fools, or we can be prepared.

Concerns about being legitimate representatives of the Asian American community, developing a multiethnic coalition, and establishing that the diverse groups constituted a cohesive Asian American political community were strongly expressed at meetings of the San Gabriel Valley and Los Angeles–area groups. At an early meetings of the San Gabriel Valley Coalition, for example, a Chinese woman mentioned that most of those present were Chinese Americans. She asked whether the organization was trying to reach out to other ethnic groups: "What about Koreans, Japanese, and other groups? Most of us here tonight are Chinese." Another Chinese person responded, "We're at the point where we have to get as many groups involved as possible. Political cohesion is developing among the different Asian groups." It was not always clear, however, exactly who—in terms of ethnicity—was present. For example, although the woman thought that everyone was Chinese, some were in fact Japanese. A Japanese man talked to her later, and she repeated her comment, saying, "We are only Chinese here." He said that there were also some Japanese, "Like me." She said, "I thought you were Chinese." A Chinese man joked, "You've been spending a lot of time with Chinese [as if the Japanese man had begun to look Chinese]." Everyone laughed.

Beyond these moments of levity, coalition members seriously devoted themselves to the task of becoming the legitimate representative of the community and involving as many individuals and groups as possible. Letters, telephone calls, and press conferences were some of the methods used to solicit participation. For example, Japanese Americans were the second-largest Asian American group (after the Chinese) in the San Gabriel Valley, so their involvement was particularly important. Members of the East Lost Angeles chapter of the Japanese American Citizens League (JACL), which meets in Monterey Park and has many members from the city, were contacted, and several officers attended the early meetings to learn about the redistricting effort. Gaining their interest, one of the members of the San Gabriel Valley coalition went to a JACL board meeting in March 1991 and asked for and received the organization's endorsement.

The Los Angeles group made a conscious effort to create an atmosphere of cooperation and explain why the various Asian American ethnic groups had a stake in redistricting. As one way of doing so, the coalition met at different locations—the ethnic-specific organization headquarters, for example, of the Korean American Coalition, Japanese American Citizens

League, Chinese American Citizens Alliance, and Search to Involve Pilipino Americans. Later, all meetings were held at the Legal Center because of its central location and—so important in Los Angeles—free and available parking.

The differences in opinion that occurred reflected the varied backgrounds and experiences of participants. A major issue surfaced among some Nisei in their fifties and sixties, perhaps as a result of their long history as a small minority fighting to integrate themselves into the political and economic mainstream. Perhaps, they suggested, part of the reason that Asian Americans had so few elected officials was that they did not have a history of people running for office. The Nisei knew of a number of Japanese Americans who had won elections in areas where Asian Americans formed a small percentage of the population. George Ige, for example, was elected to the Monterey Park City Council, Robert Matsui and Norman Mineta were elected as members of Congress in California, and Warren Furutani was elected to the Los Angeles School Board. What, then, was the need for an Asian American coalition for redistricting if Asian Americans have won in the past and could do so again if they ran good candidates? That potentially divisive issue was settled by combining both views. Better-qualified candidates were needed, and perhaps their chances for winning elections would be improved in districts with more favorable demographics.

Another concern was expressed by Asian Americans in their twenties who worked for white elected officials. They believed that white racism against Asian Americans was less than against African Americans and Latinos. That view would be significant in future discussions of potential configurations of political districts. As one Asian American man in his late twenties said, of the voting trends of whites, "Liberal, well-educated, sophisticated people will vote for an Asian. That's what helped Mike Woo win [a Los Angeles City Council seat]."

That point of view had been expressed by others as well. A Chinese American woman in her forties and a Japanese American man in his thirties joined the discussion. "We may benefit from some of the stereotypes," she said. "That is, Asians are seen as more conservative than African Americans or Latinos." "And the stereotypes about Asians being hardworking," he added. Others disagreed, however, saying that whites would only vote for an Asian American if there were no strong white candidates. One person explained, "For example, in polls, Hahn, the city attorney, and Mike Woo do very well. But Woo does well because they ask, 'Do you like Mike Woo? Do you like Hahn?' They don't ask, 'Who do you like better, Woo or Hahn?'"

Increasing numbers can change from accepting one or two neighbors to concern about economic and political competition (Lieberson 1980). The issue is especially relevant in California because Asian Americans have been elected in districts where they make up few of the population yet not in districts that have large Asian American populations. One person suggested that as the Asian American population grows race becomes more important:/"In a district with few or no Asians, maybe the voters can focus on the person and the issues. But when the number of Asians starts to rise, like in Monterey Park, then non-Asians wonder if an Asian candidate will represent only Asian interests."

Answering questions before the assembly committee on redistricting on April 23, 1991, a San Gabriel Valley coalition member mentioned the misconception that Asian Americans automatically received a high cross-over vote from whites. For example, in the 1990 city council elections in Monterey Park strong anti-Chinese feelings had been expressed by a white precinct worker: "As we were conducting part of the exit polls of city council elections, it was clear through the anecdotal evidence that we got, that there is a strong fear of Asians. . . . when one Chinese-American was running for city council and one of the Anglo persons involved in our poll came to the precinct, one of the poll workers said, 'These Chinks are voting for this Chink,' and so there's a strong feeling that's out there that I think the public is unaware of."

Opinions also differed about what would be acceptable in terms of the final achievements of the Asian American coalition. Some members, especially the newer immigrants, felt that education was a major goal. It would be a major accomplishment to prepare a strong base of knowledgable, experienced Asian Americans for the next redistricting battle ten years later. Others felt that anything less than a "good district" would be a major disappointment. Perhaps the two views reflected differences in political history. For immigrants, making the change from homeland to U.S. politics was a major shift in orientation. For native-born Asian Americans focusing on their history of little or no political representation, the goal was increased representation. As one Chinese American replied when asked why he was so heavily involved, considering that he had so little spare time because his job often kept him busy days as well as evenings seven days a week, "Asians have been screwed for too long. I want to make sure that we finally get something."

The debate around political education versus influencing district lines could have been divisive if decisions regarding resources had been divided about which goal to pursue. In practice, however, the two were intimately linked because the support of the community, which could only be obtained through outreach and educational activities, was necessary to give legitimacy to the political work surrounding the creation of districts.

Laying the Foundation for an Alliance: Asian Americans and Latinos

The Asian American San Gabriel Valley group met in April 1991 at UCLA to begin the task of planning new districts. A computer program was set up, with data arranged by city and census tract to examine such factors as race, political party affiliation, and the vote in the 1990 election for secretary of state, which featured the Democratic incumbent March Fong Eu against Joan Milke Flores, a Republican. Throughout the process the group was unable to obtain current Asian American voter registration data for the state.[8]

From the 1990 census data it was clear that the area of highest Asian American concentration and growth in the Valley centered on the four contiguous cities of Monterey Park, Alhambra, San Gabriel, and Rosemead. Demonstrating the extreme political fragmentation experienced by Asian Americans in the region, those four cities were in three separate assembly districts: Alhambra and Monterey Park were in District Fifty-nine, Rosemead was in Sixty, and San Gabriel was in Forty-two.

A population of 372,000 was required to create even the smallest political (assembly) district—140,000 more than the four cities' total population of 231,600. Cities in the San Gabriel Valley are racially mixed. Even Monterey Park, which has a majority Asian American population (57.5 percent) has a large Latino population (29.6 percent) and is 11.7 percent white. Yet the pattern of residential segregation in the valley—Asian Americans are concentrated in the four "core" cities, whites in the cities to the north, and Latinos in the cities to the east, west, and south of the Asian American core—created a number of possibilities for fashioning political districts. One alternative was to include the cities to the north, populated primarily by conservative, white Republicans but with a growing Asian American population. Another possibility was to attach cities to the south and east, areas populated primarily by Latino Democrats.

The voting record in the 1990 election for California secretary of state provided insight into the politics of the region. Flores, a white Republican, was a member of the Los Angeles City Council for the southern area of that city and unknown in the San Gabriel Valley. It is possible that Latinos may have thought she was Latino because of her surname, acquired through marriage. She won by a wide margin in the Republican northern cities such as San Marino, whereas Eu won by a wide margin in the Democratic Latino cities. The group thought that was meaningful because even though Flores had a Latino last name, incumbency and political party seemed to be more important. The group was concerned about the northern cities and wondered what it meant when a popular moderate Asian American Democrat could not win. After all, Eu had won previous elections with the highest vote totals of anyone running for a California statewide office.

Throughout July the coalition held a number of meetings. Examining the areas of population concentration and growth collided with several political realities. Serious thought was given to adding the northern cities because those areas were experiencing heavy Asian American growth, including an affluent segment that could donate heavily to political campaigns. A number of people raised concerns about anti-Asian activities in the area, however, One mentioned that Asian American homes were frequently vandalized and a recent newspaper article in the *Los Angeles Times* had listed a number of incidents, including cross-burnings on lawns, a strong reminder of the hate crimes that plagued Asian Americans.

The other alternative was adding cities to the south and east, areas populated primarily by Latino Democrats. The question raised at one meeting brought out a major reason for working with Latinos: "Will our interests be served best by someone responding to the interests of conservative whites or moderate to liberal Latinos?" Discussion focused on whether Latinos would have more in common with Asian Americans on issues such as immigration policies and bilingual voting materials (Erie and Brackman 1993).

Another issue concerned the practical matter of the more politically active voters in the north versus the less active voters in the south and what that might mean for Asian American candidates. A group member summed up the major points: "If we go north, we get Republican, high-propensity voters, people who may not vote for an Asian. Going south or east, we get Latinos, Democrats, they may not vote for an Asian either, but even in areas like Montebello which are considered middle-class Latino strongholds, their voting frequency may be less than in northern areas. Because their voter turnout is less, it may be better to go south than north."

Although opinion moved in the direction of working with Latinos, there were major problems to overcome in the development of an alliance between the two groups. Asian Americans were well aware, even though their population was growing rapidly, that Latinos still far outnumbered them in the San Gabriel Valley. For their part, Latinos had made major steps even though they were still working on establishing a strong political base, as demonstrated by the fact that they held elected positions—the Los Angeles County Board of Supervisors, state assembly, state senate, and Congress—that included Monterey Park. Asian Americans were concerned that their issues could be easily overwhelmed in an alliance.

For Latinos, the valley was seen as a place of growing political power. Richard Martinez, then director of the Southwest Voter Registration Education Project, described the valley as "the greatest bloc of potential Latino voting strength in the southwestern United States" (Newton 1990). Some Latinos were concerned about the rapidly growing number of Asian Americans and the threat that posed to Latino politics. The idea of Asian Americans as a monolithic group, strongly united with an organized and well-financed political machine, was mentioned by one Latino coalition member: "Whenever we [the Latino valley coalition] meet, there is always talk about 'the Asians, the Asians.'" As long-established residents of the valley, some Latinos felt that new Asian American immigrants were intruding on their territory.

Despite their differences, however, several factors encouraged the development of an alliance. Each group recognized the strengths of the other. As newcomers to the process, Asian Americans were acutely aware that they could learn a great deal from Latino organizations that had gained political and legal knowledge through such landmark court victories as *Gomez v. City of Watsonville* and *Garza v. County of Los Angeles*. Not only was the *Garza* decision a key factor in the Asian American interpretation of the Voting Rights Act and the *Thornburg v. Gingles* case, but it also demonstrated the importance of redistricting for electoral success when Gloria Molina was elected in the district created as a result of the decision. It was the first time in 115 years that a Latino was elected to a position on the Los Angeles County Board of Supervisors.[9] Latinos also had the support of organizations with much larger budgets, such as Mexican American Legal Defense and Education Fund and the Southwest Voter Registration Education Project, to back their efforts.

Considering that the Latino redistricting effort was spearheaded by established and experienced organizations and that organizing the diverse Latino population in the southwestern United States and forging a common agenda among Latinos in itself would be major tasks, the question is, Why would Latinos further complicate the process by working with Asian Americans? Clearly, they had little to learn from this inexperienced group, and a complex process is made even more complicated if a close working relationship with another group and their interests is added to the mix.

Latinos working on the redistricting project were well aware that the Asian American population in the state and San Gabriel Valley had grown, as documented by the 1990 census. That growth, they realized, was translating into an emerging Asian American political force in the valley, as demonstrated by successful campaigns to elect Asian Americans to local city councils and school boards. The growing Asian American population was not necessarily negative in terms of Latino political efforts. Latinos appreciated the fund-raising capabilities of Asian Americans, and the fact that such money could also flow to Latino candidates had already been demonstrated by fund-raisers Asian Americans had held for State Senator Art Torres and Marta Maestas and Xavier Becerra in their state assembly campaigns.

With their court victories based on the Voting Rights Act, Latinos realized that they could not violate the rights of other groups with their redistricting plans. In addition, the added legitimacy of a set of plans backed by both groups could be important if lawsuits were required when redistricting ended. These points were emphasized by Rita Moreno, a Southern California Latina organizer who worked for SVREP: "The idea was to be able to put something together that we could all support. You can't go in and expect to win a lawsuit on civil rights when you're violating someone else's. It makes for a poor argument."

Perhaps the most important factor favoring a joint effort was that Latinos and Asian Americans faced a common enemy—the political establishment. All too familiar with the history of political gerrymandering that fragmented Asian American and Latino communities, both groups understood that, in general, the state legislature was more interested in creating districts to ensure reelection than to protect the political rights of ethnic communities. Asian Americans and Latinos knew that they should combine the political clout of both groups through the support of one set of redistricting plans; such action would greatly increase the political and legal legitimacy of the plans. They also knew that if Asian Americans and Latinos were pitted against each other in the process both groups could lose in the end. As Moreno put it:

> If we are the only ones applying pressure, that won't work. But if in addition to Latinos, if there are Asian Pacific Americans and other groups, then that changes the whole game. They have to listen if all those groups, all those voters, are lobbying. . . . The plan was, let us work together with Asians, Pacific Islanders, and blacks and see if we could come up with something that we could all support because we didn't want to fight against one other and then have the state legislators say, "Well, you guys can't even get together among yourselves. Why

are we going to support one plan over the other? And if we support yours we violate their civil rights." Then we all come up losing.

The first meeting between the Asian American and Latino statewide coalitions occurred on May 24, 1991, in the MALDEF building in downtown Los Angeles. Discussion centered on each group's general concerns about increasing political strength through favorable districts. As with all groups that meet for the first time, people were cautious about what they said, but the general tone was remarkably cooperative and friendly, likely because of the previous relationships among the participants. In addition to Antonia Hernandez and Stewart Kwoh's acquaintanceship from their law school days, one of the main attorneys for the Asian Americans, Robin Toma, had worked for the American Civil Liberties Union and participated in its efforts in support of the *Garza* case. The primary demographers used by Latinos and Asian Americans (Leo Estrada and Paul Ong) were also professors in the same department at UCLA; their offices were right across the hall from one another. There were many exchanges of humor during meetings, and genuine laughter came easily. For example, Hernandez stressed that redistricting is a long and difficult process and it would be necessary for the two groups to keep in close contact to facilitate the developing partnership. "We have to communicate. Leo and Paul are talking to each other, probably by computer." The image of the researchers communicating through their machines brought loud laughter.

Asian Americans clearly understood that Latinos were the senior partner in terms of knowledge and experience, and they looked to them for guidance. Filipino American Tony Ricasa, for example, had worked for a number of years as a senior staff person for Warren Furutani, a Los Angeles School Board member, and was experienced in politics. He realized, however, that he had little experience with redistricting and that he and the Asian American organization would benefit from a relationship with Latinos. "Asians and Pacific Islanders are at an early stage," he said. "We look to the Latino community for help. We want to nurture the relationship; I am encouraged by the sensitivity expressed at this table. We would appreciate your guidance, steps we should take, direction to go in, it's a new process for many of us. Someone else added that we [Asian Americans] are where Latinos were in the 1960s or 1970s."

At the end of the first meeting people were positive about the cooperative atmosphere, the similar goals expressed by each group, and the prospect of working together. One thing clearly emerged from the meeting: Latinos and Asian Americans would benefit by a cooperative effort in their

dealings with the state legislature over redistricting. The two groups understood the historic importance of Latinos and Asian Americans working
together in a coordinated and formal way for the first time, and the potential political influence of such efforts was expressed in the discussion that
closed the meeting. "Planning a date for the next meeting, someone mentioned the assembly hearings and that we [the committee] should meet to
discuss and coordinate our activities. Someone suggested a meeting right
before the hearing. A Latino joked, 'We should all [African Americans,
Asian Pacific Americans, and Latinos] enter the room together, talking and
laughing, they'll [the members of the senate committee] shit.' Everyone started laughing. An Asian American added, 'Maybe we could enter singing,
"Kum Ba Yah."' The Latino replied, 'Or singing "We Shall Overcome."'"

To ease into the delicate process of balancing Latino and Asian American interests, districts and issues were discussed in general terms. Building a working relationship between Latinos and Asian Americans was
facilitated by existing relationships among the leadership and further developed through regular monthly meetings throughout the process, fre-
quent telephone contact among staff, and additional meetings scheduled
before public hearings and deadlines for district proposals. Building relationships was also promoted by the goals of the redistricting process—
creating favorable electoral districts—and the political experience of the
participants. They were generally professionals, such as attorneys, educa-
tors, or people skilled in dealing with government agencies—employees of
social service organizations and staff of elected officials, for example. Their
political experience had taught them the necessity of putting aside differences to focus on common issues. Concrete objectives had been laid out,
and committee members realized the major obstacles they faced.

Aware of their shared history of political fragmentation, constructing a
common culture as aggrieved groups was achieved despite the media's
depiction of Asian Americans as a "model minority." Latino leaders also
knew of the widespread forms of discrimination that Asian Americans
faced, including the lack of elected Asian Americans in the state legislature, the increasing numbers of hate crimes directed at Asian Americans,
and employment discrimination.

As Richard Fajardo, a MALDEF attorney, said during a discussion of
voting rights law, "When the Latinos were going through historical documents and came across things such as the Japanese American internment
and immigration restrictions, it was clear that things were as bad, if not
worse, for the Asian community. There is a tendency to believe that discrimination against Asians is not there or not very important; you have

the evidence to refute that." Richard Martinez also stressed the importance of having a history of working together and developing trust in the process of building links so that the participants could "humanize relationships and act together on common issues." Still another Latino leader observed, "It is much harder [because of damage to long-standing political relationships and personal links] to screw someone who you know and are close to because you have a history of working together."

San Gabriel Valley Latinos and Asian Americans

The first meeting between the Latino and Asian American San Gabriel Valley organizations was held in July 1991. The goal of the event was to meet and get to know one another and lay out general plans, and it was clear from the discussion that the groups were eager to work together and not allow Asian Americans and Latinos to be pitted against each another in the redistricting process. As with the initial meeting between the statewide coalitions, those who attended nodded at each other as they gathered, a result of existing ties stemming from community and campaign work that had previously brought them together.

After months of discussion, ideas for a final plan emerged. The Asian American group studied the existing Fifty-ninth Assembly District and discussed ways to modify it. Adding Rosemead and San Gabriel to Monterey Park and Alhambra would unite the core Asian American population, but Latinos were concerned about how that might affect the area's Latino assemblyman. As one put it, "Is there going to be a united, strong Asian American campaign to elect an Asian American? Or are Asian Americans going to offer him [Xavier Becerra] support? Maybe in the future, we can help an Asian American candidate."

In return for support of a plan that united the core Asian American population, Latinos urged Asian Americans to help build and strengthen political links between the two communities. Stressing the benefits of future coalitions, one Latino said that both groups still lack representatives in local elected offices although they were the majority of the population. Rosemead (which had an all-white city council) was a prime example. By combining what he perceived to be the strengths of the two communities—the Latino population and the fund-raising capabilities of Asian Americans—they could increase their political power. "Working together," he said, "Asians and Latinos can offset the disproportionate amount of political power held by Anglos. The perception among Latinos is that Asians have a lot of money, are organized. The newspapers have given this a lot of coverage. I have all the articles since this began. We can pool our re-sources, Asians have money and we have numbers."

An Asian American representative responded by saying that they were committed to working together because of common issues. Besides, the demographics of the region dictated that Asian Americans must work with Latinos, and they had a long history of doing so:

> Asians are committed to working with Latinos because the political reality is that Asians need Latinos more than Latinos need Asians because our population is smaller and we have a low number of registered voters. We know we need Lati-no support to win. In fact, we have already started making links. Tomorrow, the local Asian Pacific Democratic Club, many of the members of the coalition are part of that, are meeting with the San Gabriel Valley LULAC to discuss re-districting. The local Asian Democratic Club volunteered on Xavier Becerra's campaign. Asians volunteered for Art Torres and held fund-raisers for him and Becerra. [One of the Latinos replied that this was true. He had worked on Becer-ra's campaign and was impressed by the Asian turnout.]

The Latinos were not dealing with abstract possibilities for hypotheti-cal elections; they were concerned with concrete plans. In the round of elections that would follow redistricting, three members of the nucleus of the Latino group would run for office. Bonifacio "Bonny" Garcia ran for Congress, losing to Matthew Martinez, the Latino incumbent. Hilda So-lis ran successfully for the state assembly in a district where the white in-cumbent, Sally Tanner, decided not to seek reelection. And, in perhaps the most dramatic story emerging from the coalition, Joe Vasquez ran for the Rosemead City Council, a race he had lost previously by only fifty votes. In the 1992 city council election, Vasquez won, unseating a long-time in-cumbent, Jay Imperial, by just thirty-one votes. His contact with Judy Chu had increased through redistricting, and, unlike the previous race, Chu had publicly endorsed Vasquez. Although it is impossible to say whether Asian Americans proved the deciding factor in the election (Rosemead is 33.5 percent Asian American, 49.7 percent Latino, and 15.9 percent white) and Imperial also had support from Asian Americans, although none as well known as Chu, the involvement of Asian Americans in support of Vasquez cannot be discounted.

Uniting the four cities of Asian American concentration and growth and adding cities to the south would create a district in which Latinos remained in the majority, preserving a strong base for the Latino incumbent. Asian Americans agreed that Latinos could fine-tune the boundaries to adjust for the requirements of neighboring districts. Although such a district would favor Latino candidates over Asian American candidates, Asian Americans would benefit by having their core population united. The district thus created would end the fragmentation of their community and provide them with a strong political presence. The long-term gains achieved from developing a working relationship with Latinos and creating a district from which an Asian American might be elected as that population increased were more important than struggling to create a district that would have more favorable demographics immediately. Because of the relative size of the Asian American population in the region and its lower-than-average rates of voter registration, an Asian American would not likely soon be elected in the San Gabriel Valley.[10]

On August 30, 1991, the Latino and Asian American groups held a press conference in the Monterey Park city hall to announce their agreement on plans for voting districts. Coincidentally but reinforcing the importance of cooperation, that same morning an article had appeared in the *Los Angeles Times;* Assembly Speaker Willie Brown had "conceded Thursday that the desires of incumbent lawmakers will come first as the Assembly draws new district lines" (Weintraub 1991). In September a group of Latinos and Asian Americans went together to Sacramento and met with a number of elected officials to lobby for the joint plan.

The Republican governor of California, Pete Wilson, vetoed the plans submitted by the Democratic-majority state legislature. The state supreme court then took over the redistricting task and appointed a three-member "special masters" committee to determine new districts. After holding a new set of hearings (at which San Gabriel Valley Latinos and Asian Americans testified), the special masters filed their report on November 29, 1991. They created a new assembly district, Forty-nine, which followed the recommendations of the valley coalition by grouping the four cities of Asian American concentration. It changed the other cities recommended by the coalition for an assembly district but retained a Latino majority. Discussing the results with Latinos, an Asian American reported that they felt that even though the districts "weren't perfect, they could live with the results." Citing the importance of the coalition recommendations, the report stated: "District 49, centered on Monterey Park, Alhambra, San Gabriel and Rosemead, has only 55 percent Latino population, but the Latino registration appears to be over 44 percent. The district also had a large Asian presence—over 28 percent—and both Latino and Asian groups requested that this district include the four cities that form its basis" (Special Masters on Reapportionment 1991, p. 62).

The California supreme court adopted the new plan on January 27, 1992. The San Gabriel Valley was unique among Asian American communities participating in the redistricting process. Its regional group was the most organized and active, as suggested by their fund-raising efforts, and they had the closest working relationship with Latino counterparts. The value of the work was validated by the fact that the San Gabriel Valley was the only area in California where Asian Americans were successful in lobbying for a district that kept their core population intact.

Conclusion

Redistricting exemplifies the way government policies have defined and reflected racial categories and the social, political, and economic implications. The struggle for political inclusion, mediated and constrained by a political and judicial system that historically has served to disfranchise racial minorities, shows the contradictions and structural impediments of efforts to enfranchise minorities. Redistricting is a critical site through which subordinate groups understand, negotiate, and contest the meaning of their position as racialized minorities, the material consequences, and structures of domination. As Steven Gregory (1994, p. 365) writes about African American community residents, neighborhood struggles show how activists "selectively appropriate, contest, and transform racial meanings, forming oppositional identities and ideologies."

Doug McAdam's (1982) political process model emphasizes the importance of political opportunities and political consciousness for collective action in the civil rights movement. For redistricting, a unique confluence of national and local events created a period in which significant political change appeared likely. The judicial climate favored minority enfranchisement with recent landmark Voting Rights Act court cases. Practical matters included the tremendous growth of the Asian American and Latino populations during the 1980s, advances in computer hardware and software, and availability of demographic and political data. For the first time, nongovernment groups could carry out sophisticated data analysis.

In the San Gabriel Valley, ethnic groups share the same geographic, social, and political space. That fact is reflected by the mixed school (from elementary through high school) populations and required by the at-large election systems of the local city council and school board elections. These conditions often result in conflict as groups compete for scarce resources.

Four major factors were involved in the development of interracial ties between Latinos and Asian Americans in the case of redistricting in the San Gabriel Valley. The first was that the groups had similar histories of being discriminated against. Especially relevant was the history of gerrymandering that had resulted in inadequate political representation and the fragmentation and dilution of political power. Latinos and Asian Americans were well aware of the history of redistricting. In general, members of the state legislature had been more concerned about creating districts that would enhance their chances for reelection rather than considering the political rights of ethnic groups. That situation created a common enemy. The second factor was that the groups shared common issues of concern such as immigration legislation, bilingual education, employment discrimination, and hate crimes. The third factor was the importance of organizational scale and developing political influence by combining populations and resources through alliances. Finally, there was the fact that a number of Latino and Asian American individuals and organizations had a history of working together. The difficult task of building working relationships was made easier because of that history.

Despite such victories, racial minorities continue to fight an uphill battle for political rights, and Supreme Court decisions have threatened to undo some of the gains since the 1980s. The Court's rulings represent a strong setback in the fight for political representation and create uncertainty for the future efforts of Asian Americans, Latinos, and African Americans. The legal and political gains based on the Voting Rights Act are fragile, temporary, and under constant attack.

Shaw v. Reno (1993), for example, ruled that the Constitution does not allow states to draw odd-looking, or "bizarre," districts "solely" for racial reasons. The case dealt with a congressional district in North Carolina created during redistricting efforts after the 1990 census. The remapping had resulted in an African American winning the congressional seat. In another decision, *Miller v. Johnson* (1995), the Court decided that the Constitution does not allow for the use of race as the "predominant" factor when drawing up districts. At the same time, across the nation oddly shaped districts drawn to protect white incumbents and their predominantly white constituencies were left untouched. In Texas, one of the judges— Edith Jones—who had ruled that congressional districts drawn on the basis of race were unconstitutional because they "bear the odious imprint of apartheid" had, according to a *Los Angeles Times* article, "upheld white-majority districts on the theory that 'incumbency protection' is a time-honored tradition in redistricting but creating districts to represent minorities is not" (Savage 1994, p. A18). In other words, the defense of whiteness—racial privilege and hierarchy—is a "time-honored tradition" in the United States. Because the districts created in the San Gabriel Valley were constructed according to a number of factors (e.g., compactness and contiguity) in addition to race, they should not be at risk. And *Rural West Tennessee African-American Council v. Sundquist* (1995) upholds a lower court ruling that "majority-minority" districts need not be created to satisfy the Voting Rights Act. "Influence" districts of at least 25 percent of a minority group are sufficient to fulfill the requirements of the act, a decision that allows geographic concentrations of racial groups to be fragmented and dilutes their political power.

Conclusion: Progress?

In the fall of 1992, soon after I had completed the major portion of my fieldwork in the San Gabriel Valley, I moved to San Diego and quickly discovered how people who would never consider themselves racist nevertheless used race to make false and stereotypical judgments about Asian Americans. Race was used to categorize me as a foreigner, even when personal characteristics such as my accent, which had been molded by my youth in California, suggested otherwise.

I had gone to Mesa Community College, located in a multiracial neighborhood a few minutes from my new San Diego home, to gather information about enrolling in a class. Walking into the counseling services office, I was greeted by a friendly white woman, perhaps in her forties, who enthusiastically answered my questions. I told her that I wanted to take a foreign-language class in the evening and asked how I should go about enrolling and obtaining a parking permit and the cost of these items. After we talked for ten or fifteen minutes, she pulled out a schedule of classes, ran her finger down a page, and said, "We have an English class that meets on Tuesday and Thursday evenings. How does that sound?" For a second I stood there, silent and a little confused. Then I realized that I had told her that I wanted to take a foreign-language class and had not specified the language I wanted to study—Spanish. Even though we had been talking for a while and she could clearly hear that I was a native speaker of English, she ignored what her ears told her and focused on what she saw and what being Asian meant to her.

These kinds of racialized everyday experiences are commonplace in the lives of racial minorities, yet the whites who participate in them are often unaware of how their thoughts and actions support whiteness and are a part of the constant negotiation and reconfiguration of the content and consequences of racial identities for all groups (Omi and Winant 1986). The encounter clearly pointed out to me that although I was in a new location race continued to be a major factor in the way people judged and categorized me.

Although the event was minor, and had no material impact on my life, it reminded me of the ways race enters people's lives and affects their life chances, a situation that has existed from the very beginning of American history, when political policies and everyday practices produced and supported privileged access to power and opportunities for whites (Lipsitz 1995). Explicitly racialized government policies included the right to vote, which was limited to white men of property; the right of naturalization, which was denied to Asian immigrants; and federal housing and mortgage policies, which ensured segregated neighborhoods.

The San Gabriel Valley, with its Asian American and Latino population, offers a window into the future of race relations and politics in the United States. The two groups, the fastest-growing in the country, will play increasingly prominent roles: Latinos, with a U.S. population nearly three times that of Asian Americans, are expected to surpass African Americans in number by 2020 (U.S. Bureau of the Census 1996). The San Gabriel Valley may be appear to be overshadowed by the towering presence of nearby Los Angeles, yet it exemplifies how international, national, and regional factors coalesce with the historical experiences of individuals and groups to bring into play a complex and constantly changing set of conditions. The valley is the center of the largest Chinese ethnic economy in the United States and a node of migration, capital, and production in the global economy.

In other parts of the United States the political and economic power of whites is uncontested, and whiteness need not be explicitly expressed and protected. In Monterey Park, however, the political and cultural hegemony of whites has been eroded by the demographic and economic ascendancy of Asian Americans and Latinos. A new way of "seeing" race and ethnicity is being developed by Asian Americans, Latinos, and whites as they renegotiate the content, meaning, and political consequences of those categories. The comments of white city workers about a proposed statue of George Washington for the front lawn of city hall—residents would be able to point to the statue and tell their children that white people like Washington had once lived there—contain a grudging acknowledgment of the imperiled state of whiteness.

In contrast to studies on ethnic and racial political mobilization and alliances that consider racial and ethnic group identities as fixed and unchanging, I stress the problematical nature of group boundaries. For example, in the study by Browning, Marshall, and Tabb (1984) on coalitions among African Americans, whites, and Latinos, the development of a Latino identity for political purposes was not addressed adequately. That process is fluid and uncertain (Padilla 1985).

The Neighborhood: Connecting Histories, Constructing Identities, and Building Alliances

The historical and contemporary expression of racial hierarchy and privilege for whites and the concomitant experience of exclusion and segregation for Asian Americans and Latinos set the context in which people live their everyday lives and fashion, negotiate, and struggle over individual and group identities and politics. Just as the construction of racial and ethnic identities and political mobilization occurs within particular regional contexts, however, individuals and groups in the San Gabriel Valley bring into play a wide variety of experiences rooted in multiple geographic and historical settings.

Asian Americans born in the United States bring a different set of memories, experiences, and resources to the region than do recent Asian immigrants. For example, Sansei (third-generation Japanese Americans) possess an understanding of race shaped by their knowledge of the incarceration of Japanese Americans in U.S. concentration camps during World War II, the loss of accumulated capital and the violation of constitutional rights in the process, and the irony of knowing that Nisei men were drafted from the camps to fight for human rights in Europe while their families suffered behind barbed wire at home. They also share the local and more recent experience of restrictive covenants encountered when their parents bought homes in the San Gabriel Valley. In contrast, Chinese immigrants from Hong Kong—relatively homogeneous in terms of race— with access to large amounts of capital entered in 1996 to find real estate agents fighting for their dollars and construction companies building homes with features geared toward Asian customers.

How people make sense of their racialized experiences emerges from these disparate backgrounds, experiences, and ever-changing circumstances. Research on resource mobilization and panethnicity tends to emphasize structural factors and overlook the importance of everyday activities and events that contribute to the importance of race for political mobilization, how these everyday matters illuminate varying individual and group conceptions of ethnicity, and the cultural practices that are part of the process of constructing racial and ethnic identities and legitimating political action (Omi and Winant 1986).

In the San Gabriel Valley a range of reactions emerged in response to the growing numbers of Chinese immigrants and their capital investments. Some—such as the Nisei woman whose arm was twisted in a fabric store during an unprovoked attack by a white woman—responded to hate crimes by dreaming about fleeing the city. Others considered disidentification with the new Chinese immigrants, as occurred among Asians during earlier actions of extreme discrimination such as the 1882 Chinese Exclusion Act and the World War II incarceration. This tendency emerged from complaints by long-term Asian American residents about the "Asian flack" that affected all Asians, supposedly because of the ostentatious way that Chinese immigrants displayed their wealth. Disidentification was also evident in a Sansei's bewildered response to the changes in Monterey Park on his return to the city after being absent for a number of years: "Goddamn dad, where the hell did all these Chinese come from?"

Another option was building a panethnic identity as Asian Americans through the process of cultural construction and the employment of collective memory as diverse groups recognized the circumstances they shared and developed new identities in the United States (Lowe 1996). Major historical events such as concentration camps, exclusionary immigration laws, and restrictive covenants were combined with the very personal and painful insults of everyday life—such as racial epithets and hate crimes—in the process of racial formation. Race and ethnicity became the foundation for new, more inclusive levels of identity for people of varying backgrounds—based on such factors as class, gender, place of birth, and ethnicity—because of the way differential forms of treatment were racialized and embedded in their economic, political, and social relationships.

Constructing ethnic identities and interethnic alliances are not simply "things" that emerge when the right mix of "ingredients" are present, as suggested by research that highlights structural factors while neglecting everyday activities. As demonstrated by the confrontation between Latino farmworkers and Nisei farmers in the San Gabriel Valley's berry fields in the 1930s and California's central valley in the 1970s, the immediate clash of interests posed by employee-employer relationships displaced the common racial interests of these racially subordinate groups. In contrast, with racial and class interests overlapping, Asian and Latino immigrant laborers were able to find common ground and form the Japanese-Mexican Labor Association in Oxnard and the United Farmworkers in the central valley.

Panethnic identities and interracial alliances are the result of a long process of discovery and analysis—cultural construction—that may lead to the development of identities and alliances based on an understanding that a common experience exists while important issues of difference and disagreement remain. Ethnic identities are not monolithic and unvarying but may be based on different things for each individual: cultural factors such as language or religion or imposed identity as a result of circumstances generated by such factors as the census, hate crimes, or occupational and residential segregation. I have explored and documented the process of moving from specific identities and toward more inclusive panethnic identities and the construction of interracial alliances.

There is a difference between culture transplanted by immigrants to the United States, such as language and religion, and cultural construction that takes place as individuals and groups create a political culture and movement based on histories and experiences linked to the United States. Traditional elements may be part of the culture created; for example, Japanese Americans often begin community meetings with a *taiko* drum performance, an art form from Japan. The performance is not simply the result of culture passed on from the immigrant generation to those born in the United States, however. Rather, it is a conscious attempt to reclaim a part of a cultural heritage and assert an ethnic and political identity. It shows how the cultural content of ethnicity is continuously transformed as it is informed by historical and current events and used to support political goals. For example, a *taiko* performance at a Los Angeles community meeting in the 1990s to commemorate the successful redress and reparations movement of the 1980s marked the participants and spectators as Americans who had a unique experience related to their ancestry. It was also an experience squarely rooted in a history of discrimination experienced by people of color in the United States.

Similarly, the reimagined Aztec dance performed by Chicanos at a celebration marking the anniversary of the founding of the Centro Cultural de la Raza in San Diego to honor community activists who worked to reestablish and claim a cultural and political space in the city recognizes the Native American heritage of Mexican Americans. The irony and tension involved in reclaiming a space that rests within territory once belonging to one's ancestors, with the meaning and legitimacy of ownership transformed by the formation of nations and borders, is proclaimed by a popular slogan on T-shirts worn by many at Chicano community events: "The border crossed us, we didn't cross the border."

The first step in building an identity as Asian Americans or Latinos and using those identities as a basis for political mobilization is to recognize that race has material importance. The second step is to translate that identity into a political force through the development of networks and organizations to negotiate the political, economic, and social consequences of race and ethnicity. Although panethnic terms are applied analytically to all individuals within a category, in the case of the U.S. census, for example, it is a very different matter for those people to think of themselves as members of the panethnic group and engage in political action based on that identity.

Some persons, both immigrants and native-born, may never develop an ethnic identity that extends beyond a selective group identity (for example, Taiwanese, Okinawan, or Mexican) based on factors such as region of origin, kinship, religion, or language. Others may attempt to define themselves simply as Americans, without reference to race and ethnicity, in recognition of how their lives are rooted in the United States and with the hope of being accepted as Americans. They are thus shielded, they believe, from racism and xenophobia even as racial identities are imposed on them. For example, the Japanese American woman who lived in a home in Monterey Park that contained no references to her ancestry and was assaulted by a white woman who yelled "go back to China" in a fabric store redoubled her efforts to think of herself as an American.

Research on panethnicity clearly points out the problems that divide potential members of a panethnic group. Yet the first comprehensive studies (Cornell 1988; Espiritu 1992; Padilla 1985) overemphasized the extent to which panethnic identities exist by not sufficiently describing the varying levels of political activity that represent different degrees of attachment and commitment. Nonactivity, or active disidentification, compared to donating money, voting for a political candidate, or active involvement in an organization represents different levels of commitment, attachment, or identification. In the case of redistricting in the San Gabriel Valley, as with many political activities, only a small percentage of the Asian American population was aware of the process, and even fewer participated in the negotiations. The fact that few may take part in the activity is not to downplay the importance of such events for the entire Asian American population. Yet it is important to be clear about who participates, and the extent of that involvement, in political actions.

Morris (1984) has stressed in his study of the African American civil rights movement that many different interests within the group impeded political mobilization. Despite the problems involved in forging a common agenda due to these different interests, however, Morris does not need to examine whether or not they have a common racial or ethnic identity as African Americans. That is taken as a given. The situation is fundamentally different for the various groups that attempt to unite in panethnic categories where such identities are always problematic and never include all the individuals or groups that such categories claim to represent. Panethnic categories continually need to be constructed and reconstructed, as in the case of Chinese and Japanese Americans uniting to elect Asian Americans in the San Gabriel Valley.

Identities are highly situational and multilayered, and when individuals and groups come together politically as Asian Americans it does not erase their other identities. As an example of how conflict can emerge from these various identities, the day after the Asian American redistricting fund-raising event in Monterey Park, which many had attended as members of ethnic- and gender-specific organizations, I received a telephone call from a Japanese American woman who had attended as a member of the Japanese American Citizens League. She was troubled because George Ige, a former Monterey Park council member, had not been acknowledged as were other dignitaries present. As she saw it, the emphasis was on the Chinese, and the many contributions of Japanese Americans in the region had been ignored. She supported attending an event that pushed an Asian American agenda and was willing to recognize the growing prominence of the new Chinese immigrants, but only if the long history of Japanese Americans was given its due and not eclipsed in the process.

The complexity of the lives of individuals is reflected by the wide and sometimes contradictory range of interests that their professional, personal, and political concerns generate. For example, Sophie Wong, a Chinese American, was involved in organizations based on her gender, livelihood in real estate, and political ideology. Committed to meeting the unique educational needs of a diversified student population and helping other immigrants adjust to the United States, and as a staunch Republican and member of the Alhambra School Board, she worked to serve her constituency and moderate the Republican Party's attempts to cut off benefits to immigrants.

Interracial Alliances

Understanding that panethnic identities and political mobilization are driven in large part by the need for resources, networks, and organizations necessary to engage in effective political action recognizes the links between research on panethnicity, resource mobilization, and racial and ethnic politics. It also recognizes that the ongoing construction of ethnic identities and political alliances are related and emerge from similar factors. Likewise, the development of interracial alliances is driven by the same factors, aided by the process of cultural construction and collective memory as various groups establish common goals and a basis for collective action.

Latino and Asian American identities have been shaped by similar forces and events. The two groups share the same neighborhoods because they have been affected by, and have fought against, the same political and economic forces of exclusion and discrimination. They have endured tragedies and shared victories together, experiences still vivid in the memories of area residents. They have battled segregation and restrictive covenants, and even the tragedy of the concentration camps affected both groups. A Latino told the poignant story of his wife, a Latina, who drove her best friend, a Japanese American woman, to the station, where they cried and said their goodbyes before the friend boarded a train to begin imprisonment in a concentration camp. The lives of Latinos and Asian Americans in the Los Angeles area have been intertwined for many years, and their contemporary identities and political goals and alliances are facilitated by that history.

Redistricting in the San Gabriel Valley demonstrated that the need to institutionalize a political base to participate in the process effectively was a major driving force for Asian Americans organizing along panethnic lines. Redistricting also showed the importance of developing interracial alliances for the same reason. It demonstrated the need for building a relationship based on a shared understanding of similar histories of discrimination and political goals and the realization that working together would greatly improve the chances of influencing the outcome of the redistricting process. At the same time, Asian Americans and Latinos recognized their differences (Latinos, for example, held advantages in terms of registered voters and experience in voting rights court cases) and acknowledged that they shared the same geographic space and thus competed for the same electoral offices.

The development of ethnic- or race-specific organizations has been criticized by both liberals and conservatives for defining boundaries and creating barriers, preventing cooperation with groups outside those boundaries, and balkanizing American society (Schlesinger 1992). Yet the history of constitutional amendments, court decisions, and federal legislation to remove barriers to citizenship, naturalization, and voting is a history of political pressure, of challenges raised by groups that demonstrate the need for political action and the importance of organizations to support such efforts.

The alliance between the Chinese PTA and LULAC over student conflict in the Alhambra School District and the multiracial redistricting coalition illustrate that establishing political groups with defined issues and goals can create an institutional base from which negotiations among organizations can proceed. There is a possibility of alliances built on common issues and goals. Such battles for equality on the part of racial and ethnic organizations are not divisive. Indeed, as Gary Okihiro (1994, p. ix) reminds us, these struggles help "advance the principles and ideals of democracy" that the United States strives to achieve as the groups work for inclusion.

The rise of Asian American and Latino political influence in the San Gabriel Valley also points out the need for racial minorities to develop independent networks and organizations, an "indigenous" foundation (Morris 1984) to institutionalize a base that can create and support an agenda that meets their unique political interests. That is in contrast to research that emphasizes the importance of whites and their role in multiracial coalitions (Browning, Marshall, and Tabb 1984, 1990). Clearly, alliances with whites are important, as in the cases of Judy Chu and her multiracial foundation and the defeat of Sam Kiang that was attributed to voter perception of him as the candidate of Chinese immigrants.

For elected officials to be accountable to an Asian American constituency, however, and to have organizations that can advocate for the interests of racial minorities, groups must establish their own organizations from which they can participate in politics from a position of power instead of as subordinates (Carmichael and Hamilton 1967). Organizations may be relatively permanent, serve a region or larger area, and have fundraising capabilities and a paid staff. Such groups provide essential resources for the community. For example, the Asian Pacific American Legal Center of Southern California and the Mexican American Legal Defense and Education Fund were essential for redistricting. They provided legal analyses of the Voting Rights Act and the staff for day-to-day and long-range organizing. Ad hoc groups that arise to handle a specific issue, such as CARE in the case of the redevelopment of Atlantic Square, are also critical, especially at the local level.

The influence of such neighborhood groups does not end when they disband. It is not the organizations per se that are essential; instead, it is the working relationships among individuals and groups that such organizations nurture and support. Even though community organizations come and go, the same individuals and networks often play leadership roles in different organizations and maintain relationships within and among other ethnic and racial groups. Mike Eng, for example, played prominent roles in the Asian Pacific Democratic Club, the San Gabriel Valley redistricting group, and in public hearings around the issue of language on business signs. And Jose Calderon was active in LULAC, the sign issue, and the parents' multiracial coalition in the Alhambra School District.

Individual relationships are also important for building alliances among regional organizations. The example of the Latino and Asian American statewide redistricting alliance illustrates the influence of preexisting ties. The executive directors of MALDEF and APALC, Antonia Hernandez and Stewart Kwoh, respectively, attended law school together, and Leo Estrada and Paul Ong, the two main demographers used by Latinos and Asian Americans, were professors in the same department at UCLA.

The growing organizational scale of politics provides a major driving force for the construction of panethnic identities and interracial alliances. Cultural construction and collective memory create strategic communities of shared interests and histories. Can the process of inclusiveness move beyond panethnicity to a panracial level? Have the boundaries separating Latinos and Asian Americans disappeared under certain circumstances? Laura Pulido (1997) proposes that a panracial identity has formed among those in the environmental justice movement. That identity is actively constructed by primarily working-class racial minorities based on their opposition to subjugation and environmental racism. On some occasions, Asian Americans and Latinos have worked together to fight white racial privilege in the San Gabriel Valley (for example, redistricting in the 1990s or contesting the English-only movement), and their identity as racialized minorities has bound the groups, existing simultaneously with more particularistic groupings. At this point, the term *people of color* moves from a descriptive phrase to one of common identity.

The Next Whites? or, The Many Faces of Hate

Based on the impressive economic and social gains that Asian Americans have made in U.S. society, some social scientists have suggested that they may follow the racial trajectory of Southern and Eastern Europeans and move from a non-white to white racial category (Gans 1994). Considering, however, that an Asian American identity has such strength among affluent entrepreneurs and professionals, those who have made the greatest economic headway into the mainstream, the experience of these individuals shows that what has changed are the forms and sites of discrimination rather than the disappearance of the importance of race and racism. To an outsider, the large number of Japanese American engineers is certainly a sign of progress compared to the days when graduates of the University of California, Berkeley worked at their parents' roadside fruit stands because no engineering company would hire them. Yet interpreting the large number of Japanese American engineers as a sign that discrimination has disappeared ignores the glass ceiling these engineers face as they are denied entry into the executive and managerial ranks and experience income differences from their white counterparts.

In some instances, the discourse on Asian Americans as the next "whites" shifts attention away from the forms of discrimination that persist, and by doing so it supports white racial privilege. In the debate on affirmative action, for example, supporters of Proposition 209 cite the case of Asian Americans and the way affirmative action in college admission programs supposedly hurts Asian Americans. However, by ignoring the way discriminatory practices in admissions favor whites to the disadvantage of Asian Americans, this argument does not address major forms of inequality in the admissions process (Nakanishi 1989; Takagi 1993). Rather than bringing equity and fairness to admissions, attacks on affirmative action eliminate gains made by racial minorities while leaving practices in place that support white privilege.

The tensions that have erupted among long-term residents and the new immigrants in the San Gabriel Valley reveal the fragile and impermanent nature of whites' acceptance of Japanese Americans in particular and Asian Americans in general as "good neighbors and citizens" of the community. The Nisei woman who was assailed in a fabric store, for example, had both her ethnicity and nativity cast aside by the woman who attacked her and categorized her as a recent Chinese immigrant. At the moment of the attack the woman had no control over her position in U.S. society, and the assailant may not have cared whether her target was a Nisei and not a Chinese immigrant. The operative category may well have been "Asian" and thus equally guilty of not being American, as discussion over architecture and restaurants pointed out in the case of the redevelopment of Atlantic Square.

Although violence affects everyone in the United States, hate crimes that threaten racial minorities create a public risk that whites do not experience. Hate crimes transcend class lines. Affluent Asian Americans learn that their wealth is not a barrier to prejudice; it and success become targets as homes, churches, and businesses are vandalized. Although intensely experienced by those afflicted, most hate crimes go unnoticed except for those instances when lawsuits are filed or publicity ensues. One tragic example of a violent act directed against Asian Americans occurred in Stockton, California, in 1989. Patrick Purdy—white and armed with an AK-47 assault rifle—entered an elementary school playground and fired on the children there. Five, all Southeast Asian, were killed, and thirty others were wounded. Purdy then used the rifle to take his own life. The chilling conclusion of the report issued by the California attorney general, that Purdy chose the school "in substantial part because it was heavily populated by Southeast Asian children," is a shocking reminder of the extreme forms of racism that exist in the United States (U.S. Commission on Civil Rights 1992, p. 31).

That hate has many levels and creates many extreme events should not blind people to the increasingly subtle and sophisticated forms of discrimination that exist and the fact that new types and sites constantly appear. Race is given meaning, and discrimination results, in labor market discrimination and glass ceilings; differential access to public places for businesses, as in the case of Atlantic Square and the insistence on American restaurants; nativism and racism disguised as anti-development in the slow-growth movement in Monterey Park; steering practices by realtors that maintain segregated neighborhoods; immigration legislation designed to cut down on the number of immigrants from Asia and Latin America; media scrutiny and criticism of Asian political contributions while ignoring those from Canadians or Europeans; and, on a personal level, people like the counselor who offered to enroll me in an English-as-a-second-language class.

The racial hierarchy contained in whiteness is difficult to dismantle, partly because those who engage in practices that support it are often unaware of the ways in which their actions support discriminatory procedures. Racism is rarely as blatant and pernicious as the killings committed by Patrick Purdy. The Monterey Park residents who participated in the public debate over the architectural design of Atlantic Square and the counselor who offered me assistance would vehemently deny that they engage in racist practices.

Progress is not inevitable. In fact, there are many signs that gains are often temporary. George Ige, describing his campaign for his first election to the Monterey Park City Council in 1970, spoke fondly of the unsolicited support he received from a group of Issei (first-generation Japanese immigrants) from Los Angeles who had read about his campaign in one of the local Japanese-language papers and offered their help. The group became one of the major financial supporters of his campaign. "One of the really surprising and enlightening and really fulfilling experiences I had," Ige said, "was that a group, members of the Okinawa Kenjinkai [prefectural organization]" provided support.[1] "They were very astute. They knew the political game. They were very aware that finances were going to play a very important part in the political game." Ige discussed the history of immigrant groups supporting co-ethnics in the United States and said that when the "Irish first came to New York or Boston, they were very cohesive," similar to his experience and that of Judy Chu and the contemporary Chinese community. Although Chu could publicly acknowledge her support from the Chinese community, however, Ige could not. The changing racial climate made it possible for her to have large fund-raising banquets at Chinese restaurants in Monterey Park and not alienate Latino and white supporters whereas Ige had to keep his support from the Issei private.

Although the difference between the way Chu and Ige could publicize their bases of financial support points to progress in race relations, it belies the underlying tension that continues to inform political relationships in Monterey Park and crop up whenever Latinos and Asian Americans make significant gains. When Lily Chen, David Almada, and Rudy Peralta were elected to the council in 1982, for example, the city had its first majority Asian American and Latino council. The three lost in their bids for reelection, however, in a hotly contested election in which nativism and racism were disguised as anti-growth (Fong 1994). An offensive and explicit expression of racism occurred on election day in 1990. A white member—a male who appeared to be in his late fifties—of the research group conducting an exit poll entered one of the polling places and asked the volunteers running the site, "How are things going?" "They're [Asian Americans] voting for the Chink!" a white female volunteer responded, apparently believing that his age and race would align him with established residents (Horton 1995, p. 139). The racism exposed by her comment claimed more voters in 1994, when Kiang was running for reelection and a number of other Chinese American candidates were also on the ballot. That prompted local newspapers to discuss the possibility of a Chinese majority on the council. None of the Chinese won, including Kiang, very likely a backlash against the growing Chinese presence in the city.

At first glance, the multiracial character of the San Gabriel Valley suggests that racial integration is well underway, supporting the idea that Asian Americans are making social gains. Rather than a large-scale change in settlement patterns and white tolerance of racial minorities, however, in the long run only minor adjustments have occurred. Throughout U.S. history, housing patterns show that whites generally avoid large concentrations of racial minorities; in general, African Americans of all economic

levels have faced the greatest obstacles to settlement in white communities (Logan, Alba, and Leung 1996; Massey and Denton 1993). Although
middle-class Latinos and Asian Americans have gradually penetrated white
suburbs in the San Gabriel Valley, reracialization in the form of segregation rather than integration returned to the valley.

Following the trajectories of San Gabriel Valley communities through
time reveals two patterns. First, what I call the "desegregation and reseg-
regation" of communities occurred, with Monterey Park as the example.
After experiencing integration, or desegregation, in the late 1950s, the
community became resegregated in the 1980s as white flight continued and
the numbers of Asian Americans and Latinos grew by 1990 to compose
87.1 percent of the population. The second pattern has been exhibited by
the city of San Marino, which in 1990 was 62.4 percent white, 32.1 percent Asian American, 5.1 percent Latino, and .4 percent other. The fact
that San Marino, one of the oldest and wealthiest communities in Los
Angeles County, contains a historical and cultural treasure, the Hunting-
ton Library and Botanical Gardens, suggests that whites are reluctant to
leave communities that have strong amenities such as excellent cultural
institutions, well-maintained and exceptional housing stock, and well-func-
tioning city services. The continued presence of whites also suggests the
importance of economic class in cities surrounding San Marino that act
as buffers from the large concentrations of low-income African Americans,
Latinos, and Asian Americans in Los Angeles County and the relative tolerance that whites have for high-income Asian Americans compared to
African Americans.[2]

How is progress measured? In many real ways the situation of Asian
Americans is better than it once was. There was a time, for example, when
the state used its power to enforce restrictive covenants, and immigrants
could not own land in California. Progress is a difficult thing to measure,
however, for discrimination is not easily quantifiable. It is found instead
in constantly changing forms and sites. On the one hand, Asian Americans with college degrees are entering professions once closed to them. On
the other, they can expect to receive lower returns—in terms of income—
on formal education than whites. Asian immigrants can also now become
naturalized citizens and vote. The meaning of that vote, however, is lessened when election procedures such as at-large voting schemes render votes
meaningless in the decision-making process.

Does that mean that the political work—past and present—for which
Asian Americans have so strenuously labored has accomplished little or
nothing? Asian American and Latino political activists in the San Gabriel

Valley are not working toward radical transformation of U.S. institutions. As members of the professional-managerial class (Ehrenreich and Ehrenreich 1979) they have careers that have provided their families with comfortable homes in the suburbs and access to good schools; in some ways the system has worked for them. Their class position has influenced their politics; it is a mainstream, within-the-system approach as opposed to politics of protest working toward radical change. When their political goals operate within institutional parameters, one issue that analysts of social movements pose is whether such movements are inherently limited and unlikely to produce major social change (Eisenger 1980).

San Gabriel Valley activists, however, were involved in various types and sites of grass-roots activities as well as electoral politics that have generated changes in the political, economic, and social institutions in the area and created room for reform. The importance of these changes should not be underestimated. Stressing the way in which such movements emerge from, and are a dialogue with and contestation of, the material conditions activists face every day, George Lipsitz (1988, p. 233) recognizes that these activities "win concessions and transform the terms of political debate within the hegemony that exists." The activists are creating changes that improve the conditions of their lives, working environment, and local politics. To not recognize the importance of such changes is to ignore the emotional and physical violence of discrimination, the salience and impact of race in daily lives, and the importance of work that contests and reconfigures the content and consequences of such identities and their relationship to concepts of community and citizenship and the negotiation of membership.

Latinos and Asian Americans' growing numbers in the region have enhanced and solidified the political inroads they have made. The 1996 U.S. Census Bureau population growth projections show that the nation's Asian American population will double by the year 2010 and the Latino population will double in the following decade. California will continue to be a major center of population growth for both groups. Signs of the growing political influence of Latinos are apparent in the ascendancy of Cruz Bustamante to the assembly speaker's position and in the fact that Latino voters in Los Angeles outnumbered African Americans in the 1997 mayoral contest.

How will the continued growth of the Latino and Asian American populations affect politics in the San Gabriel Valley? Just as the need for resources generated a powerful reason for alliances along panethnic and interracial lines by groups too small to influence politics on their own, expanding numbers can lead to fractured political communities as organizing along the lines of more exclusive identities is made possible by the tremendous growth of particular groups. The 1991 conflict that arose between supporters of Sam Kiang and Judy Chu over the firing of the Monterey Park city manager and the hiring procedures for bilingual operators exposed divisions among immigrant and native-born Chinese Americans. The proliferation of ethnic-specific organizations—such as the Taiwanese American Citizens League—is also evidence of increasing segmentation.

In the case of redistricting in 1990 and 1991, Latinos agreed to the Asian American request to group the four cities that contained their core population within districts. The Latinos were confident of being able to continue to maintain control of elections in the region. Although they far outnumber Asian Americans in the San Gabriel Valley, as the latter group grows in number and its voting power in specific districts begins to alter the balance of power, the kind of cooperation that existed in 1990 and 1991 will be much more difficult to orchestrate. Clearly, the formation of intra- and interracial alliances will be increasingly problematic as Latino and Asian American populations continue to grow and the groups shift from being the underrepresented minorities to established powers.

Countering the tendency for increasing fragmentation are glaring reminders of the racially discriminatory and anti-immigrant forces that Latinos and Asian Americans must continue to battle—for example, the passage of the anti-affirmative action Proposition 209 and federal cuts in the benefits of documented immigrants. As in the case of the Multi-Cultural Community Association and the Alhambra School District, the threat of violent and potentially fatal interracial confrontations that would endanger children's lives creates an issue that transcends ethnic and racial lines and forms the basis for an alliance between specific ethnic groups.

Finally, as Latinos and Asian Americans gain positions in significant numbers in institutions that historically have been used to protect the interests of those in power and exclude and disfranchise racial minorities, the challenge will be to avoid replicating the discriminatory practices of the past. It will be necessary to create a system that is responsive and equitable. Considering the complexity of the Asian American population and the record of strife that exists, the challenge of serving the needs of this complex population will continue. Yet the record of activists and individuals in organizations such as the Asian Pacific American Legal Center and MALDEF, who strive to advocate for the most disfranchised members of society and use tactics such as multiracial alliances to do so, indicates a politics that will be inclusive rather than exclusive.

An Overview of the Analytical Framework

Based on events in the San Gabriel Valley involving the construction of racial and ethnic identities, political mobilization, and interracial political alliances, I developed an analytical framework for examining these issues in a community setting (figure 2). I suggest that these areas are connected and, at times, interrelated parts or phases of the same process. By identifying these links and studying the areas together, three substantive and theoretical areas traditionally studied separately— panethnicity, resource mobilization, and ethnic and racial politics—can be connected. Doing so generates descriptions and analyses of the origins, development, and purpose of these processes that reveal how they develop and are related rather than conceptualizing and examining each topic as self-contained and independent.

Key Areas of Study

Historical, Contemporary, and Structural Circumstances

Events in the San Gabriel Valley demonstrate the importance of considering how international, national, regional, and local factors converge and create a regionally specific context for race, ethnicity, and politics. Racial and ethnic identities do not develop in a vacuum. Rather, they are highly situational and multilayered. They emerge from a particular local context where they simultaneously have personal, individuated meaning and are linked to larger social and economic systems that give them material meaning and consequences.

The demographic and economic context of the valley has been shaped by U.S. government policies, for example, on mortgage programs, infrastructure construction, and immigration, that have directly affected its racial character. These policies have interacted with local procedures such as restrictive covenants, redlining by financial institutions, and steering practices by realtors. Combined with international factors such as the emigration patterns of individuals from Hong Kong and Taiwan (influenced by their relationships with China), the global flow of capital, and the internationalization of the production process, they have led to the San Gabriel Valley becoming important in the global Chinese economy.

Through U.S. government policies, the state has been a major site of conflict as groups struggle over racial policies and resources. Asian immigrants and Asian Americans have had a long history of conflict with the U.S. government over the classification and consequences of their racial identities. Areas of concern have included policies regarding the right to own property (the Alien Land Laws) and choose marriage partners (miscegenation laws), along with naturalization and immigration policies. As Michael Omi and Howard Winant (1994) point out, racial categories are constructions, and their boundaries and social, economic, and political significance are continually shaped and transformed through negotiation and conflict in a process of "racial formation."

In terms of the way these issues are contested in a community setting and shaped by local factors, mediating institutions such as school systems and local governments structure relationships among groups in the way they institutionalize and order forms of interaction (Lamphere 1992). On a regional level, for example, the political structure of East Los Angeles, a low-income, unincorporated area of the county, offers few opportunities for involvement, in contrast to Monterey Park's variety of institutionalized programs (Pardo 1990). This points out the importance of recognizing the complex relationships among structural factors—such as institutions, laws, and policies—and how they create unequal and discriminatory situations while affecting the sorts of actions possible, allowable, or legal in a community setting.

In these local settings, conceptions of identity, race, and politics are extremely heterogeneous within ethnic and racial groups, in part because individuals bring a variety of personal and group histories to each setting (Lowe 1991). With the movement of people domestically and internationally, the concept of race has different meanings for native-born Americans, who grow up in a highly racialized and racially heterogeneous society, than it does for immigrants from regions where the racial mix is less varied and particular ethnic histories are more meaningful. One example is the division between native Taiwanese and the wave of Nationalist Chinese who came to Taiwan in 1949 after the communist revolution.

For immigrants from Asia, notions of race and ethnicity may be radically transformed in the United States, where, as Asians, a fundamental change in their racial position occurs and they suddenly become part of a minority group. Simultaneously, their U.S. interests and identities are combined with their position as transnational immigrants who have political, economic, and familial concerns that cross national boundaries (Schiller 1992, 1994).

Notions of race and ethnicity in the United States are formed before people arrive there (Abelmann and Lie 1995; Kim and Yu 1996). Immigrants' understandings of the nation and its racial and ethnic groups are influenced by media images. For example, the practices of Asian entrepreneurs in the San Gabriel Valley are influenced by images of U.S. capitalism. Likewise, the history of conflict between

Korean immigrant shopkeepers and their African American clientele in Los Angeles begins in Korea, where people are first exposed to media images of Los Angeles. Similarly, African Americans in the United States experience the nation's stereotypes about immigrants and Asians.

Events from each era must also be considered, understanding that people in a particular region bring different experiences to a setting. Some immigrants from Japan entered the United States when naturalization was impossible, were incarcerated during World War II in U.S. concentration camps, or experienced restrictive covenants when they first tried to move to the San Gabriel Valley. They have a completely different experience than recent Chinese immigrants who have entered a city where they are part of an Asian American majority population, encounter real estate agents and building contractors who cater specifically to their interests, and can become U.S. citizens.

The "historical, contemporary, and structural circumstances" and forces of figure 2, part A represent the context—in terms of international, national, state, and local factors—from which racial and ethnic identities and politics emerge and, in turn, negotiate, transform, or contest such factors in a regional site. To study identity formation and political mobilization in a community setting recognizes that individuals are embedded in complex patterns of gender, racial, class, and political relationships that are highly influenced by the regional historical and contemporary context.

Organizational Scale

Economic and political modernization is a driving force behind the increasing scale of racial and ethnic organizing (Hannan 1979). The growing scale of the state and the corresponding growth in organizations that confront it provide a central dynamic for ethnic political alliances. Although U.S. government policies have always been racialized, for example, in the way race circumscribed citizenship and suffrage rights, the civil rights movement contributed to a critical change in that process. A formal shift in government ideology and practice recognized racial and ethnic groups in addition to the individual as legitimate units of analysis for calculating the distribution of resources and effects of discrimination. As the government grows in scope and scale and groups struggle over government-controlled resources and policy formation, such groups must also grow in size to support their interests effectively (Enloe 1981; Nagel and Olzak 1982, 1983; Nielsen 1985; Olzak and Nagel 1986).[1]

Showing the importance of organizational scale for the construction of new racial and ethnic groupings are works that examine panethnicity, that is, the development of ties and cooperation among groups of different national origins and the formation of larger, more inclusive associations as Asian Americans, Latinos, or Native Americans (Cornell 1988; Espiritu 1992; Lopez and Espiritu 1990; Nagel 1996; Padilla 1985; Trottier 1981). Interaction with government agencies is seen as the central dynamic driving that process. Racial groups recognize the need for

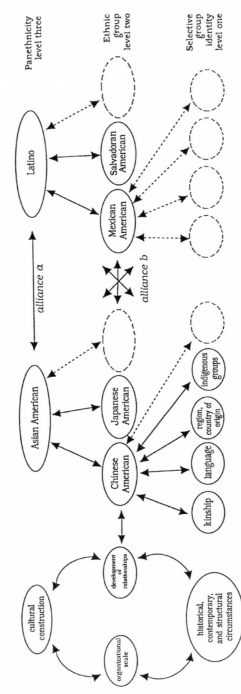

Figure 2. An Analytical Framework for Studying the Construction of Racial and Ethnic Identities and Political Alliances in a Community Setting

ethnic subgroups to organize in order to negotiate policy and resource allocation with the government.[2]

Research on resource mobilization recognizes the importance of resources, group interests, political opportunity, and social structure (Gamson 1975; McAdam 1982; McCarthy and Zald 1977; Morris 1984; Oberschall 1973). Such works demonstrate that a group's ability to mobilize resources in the pursuit of common goals is a critical factor for initiating and sustaining a movement. Resources include both material and nonmaterial items: money, leadership skills, labor, organizations, and networks (Oberschall 1973). The stress on resources is also the basis for a number of studies on interracial political alliances (Browning, Marshall, and Tabb 1984; Sonenshein 1993).[3]

In the San Gabriel Valley, native-born Chinese Americans, Japanese Americans, and recent Chinese immigrants understood that alone each group lacked the numbers and resources required to be effective in the political arena. The construction of an Asian American identity and its translation into a political movement to create and institutionalize a political base demonstrate the dynamics of organizational scale, the importance of resources, and the exigencies of electoral politics. Organized as Asian Americans through politics, these individuals work to negotiate and reconstruct the economic, political, and social consequences of race and the criteria for membership in the local and national community as Americans.

The construction of racial and ethnic identities is an integral part of the process of building interethnic political alliances. As emphasized by panethnicity theory and resource mobilization theory, the growing scale and complexity of the state requires a corresponding growth among groups that interact with the government and its agencies. Groups competing for government resources and policy formation must organize on a level to match their competitors. The escalating level of resources required to participate in electoral politics at all levels also encourages increased organizational scale (Browning, Marshall, and Tabb 1984). The importance of relationships with government agencies and the requirements of politics for the development of ethnic identities and political alliances are represented by "organizational scale" in figure 2, part A.

Cultural Construction

Structural conditions and historical circumstances alone cannot explain how individuals and groups construct ethnic and racial identities and political alliances (Morris and Mueller 1992). Through ethnography, I emphasize the importance of everyday life as a site of analysis because of the way lived experiences reveal the role of social forces, such as government institutions and racism, and in turn how individuals enact cultural practices that show their interpretations and contestation of such institutions, a perspective embodied in the research of the "new" social movements (Johnston, Larana, Gusfield 1994; Johnston and Klandermans 1995).[4] In contrast to "old" social movements based on class conflict in industrial economies, Robert Fisher (1993, p. 4) describes new social movements emerging in the post-industrial economy based on communities of interest not directly linked to the work place, for example, or to the environmental, feminist, or peace movements.

Examining the details of everyday life also shows the way history and culture are used in the construction of racial and ethnic identities and political mobilization. Joane Nagel (1994), recognizing the mutability of culture (Barth 1969), has examined how historical and contemporary experiences are used in the process of "cultural construction"; the symbolic significance and cultural substance of ethnicity is produced by individuals and used to support, and give meaning to, ethnic identities and group boundaries.[5]

As George Lipsitz (1988) explains in his work on African American activists, "collective memory" in terms of an understanding of a shared history can legitimate contemporary social movements. Collective memory, which activists strategically employ, is a historical source; when it is combined with contemporary issues, purpose and goals can be extracted and used to bind people together and create a sense of group membership and legitimacy.[6]

Efforts to counter the move to ban the use of foreign languages on commercial signs in Monterey Park illustrated the process of cultural construction. Mike Eng's organization of immigrants to monitor city commission meetings and Jose Calderon and Kathy Imahara's explanation of constitutional rights and the history of the civil rights movement are examples of efforts to create links among the experiences of recent immigrants and established residents through shared history and struggle.

"Cultural construction" (figure 2, part A) recognizes the importance of everyday activities and culture in the process by which individuals produce the symbolic significance and cultural substance of ethnicity as they construct ethnic identities and group boundaries, establishing a foundation for the development of community and a basis for political mobilization (Nagel 1994). The cultural content of ethnicity is constantly changing as local and national histories are reinterpreted and reconstructed in combination with contemporary concerns to create, sustain, and legitimate political movements (Lipsitz 1988).

The Development of Relationships

The importance of long-term interaction among community leaders for the development of working relationships and coalition-building is a critical but often neglected area of research, as pointed out by Raphael J. Sonenshein (1993) in a study of political alliances between African Americans and whites in Los Angeles. A working relationship, a sense of trust, and a culture that legitimizes the links among ethnic and racial groups all create a foundation for alliances. Chinese and Japanese American activists, for example, met while working in their respective communities in Los Angeles's Little Tokyo and Chinatown during the 1970s, developed relationships as they created networks to engage in politics in Los Angeles, and eventually established the West San Gabriel Valley Asian Pacific Democratic Club in 1985. And the Latino and Asian American redistricting alliance was facilitated by the long working relationships of Antonia Hernandez and Stewart Kwoh, directors of the legal organizations that guided the redistricting effort and conducted the voting rights analysis, and UCLA professors Leo Estrada and Paul Ong, who supervised the examination of demographic data.

Long-term interactions among community leaders create working relationships that lead to coalition-building (represented in figure 2, part A by "development of relationships") both interethnically, in the case of panethnicity, and interracially. Organizations facilitate and sustain long-term interaction among community leaders and create working relationships that lead to coalition-building.

These four areas—historical, contemporary, and structural circumstances; cultural construction; organizational scale; and the development of relationships—form the context and key forces that drive the development of racial and ethnic identities on multiple levels, political mobilization, and interracial political alliances. That individuals and groups also exert an influence on structure and context through their political practices is indicated by arrows in figure 2, parts A and B.

Multiple Levels of Identity and Interracial Alliances

Research on panethnicity in the United States suggests that the construction of ethnicity contains three levels with increasing levels of inclusiveness. First, in what I call "selective group identity" (figure 2, part B, level one), groups are formed based on criteria such as kinship, language, and region of origin (Hannan 1979) or, in the case of indigenous groups, ancestry and territory. On the next two levels, cultural construction takes place in which historical and contemporary events in the United States create commonalities that extend beyond a selective group identity and contribute to more inclusive levels of ethnic identity (level two), as discussed in research on panethnicity and racial formation that examines the constructed nature of ethnic identity, the fluidity of boundaries, and multiple levels. At the second level, identity as an ethnic group is constructed. Just as an "Italian American" identity is formed in the United States not in Italy (Gans 1962), the same is true for other groups such as Japanese Americans, Chinese Americans, or Mexican Americans.[7] Then, a panethnic identity such as Asian American or Latino occurs (level three).

Ignoring differences among Asian Americans reinforces racism and discrimination based on an essentializing discourse that constructs a homogeneous image of all members of the group (Lowe 1991). Recognizing differences within a panethnic group not only works to dismantle stereotypes and address racism but also allows for political action within that group based on an assessment of the particular issues of subgroups. Lisa Lowe (1991) points out that recognizing the heterogeneity within a panethnic group while simultaneously identifying common issues opens the possibility of creating political alliances with other groups that may differ in class, gender, or race. It establishes alliances based on similar political interests while acknowledging differences.

Three areas critical for panethnic relationships also play key roles in the development of interracial alliances: the development of organizations, relationships among leaders, and cultural construction. The importance of developing networks, organizations, and resources to participate effectively in negotiations with the U.S. government and its agencies over policy formation and resource allocation and to compete in electoral politics at local, state, and federal levels also provides a major dynamic for the development of interracial political alliances.

The structural demands of politics and similar ideologies, however, are not enough for the development of interracial coalitions. The groups' self-interests must be advanced through a coalition (Carmichael and Hamilton 1967; Sonenshein 1993). Likewise, organizations are critical not only for gathering resources and coordinating activities but also because, to benefit individually, a coalition's participants must each have a base of power and resources from which they can participate as partners rather than subordinates (Carmichael and Hamilton 1967).

The importance of organizations is clearly illustrated in Morris's (1984) study of the U.S. civil rights movement, in which he examines the origins of the movement and its strategy to address the economic, political, and social discrimination faced by African Americans. Emphasizing local participants, Morris (p. 282) focuses on the activities of organizations, developing an "indigenous perspective" for the study of aggrieved groups that examines the elements he believes vital for social movements: resources, activists with ties to local organizations, and sound tactics and strategies. Rather than a reliance on outside elites, Morris shows how indigenous organizations spearheaded the movement.[8]

Cultural construction takes place during the process of building interracial alliances, as it takes place in the construction of an ethnic identity. Latinos and Asian Americans have shared geographic and political spaces, from the agricultural fields of Oxnard to the urban communities of Boyle Heights and Monterey Park, and have established common ground through their struggles for equality. Perceptions of discrimination can help build links among racial groups, establishing a basis for alliances as leaders actively use history and contemporary events to develop goals and legitimate efforts. Carole J. Uhlaner's (1991) research supports this point. She recognizes that persons who believe discrimination exists against their own group are more likely to accept its existence against other groups, and that awareness can contribute to ethnic and racial alliances. Latinos and Asian Americans have been racialized differently in the United States. Unlike early Asian immigrants, for example, Latin Americans were eligible for citizenship. Despite such differences, both groups recognize their subordinate position in a U.S. racial hierarchy that privileges whiteness. Although labor-market discrimination and the anti-affirmative provisions of Proposition 209 affect each group differently, for example, both understand how such practices embedded in U.S. society enforce privileges for whites.

The case of redistricting and the alliance between Asian Americans and Latinos illustrated the importance of developing organizations for the pursuit of political goals, how such organizations helped create a foundation for an alliance between the groups, and the need for resources and previous relationships among participants. Also critical for developing working relationships, as the case of redistricting underscored, were the importance of fostering an understanding of shared histories of discrimination and political disfranchisement and a clear idea of how working together would enhance the likelihood of realizing each groups' goals. The statewide redistricting alliance was between panethnic groups—Asian Americans and Latinos (figure 2, "alliance a"). In the San Gabriel Valley, however, the Latino organization and inhabitants of the region were primarily Mexican American, and the relationship (figure 2, "alliance b") was between an ethnic group (Mexican American) and a panethnic group (Asian American). Although these alliances dissolve, the networks among individuals and organizations live on and are reestablished as needed, as was the case of the multiracial support that grew out of redistricting for the successful Rosemead City Council campaign of Joe Vasquez.

Thus, research on panethnicity, political mobilization, and interracial politics stresses the importance of organizational, structural, and historical factors. Studies on panethnicity, however, focus only on relationships among groups within a panethnic category, such as Japanese, Filipino, and Korean in the development of an Asian American category. Such studies do not examine how factors that lead to multiple levels of ethnic identity affect relationships between racial groups. Similarly, identities in studies on racial and ethnic politics are taken as a given; they along with boundaries are seen as constants. What is lacking is an exploration of how factors such as the need for resources, networks, and organizations promote ethnic and racial identities on multiple levels. Rather than studying each separately, examining the construction of racial and ethnic identities, political mobilization, and interracial alliances in a community context, using an analytical framework that combines research on panethnicity and racial politics recognizes the relationships among these processes and that they emerge from the same forces.

Emphasizing the structural, historical, and organizational factors contained in these theories, combined with a focus on how meaning and identity are constructed by individuals out of everyday interactions and the cultural practices they generate, provides a more comprehensive understanding of the political importance of race and political relationships among different racial and ethnic groups. This analysis also reveals how individuals produce the symbolic significance and cultural substance of ethnicity as they construct identities, mobilize politically, and develop alliances.

NOTES

Foreword

1. The first use recorded in the *Oxford English Dictionary* comes from the *Butte Record* of Oroville in California's mother lode country for January 31, 1857, which told readers in a story about a New Year's celebration that "Chinatown was wild with joy."

2. See Horton (1992, 1995) and Fong (1994).

Introduction

1. The San Gabriel Valley includes many cities. I focus on a cluster of four with the largest, fastest-growing Asian American populations: Monterey Park, Alhambra, San Gabriel, and Rosemead.

2. As of 1996 the higher elected officials from this region were Gloria Molina of the Los Angeles County Board of Supervisors, District 1, Diane Martinez of the Forty-ninth Assembly District, Hilda Solis of the Twenty-fourth Senate District, and Matthew Martinez of the Thirty-first Congressional District.

Because the term *Latino* is used more often by community residents, political activists, and politicians in the San Gabriel Valley than the Bureau of the Census's term, *Hispanic,* I will use the former throughout this volume. In the San Gabriel Valley, Latinos are primarily of Mexican ancestry. Latinos have been enumerated in a variety of ways in the U.S. censuses, complicating comparisons with data before 1980, when a form of self-reporting was adopted. See Hayes-Bautista and Chapa (1987) for a discussion of terms the Bureau of the Census has used for Latinos.

3. Traditional anthropological definitions of race and ethnicity focus on the biological aspects of the former and the cultural aspects of the later (Schermerhorn 1978). Although conceptualized as concrete categories, this is problematical because race and ethnicity are both socially created constructs (Rex 1983; van den Berghe 1967). Omi and Winant (1986, 1994) explain that race is not a concrete or fixed category based on some sort of "biological fact" but rather the result of political and economic processes.

What is important for this study of racial and ethnic identities and politics is the process by which racial and ethnic categories and politics are constructed through interaction between participants and the larger society rather than the determination of whether these are racial or ethnic politics or how to categorize people. I use the terms *race* and *ethnicity* with these cautions. To reduce repetition, I sometimes use "ethnicity" or "race" rather than "race and ethnicity."

4. In the demographic tables in this book that use U.S. census data, "Latino" is developed from the classification "Hispanic Origin by Race," using the heading "Hispanic origin" and the subcategories "white" and "other race." White is from "not of Hispanic origin, white." African American, Asian American, and Native American are from those categories in "not of Hispanic origin" added to the same race from "Hispanic origin." That method gives priority to "race" over "Hispanic" classification and reflects the working definition used by Asian Americans in the redistricting case study in chapter 6. This accounts for individuals such as Filipino Americans, considered Asian American by the redistricting coalition, who checked both the Asian or Pacific Islander category under the race question and the Hispanic category.

5. See also Alba (1990), Gans (1979), and Novak (1996).

6. This is similar to what occurred during the first major waves of Japanese immigration at the turn of the century, although then the Chinese preceded the Japanese into the United States. Ichioka's study (1988) of the Issei (first generation) noted that leaders of the Japanese community were well aware of the strong anti-Asian sentiment that existed among large segments of the American population and resulted in the Chinese Exclusion Act of 1882. For that reason, they sought to distinguish themselves from the Chinese. Aware of the belief among white Americans that Japanese, like Chinese, could not be assimilated into American life, leaders of the U.S. Japanese community decided to adapt behavior and clothing to match American standards, something they believed the Chinese did not do. Of course, the Japanese were equally unsuccessful, and the passage of the Gentlemen's Agreement of 1908 banned the immigration of Japanese laborers. A reversal occurred during the incarceration of Japanese Americans during World War II, when some Chinese Americans actively sought to distance themselves from the Japanese Americans (Daniels 1988).

7. Quotations here and throughout this volume are from my fieldnotes of the event or interviews unless otherwise noted. This material was gathered between 1988 and 1997.

8. During part of this period, from 1988 to 1990, I worked on a research project directed by John Horton, associate professor of sociology at the University of California, Los Angeles. From that project I draw on fieldnotes, two exit polls for an election to the Monterey Park City Council, and formal interviews ranging in length from one to four hours conducted with approximately a hundred residents—Asian American, Latino, and white—active in local politics. Horton's study was part of a research project funded by the Changing Community Relations Project

of the Ford Foundation and the Institute of American Cultures, UCLA. The Ford Project examined relationships among newcomers and established residents in six cities throughout the United States. In addition to John Horton, I wish to acknowledge the assistance of the other members of the UCLA research group: Jose Calderon, Jerry Kimery, Liang-Wen "Wayne" Kuo, Mary Pardo, Linda Shaw, and Yen Fen Tseng.

9. My major sites of participation include the following political campaigns: Judy Chu for the Monterey Park City Council (1988), Sam Kiang for the Monterey Park City Council (1990), Sophie Wong for the Alhambra School Board (1990), and Xavier Becerra for the Fifty-ninth Assembly District (1990). I participated briefly in the campaigns of March Fong Eu for California secretary of state (1990), Art Torres for the Los Angeles County Board of Supervisors (1991), Joe Vasquez for the Rosemead City Council (1992), Richard Fajardo for the Forty-ninth Assembly District (1992), and Judy Chu for the Forty-ninth Assembly District (1994).

Because my goal is to study the process of political and ethnic formation rather than any one actual site, I followed individuals and issues throughout the region and involved myself in a number of other activities. They ranged from short events (fund-raising for Asian American and Latino politicians, Monterey Park celebrations such as Fourth of July, Cinco de Mayo, Citizens' Day, play days, and homecoming, and Historical Society and Langley Senior Citizens Center events) that involved an afternoon or evening to longer commitments on planning committees (Monterey Park Harmony Week) for special events that took a number of weeks or months to accomplish.

Chapter 1: Monterey Park and the San Gabriel Valley

1. The Los Angeles Customs District includes the ports of Los Angeles and Long Beach, Los Angeles International Airport, and airports in Ventura County and Las Vegas (Iritani 1995a).

2. Harrison and Bluestone (1988, p. 29) borrowed this phrase from Akio Morita, the co-founder of Sony, who described the loss of a major portion of the U.S. manufacturing base as a "hollowing of American industry."

3. For a more detailed discussion of U.S. immigration policy and demographic change, see Hing (1993), McClain (1994), Ong and Liu (1994), and Portes and Rumbaut (1990).

4. An extreme example of low-wage labor in the San Gabriel Valley occurred in the city of El Monte, where it was discovered in 1995 that Thai immigrants worked and lived in slavelike conditions in a garment factory.

5. Tseng cites Kotkin and Kishimoto (1988).

6. Comparing data obtained in a telephone survey of Chinese business owners in Los Angeles County with Yoon's data (1991) on Korean business owners in Chicago, Tseng examined the premigration background of the two groups (1994a, table 4.2, p. 98). Tseng found a higher level of college graduates among Chinese:

86 percent compared to 67 percent for Koreans. In terms of premigration occupation, 23 percent of the Chinese were in an executive position, compared to 24 percent of Koreans. A telling statistic is that 21 percent of the Chinese were professionals, compared to 7 percent of Koreans. Also significant is that 43 percent of the Chinese had owned a business in their homeland, compared to 24 percent of the Koreans.

7. This is according to data from the Immigration and Naturalization service for 1983–90 for immigrants from Hong Kong, China, and Taiwan (Fong 1994, table 5, p. 32).

8. In Hawaii only people designated by the U.S. government as leaders of the Japanese American community—teachers and religious leaders, for example—were sent to concentration camps. Thus, most soldiers from Hawaii were not drafted from camps.

9. The Nisei soldiers were part of a motorized unit of the 522d Field Artillery Battalion of the 442d Regimental Combat Team. They were sent ahead of the main Allied force to disrupt retreating German troops and prevent them from establishing a defensive position. For reasons never fully explained by their white commanding officers, the Nisei were told that they should not talk about the events surrounding the liberation of Dachau. Although soldiers were not normally allowed to have cameras, a few of the Nisei secretly kept cameras and took pictures of the liberation. A temporary exhibit, featuring photographs taken by the Nisei liberators of Dachau, opened in the Israeli Holocaust museum, Yad Vashem, on May 3, 1992.

10. I first heard the paradox of the Statue of Liberty and the Chinese Exclusion Act in a talk given by Shirley Hune, "Towards the Reconstruction of Knowledge and Scholarship: The Discourse of Asian-American Studies," on January 31, 1992, at the University of California, Los Angeles. Higham (1984) has described how the symbolic significance of the statue has changed from the original intents of commemorating French and American relations and celebrating U.S. independence and stability to an opposition to oppression and a celebration of diversity. It was during the latter period that Lazarus's poem, unnoticed for decades, received attention.

11. *Ozawa v. United States* and *United States v. Bhagat Singh Thind* were the Supreme Court cases involving Japanese and Asian Indian immigrants, respectively. The Immigration and Naturalization Act of 1952 (the McCarran-Walter Act) finally eliminated race as a barrier to naturalization.

12. Chan (1991, p. 47) notes the research of Dudley McGovney concerning states that followed California in the passage of alien land laws. Arizona, Washington, Louisiana, New Mexico, Idaho, Montana, Oregon, and Kansas had passed such laws before the war. During the war, Utah, Wyoming, and Arkansas, states that had concentration camps within their boundaries, also passed legislation. As Chan suggests, "Legislatures of those states apparently did not want any Japanese to get the idea they could easily settle there after the war was over."

13. Although he believed that the decision was wrong and racist, Yoneda (1983)

did not protest because he believed that the immediate task of the U.S. Communist Party was to aid the country's efforts to defeat Nazi and Japanese fascism. In retrospect, Yoneda has written that he should have protested the decision when it was made. At the 1959 and 1972 conventions of the U.S. Communist Party, he and others worked to include resolutions, which were adopted, that acknowledged the racism and wrongdoing in the actions of the Communist Party and the U.S. incarceration of Japanese Americans.

14. See United States Commission on Civil Rights (1975) and Massey and Denton (1993) for a discussion of these cases.

15. Until 1950, the National Association of Real Estate Brokers code of ethics stated, "A Realtor should never be instrumental in introducing into a neighborhood, by character of property or occupancy, members of any race or nationality, or any individual whose presence will clearly be detrimental to property values in the neighborhood" (U.S. Commission on Civil Rights 1975, p. 4).

16. A decade after the passage of Title VIII and *Jones v. Mayer* (1968), a study by the National Committee against Discrimination in Housing (1979, p. 7) concluded that the number of complaints filed relative to the number of housing deals involving racial minorities had been "infinitesimal": "Title VIII is a weak instrument, responsibility [for its enforcement] is diffuse, resources and staff have been woefully inadequate."

17. The fact that discrimination continues is not surprising. After all, the Civil Rights Act of 1866 also prohibited racial discrimination in housing transactions, but discrimination continued because no steps were taken to enforce the act.

18. Considered the center of the city's Jewish community during the 1920s, it included other European immigrant groups such as Russians, Italians, and Poles (Romo 1983). During the 1920s the area contained the largest Japanese American population in the region.

19. One of the most intriguing episodes of the concentration camp era was the case of Ralph Lazo, a Latino of Mexican and Irish ancestry who decided to enter the camps. At the time, he was a student at Central Junior High School near Little Tokyo and had many Japanese American friends. When they were sent to the camps, he decided to go with them. No one knows why he did so or why his family allowed him to go. As his sister explained, "He just came in one day and told my dad, 'I'm going to camp.'" In a 1981 interview Lazo mentioned that government officials had never asked about his ancestry. He remained in Manzanar until being drafted in 1944. Lazo died in 1992 (Barker 1992).

20. For a detailed account of the slow-growth movement in Monterey Park, see Fong (1994) and Horton (1989, 1995).

21. Lo's (1990) examination of the California property tax revolt in the 1970s, Proposition 13, recognized the highly politicized character and tradition of community activism in the city.

22. For a discussion of the language issue in Monterey Park, see Horton and Calderon (1992).

Chapter 2: Reasserting Whiteness

1. Fifteen residents were on the city council's committee. Five plans were produced and published by the committee and consulting firms: one general guide for the city and four specific plans, each focusing on one of the city's business districts.

2. As of 1995, agreements had expired between the city and developer for a project on the property. The director of the Monterey Park Economic Development Division said that the development company was concentrating its efforts on other projects.

3. According to a letter from Monterey Park's Economic Development office, three companies submitted proposals: Champion Development, Schurgin Development, and La Caze. Although information on the last company is unavailable and it was unlisted in 1996 Los Angeles County telephone directories, it appears that none of the firms were owned by Asians.

4. At an earlier CARE meeting, a city council member who was involved thought that four hundred signatures would be enough to send a strong message to the council.

5. Of course, calling the theme "Mediterranean" does not mean that it resembles, or is derived from, architectural elements from that region of the world. What is significant is that the generic term *Mediterranean,* which has European roots, was used rather than *Mexican* or *Spanish,* which have been deemed too ethnic by residents and city-funded planners.

6. The event, sponsored by the local Kiwanis Club, was titled "Salute to America's Cultural Harmony" and held on September 8, 1989, in Pasadena, the northern part of the San Gabriel Valley.

7. David Roediger's work is clearly aimed at analyzing and dismantling racial privilege and hierarchy. My argument about the emptiness of white culture is unfair in the sense that I give his work a meaning that has nothing to do with his project involving institutionalized discrimination. Work can be read in ways that are unintended by an author, however, and I acknowledge that my interpretation is at odds with the direction of his body of work.

8. Support for a Mediterranean design did not break down neatly by race. During the public hearings, some whites stated that Monterey Park should capitalize on its strength as a destination point for Asian tourists, and Latinos and Asian Americans spoke about the need for a place to "feel at home." Asian American and Latino support for a Eurocentric vision of America is discussed in chapter 3.

9. Betty Couch, Judy Chu, Barry Hatch, Chris Houseman, and Patricia Reichenberger were the council members during this period. Chu focused on fiscal issues during the redevelopment project deliberations.

Chapter 3: Asian American Politics

1. See also Morris (1984) and Robnett (1997) for studies of African Americans and the civil rights movement and Takash (1993) for a study of elected Latina

political officials for works that examine politics using an expanded conceptual framework. In contrast, earlier studies on political activity—Campbell et al. (1960), Dahl (1973), Milbrath (1965), and Verba and Nie (1972)—used a narrower set of variables and emphasized economic and education levels as well as generation to explain U.S. political activity and interests.

2. Asian Americans who have served on the Monterey Park City Council are: Alfred Song, Korean (1960–62), George Ige, Japanese (1970–780), G. Monty Manibog, Filipino (1976–78), Lily Chen, Chinese (1982–86), Judy Chu, Chinese (1988–2001), and Samuel Kiang, Chinese (1990–94). Latinos who have served on the council are: Matthew Martinez, Mexican (1974–82), David R. Almada, Mexican (1982–86), Rudy Peralta, Mexican (1982–86), Fred Balderrama, Mexican (1990–99), Rita Valenzuela, Mexican (1992–2001), and Francisco Alonso, Spanish (1992–99). Alonso was born in the United States and identifies himself as Hispanic; his parents are immigrants from Spain. (Monterey Park Seventy-fifth Anniversary Committee 1991).

3. The institute's publications include: Hing and Lee, eds. (1996), Ong (1994), Ong, ed. (1994), and Ong and Hune, eds. (1993).

4. The tenure issue is covered at length in *Amerasia Journal* 1990, 16(1): 61–169.

5. Xavier Becerra, born and raised in Sacramento, began his political career in Monterey Park, where he lived and was elected to the state assembly in 1990. When Edward Roybal retired from Congress, Becerra won that seat in 1992 and moved to the district.

6. The acronym was changed from APPCON to A3PCON when the word *policy* was added to the agency's name in 1996 to reflect its research and advocacy roles on issues.

7. For a discussion of conflict between the leadership and constituencies of social service organizations due to class, ethnic, gender, and generational differences, see Espiritu (1992), and Espiritu and Ong (1994). For a discussion on the early history of Asian American social service agencies, see Kuramoto (1980).

8. For a detailed examination of the Japanese American Citizen's League, see Chuman (1981), Hosokawa (1982), and Takahashi (1982).

9. See Horton and Calderon (1992) for a discussion of the English-only movement in Monterey Park. Hatch and another city resident, Frank Arcuri, organized a drive to have English declared the official language of the city. On August 21, 1985, they put a legal notice in the *Monterey Park Progress* to announce their intent to launch a petition to have the measure placed on the April 1986 city election ballot. The petition stated: "English is the language we use in Monterey Park when we want everyone to understand our ideas. This is what unites us as Americans, even though some of our citizens speak other languages. Let us make English our official language as a symbol of this unity." After more than 3,300 signatures were gathered, the petition was submitted but ruled invalid by the city attorney because it failed to "carry the text of the proposed ordinance" (Babcock

1985, p. A1). The issue appeared on a statewide ballot as Proposition 63 in November 1986 and easily passed, 73 to 27 percent. The proposition passed in Monterey Park but by a smaller margin: 56 to 44 percent (Ward 1986).

10. For a more detailed discussion of the 1988 and 1990 elections, see Fong (1994); for a discussion of the 1988, 1990, and 1994 elections, see Horton (1989, 1995).

11. Earlier Asian American voting preferences in California elections have been poorly documented and, as noted by critics of these works (Din 1984; Nakanishi 1985–86), are usually extracted from polls that include so few Asians that the results are virtually meaningless. The two exit polls taken for the 1988 and 1990 Monterey Park City Council elections were significant because they included large samples of Asian American voters. Horton notes (1995) that 1,390 usable questionnaires were collected from the twenty city precincts in 1988, representing 17 percent of those who voted. Because the research project focused on the Asian American population, they were oversampled.

Significant at the .01 level means that one chance exists out of a hundred that the relationship could have been due to random chance or sampling error. Thus, the results strongly suggest that factors other than chance are responsible for the relationship between race and voting behavior.

12. The 1990 exit poll was organized and run by John Horton and myself. The questionnaire was also translated into Chinese. The exit poll was conducted at all the city's precincts for four hours in the morning and again for four hours in the evening during the peak voting periods. Every third voter was approached as they left the polling place, and 974 usable questionnaires were gathered. Questions of opinion that were originally planned for the 1988 exit poll were deleted in the final questionnaire because of the concern that such questions might reduce the response rate because of an atmosphere of heightened political tension.

13. See Nakanishi (1986) for a discussion of this method.

14. The figures are from Song's campaign statement of receipts filed on April 15, 1960. Chu's contributions were from statements covering July 1987 to June 1988. Her total of $34,233 is from page 2 of her June 1988 statement.

Chapter 4: Asian American Political Issues

1. The 1986 election, held at the height of the slow-growth movement, in which the three incumbents (Lily Chen, David Almada, and Rudy Peralta) lost, drew 39.2 percent of the voters, one of the highest turnouts in city history (Fong 1994).

2. In the 1992 election, incumbent Judy Chu raised $53,927; John Casperson, $34,928; Charles Wu, $39,458; and Raymond Wu, $41,519. The 1982 and 1986 campaign totals are from the consolidated campaign statements, form 490; the 1988, 1990, 1992, and 1994 campaign totals are from the officeholder, candidate, and controlled committee campaign statement, long form.

3. The overall vote in the 1992 presidential election was 43 percent for Bill Clin-

ton, 38 percent for George Bush, and 19 percent for Ross Perot. The vote among African Americans was 86 percent, 9 percent, and 5 percent, respectively; among Asian Americans it was 45 percent, 38 percent, and 17 percent, respectively; among Latinos it was 56 percent, 29 percent, and 15 percent, respectively; and among whites it was 37 percent, 42 percent, and 21 percent, respectively (*Los Angeles Times* 1992).

4. See McCormack and Jones (1993) for work on African American candidates and Underwood (1995) for a discussion of Latino candidates and deracialized campaign strategies.

5. From fieldnotes and Nakayama (1990). In Los Angeles on December 8, 1990, a fund-raising event aimed at the Asian American community was held to support Robert Matsui's bid for U.S. Senate in 1992. He later dropped out of the race because of an illness in the family.

6. Gender and class constantly influence politics and deserve discussion throughout this book. I did not focus directly on gender and class, yet even though my data were limited, important points did emerge.

7. Eleanor Chow retired and moved to Las Vegas, where she ran for a seat on the school board. When I asked about the events that led her to do so, she explained that she had once dropped by the school district's office to volunteer her time. Asian American parents in the district, along with school officials who hoped to use her years of experience in education, urged her to run for office. Endorsed by numerous groups such as the Clark County Classroom Teacher's Association, Las Vegas Metro Police Protection Association, and Nevada State AFL-CIO, Chow ran for the school trustee position for Clark County, which covers a third of the state, made it through the primary, and was defeated in the final election in 1996.

8. Eleanor Chow was elected to the Montebello Board of Education, Sophie Wong to the Alhambra Board of Education, Judy Chu to Monterey Park City Council (her first elected office was to the Garvey Board of Education), and Alice Hwang to the South Pasadena School Board. Willard Yamaguchi of the Montebello Board of Education was the only male elected official that year.

9. Terming them the first candidates is based on available records of school board members and a study of names.

10. Koreans (Kim 1981), immigrants from the Caribbean area in New York City (Kasinitz 1992), Cubans in Miami, and Mexicans in the Southwest (Portes and Bach 1985) are examples of groups with political interests that cross national borders and that pay close attention to events in their homelands and the implications of U.S. foreign policy.

Chapter 5: On Common Ground

1. Chinese were excluded by the Chinese Exclusion Act of 1882; Japanese and Koreans by the Gentlemen's Agreement of 1908 (because Korea was under Japanese rule at the time, it also affected Koreans) and the Immigration Act of 1924;

Asian Indians by the Immigration Act of 1917; and Filipinos by the Tydings-McDuffie Act of 1934. For a detailed discussion of immigration and legislation, see Chan (1991), Chuman (1981), Espiritu (1996), Hing (1993), McClain (1994), and Takaki (1989).

2. Leonard's research (1992) shows how agriculture also brought Asians and Mexicans together in the case of Asian Indian immigrants who settled in the state during the first decades of the twentieth century. Establishing roots in the United States, the men in this group were faced with immigration laws that cut off the immigration of women from India and antimiscegenation laws and local customs prohibiting marriage to white women. They primarily married Mexican women whom they had met while engaged in agricultural work.

3. See Almaguer (1994) for a discussion of the strike and race relations in California and Ichioka (1988) for a discussion of the strike and the history of Japanese immigrants in the United States.

4. This section on Edward Roybal borrows heavily from Underwood (1992).

5. For a detailed examination of the League of United Latin American Citizens, see Garcia (1989), Gutierrez (1995), Marquez (1993), and Orozco (1992).

6. The Japanese American Citizens League gave its support to the McCarren-Walter Act because it removed the final barriers to naturalization for Asian immigrants. The league was, however, ambivalent because it was also against the act's discriminatory provisions.

7. Just as the Chinese PTA was transformed from an informational group for immigrant parents to a political lobbying group, Marina Tse's activities also broadened into community activism and later into international diplomacy. In 1993 she was appointed to the Monterey Park Library Board of Trustees. In recognition of her background as a special education teacher in the Duarte Unified School District (northeast of Monterey Park), Gov. Pete Wilson appointed her to the California Special Education Commission in 1994. In 1996 the Los Angeles County Board of Supervisors appointed her as liaison between the city of Taipei and Los Angeles.

8. See Calderon (1995) for a detailed discussion of the development of the multiracial coalition.

9. On August 27, 1989, for example, the Los Angeles chapter sponsored a forum entitled "Understanding the Fair Play Committee and Draft Resisters during World War II" at the Japanese American Cultural and Community Center in Little Tokyo. Frank Emi, a member of the Heart Mountain Concentration Camp Fair Play Committee, which had protested the drafting of Japanese Americans from camps while their constitutional rights were being violated, and Mits Koshiyama, a draft resister, were members of a panel and also spoke. Peter Irons was also a panelist. Informational packets contained copies of Fair Play Committee's bulletins and newspaper articles from the World War II era. "The FPC," said one bulletin, "believes we have a right to ask that the discriminatory features in regards to this selective service be abolished, our status be clarified, and a full restoration of our rights before being drafted. THIS ABSENCE OF A CLARIFICATION OF OUR

STATUS, RESTORATION OF OUR RIGHTS, AND THE LIFTING OF DISCRIMINATORY RESTRICTION IS THE KEYSTONE OF OUR ATTITUDE TOWARDS THE PRESENT PROGRAM OF DRAFTING US FROM THIS CONCENTRATION CAMP" (emphasis in the original).

10. Glenn Omatsu (1990b), a founding member of the Alliance of Asian Pacific Labor, AFL-CIO, cautions that organized labor's interest in recruiting Asian and Latin American immigrants may at times be more about increasing membership and strengthening unions than advocating for the specific interests of immigrant workers.

Chapter 6: The Case of Redistricting

1. Alfred Song was a member of the state senate from 1967 to 1978, the only Asian American to serve there. In the state assembly, Paul Bannai of Los Angeles served from 1973 to 1980, March Fong Eu of Alameda from 1976 to 1974, Tom Hom of San Diego from 1969 to 1970, and Floyd Mori, also from Alameda, from 1975 to 1980. Nao Takasugi, from Oxnard, was elected to the assembly in 1992 and reelected twice, serving the maximum allowed under California's term limitation regulations. Mike Honda from San Jose was elected to the assembly in 1996 (Eljera 1997).

2. The core sponsors of "The Other Side of (the) Census: Reapportionment and Political Empowerment" were the primary groups, in addition to the UCLA Asian American Studies Center, that provided the legal and demographic analysis and organizational resources for the redistricting effort. The co-sponsors were important for giving CAPAFR legitimacy in terms of support and representation among Asian Americans and for community outreach and education.

The following groups were listed in the program as core sponsors: the Asian Pacific American Legal Center, Asian Pacific Planning Council, and Alliance of Asian Pacific Labor AFL-CIO. Co-sponsors were Awareness and Support for Asian Pacifics and the Asian Pacific Women's Network, Filipino American Public Affairs Council, Indo-American Political Association, Japanese American Bar Association, Korean American Bar Association, Korean American Coalition, Organization of Chinese Americans, Organization of Chinese American Women, Philippine American Bar Association, Pilipino American Network and Advocacy, Southern California Chinese Lawyers Association, Taiwanese American Citizens League, Thai Association of Southern California, Women's Organization Reaching Koreans, Leadership Education for Asian Pacifics, Japanese American Citizens League (Pacific Southwest District), and Chinese American Citizens Alliance. Resource institutions were the Edmund G. "Pat" Brown Institute of Public Affairs, California State University, Los Angeles, and the Jesse Unruh Institute of Public Affairs, University of Southern California.

3. Art Takei was the representative from the Alliance of Asian Pacific Labor. He explained in a telephone interview on December 10, 1996, that the Los Angeles–based organization had begun in 1987 and in 1992 became part of the Asian Pacific

American Labor Alliance AFL-CIO, which was founded that year. Takei's long history with unions began in 1957 when he joined the Retail Clerks International Union. Working for the "political empowerment of the Asian and Pacific Islander community," he explained that participation in redistricting was necessary because "for those of us with experience in politics, you understand that a lot of policy is made as a result of who is in power, and reapportionment and redistricting in some ways predetermines who is going to be in power. That's why we felt that we had to have a voice in the process."

4. In 1975 the Voting Rights Act was changed to include language minority groups, including Asian Americans and Latinos. See Davidson, ed. (1984), Davidson and Grofman (1994), Grofman and Davidson, eds. (1992), Guinier (1994), and Thernstrom (1987) for in-depth examinations of the meaning and impact of the act.

5. According to the three criteria established by the Supreme Court in *Thornburgh v. Gingles,* to demonstrate a violation of section 2 of the Voting Rights Act an ethnic or racial group must show first that it is sufficiently large and geographically compact to constitute a majority in a single member district, second that it is politically cohesive or tends to vote as a bloc, and third that the majority votes sufficiently as a bloc to defeat minority candidates (Tamayo, Toma, and Kwoh 1991).

6. In 1985 the Los Angeles City Council districts were redrawn to amend discrimination against Latinos. Asian Americans became involved in the process when it appeared that Mike Woo's district might be carved up, but the death of a council member opened the process, and Woo's district was not reconfigured into a majority Latino district. Asian Americans were late-comers to the process, however, and although Woo's district was saved many Asian American communities in the city were fragmented. As one Asian American recalled, "In 1985 we participated in the city council redistricting but never organized enough to impact the redistricting process, so we get impacted, split up, fragmented."

7. In 1991, although not admitting that discrimination existed, Alhambra officials reached a settlement with the U.S. Department of Justice, pending approval by a federal judge. Up to $180,000 was to be spent by the city to settle claims. The city would also retest applicants for the police and fire departments and revise the fire fighters' test (*Rafu Shimpo* 1991, p. 1).

8. The group kept in mind the major guidelines (in descending order of priority) for creating districts according to federal and state laws. First, federal law required that districts be equal in population; second, the Voting Rights Act was to be followed and communities of interest not fragmented; and, third, state criteria requested that cities should be kept whole within a district when possible.

9. Two Spanish-surnamed supervisors were elected in 1872 and served until 1875. Yvonne Brathwaite Burke, an African American, was appointed in 1979 but defeated when she ran for the position. It appears that no women or members of

ethnic groups were elected during the twentieth century until the election of Molina in 1991 (Ferrell 1991; Simon 1991).

10. The primary concern of the Latinos (before agreeing to the plan) was whether there would be a strong Asian American challenge in the next election if they grouped the four cities. Adding new cities to the existing assembly district would increase the incumbent's campaigning in the next election because he would have to reach voters in the new cities. Although not promising anything, Asian Americans noted that the strongest potential Asian American candidate in the region (Judy Chu) was not planning to challenge the incumbent in the next election. Latinos understood that in the future the new district would eventually lead to conditions that would improve chances for the election of an Asian American, a critical need because at the time of the negotiations there had not been an Asian American in the state legislature for nearly a decade.

In the first election following redistricting, Asian Americans could mount a campaign and not violate the understanding between Asian Americans and Latinos because the incumbent did not seek reelection. Two Republican Asian Americans did run but faired poorly in the predominantly Democratic district. Diane Martinez won the hotly contested race that contained a number of strong Latino candidates. Although Chu challenged her in 1994, Martinez won and retained her seat.

Conclusion

1. Japan is divided into forty-seven prefectures (geographical units administered by governors and assemblies), and early Japanese immigrants formed associations in the United States based on the prefectures from which they immigrated.

2. In a conversation involving this topic, Min Zhou has disagreed with my belief that a number of whites would remain in San Marino because of the city's amenities. Zhou believes that affluent whites will use their resources to relocate to white communities.

Appendix

1. Enloe (1981) points out that during the twentieth century the U.S. government has dramatically increased control over the distribution of resources. For example, state institutions such as the Immigration and Naturalization Service and the Bureau of the Census have control over important areas of policy formation.

2. Cornell's (1988) study of Native Americans in urban areas and Padilla's (1985) work on Latinos in Chicago demonstrate the importance of organizational scale for politics at local and state levels in addition to the federal level stressed in the work of Enloe (1981), Hannan (1979), and Nagel and Olzak (1982). The work of Cornell and Padilla demonstrates that panethnic identities grow out of political necessity because competition for resources among many urban groups demands

a more inclusive level of organization to deal with local and state government agencies and engage in electoral politics.

3. Browning, Marshall, and Tabb (1984, 1990) studied the efforts of African Americans and Latinos to achieve political incorporation in ten northern California cities. Their work suggests that resources, in terms of population, the development of organizations, and political knowledge and skills, were key elements for political mobilization involving protest and electoral activities. By "political incorporation," Browning, Marshall, and Tabb (1984) go beyond the traditional measure of representation—counting the number of minority elected officials—to include the degree to which a minority group's interests are reflected in the development of policy and allocation of resources.

4. With few exceptions (e.g., Morris 1984), the heavy emphasis on macro-level analysis in research on panethnicity and resource mobilization neglects the importance of everyday activities and culture in terms of what they reveal about—and how they are understood and incorporated into—the development of racial and ethnic identities and interracial political alliances.

Although research on new social movements emphasizes the importance of studying everyday life and community context (Melucci 1989), few studies under that rubric have been carried out on racial identities and politics. Racial and ethnic politics are not just interest group politics in which a collective identity is developed for instrumental purposes. Treating race in such a fashion overlooks its history and fundamental importance in shaping social relationships. See Glazer and Moynihan (1986) for a portrayal of racial politics as interest group politics; see Hero (1992) and Espiritu (1992) for a discussion of why interest group politics are not synonymous with racial politics.

5. Barth (1969) has pointed out that anthropologists' overriding focus on culture ignored how ethnic group boundaries were maintained or transformed and the way ethnic boundaries can change independent of culture.

6. See Lowe (1996) and Okihiro and Myers (1996) for a discussion of collective memory among Asian Americans. Stressing the link among the activities, networks, and cultural practices of everyday life and broader economic and political factors, a group of researchers examining Latino communities in Texas, California, and New York introduced the concept of cultural citizenship to describe the process through which politically subordinate groups establish an identity and legitimate political and social claims (Benmayor et al. 1988). Swidler (1986) also emphasizes the importance of culture as a resource for developing political strategies. Especially relevant is how groups can appropriate cultural ideals such as equality to legitimate actions and goals. McAdam (1982) stresses the importance of political consciousness in his work on the civil rights movement, suggesting that challenges to discrimination occur not only when groups acquire resources and organizational capacity for effective change but also when political opportunities occur and gains are thought possible in a process of "cognitive liberation."

7. Although Padilla (1985) focused on the union of Mexican Americans and Puerto Ricans in Chicago, the process starts one level earlier. A Mexican American identity among diverse groups must also be constructed.

8. Morris's (1984) study of indigenous organizations demonstrated that African American churches were the institutional centers of the movement, providing organizational capacity, leadership, and resources. Mass protests, marches, and economic boycotts were particularly effective efforts to develop extensive grass-roots involvement and apply pressure for social and economic change. The boycotts to end segregation on buses in Baton Rouge, Louisiana, in 1953 and in Montgomery, Alabama, from 1955 to 1956 were examples of successful efforts. These achievements, however, were made possible not just through the organization and implementation of mass protests but because the effort was planned and executed by a range of grass-roots participants, leaders, and organizations able to supply the material, legal, financial, and organizational support that created a comprehensive plan incorporating the economic and legal aspects of boycotts in addition to a political and social understanding (Lipsitz 1988).

REFERENCES

Abelmann, Nancy, and John Lie. 1995. *Blue dreams: Korean Americans and the Los Angeles riots.* Cambridge: Harvard University Press.

Ackelsberg, Martha A. 1984. Women's collaborative activities and city life: Politics and policy. In *Political women: Current roles in state and local government,* 242–59. Edited by Janet A. Flammang. Beverly Hills: Sage Publications.

Acuna, Rodolfo. 1988. *Occupied America: A history of Chicanos.* New York: Harper and Row.

Alba, Richard D. 1990. *Ethnic identity: The transformation of white America.* New Haven: Yale University Press.

Alhambra City, Justice Department reach tentative agreement. 1991. *Rafu Shimpo,* June 8.

Alhambra School District. 1990. Alhambra City School District 1990–1991 ethnic survey. Nov. 1.

Almaguer, Tomas. 1994. *Racial fault lines: The historical origins of white supremacy in California.* Berkeley: University of California Press.

Arax, Mark. 1985. Lily Lee Chen, roots—and perhaps her political goals—lie beyond Monterey Park. *Los Angeles Times,* Nov. 11.

———. 1987a. San Gabriel Valley: Asian influx alters life in suburbia. *Los Angeles Times,* April 5.

———. 1987b. Nation's first suburban Chinatown. *Los Angeles Times,* April 6.

Arroyo Group. 1987. *Mid-Atlantic specific plan: City of Monterey Park.* City of Monterey Park.

Asian American Legal Defense and Education Fund. 1996. 3,200 Asian American voters in NYC polled on election day. Press release, Nov. 7.

Asian Law Caucus. 1996. Asian Law Caucus study shows voting patterns of Asian Americans in S.F./Oakland. Press release, Nov. 7.

Asian Pacific American Legal Center. 1991a. *Asian Pacific American Legal Center News* 7(1).

———. 1991b. *Asian Pacific American Legal Center News* 7(2).

———. 1995. *Asian Pacific American Legal Center News* 12(1).

————. n.d. *Leadership development in interethnic relations program.* [Brochure and application.]

Asian American Studies Center, University of California, Los Angeles. n.d. *Strategizing for the next twenty-five years.* Los Angeles: Asian American Studies Center.

Avila, Joaquin G. 1984. Equal educational opportunities for language minority children. *University of Colorado Law Review* 55(4): 559–69.

Babcock, Ray. 1985. English use petition planned. *Monterey Park Progress,* Aug. 21.

Barker, Mayerene. 1992. Japanese-Americans mourn an old friend. *Los Angeles Times,* Jan. 8.

Barrera, Mario. 1979. *Race and class in the southwest: A theory of racial inequality.* Notre Dame: University of Notre Dame Press.

Barth, Fredrik. 1969. *Ethnic groups and boundaries.* Boston: Little, Brown.

Benmayor, Rina, Richard Chabran, Richard Flores, William Flores, Ray Rocco, Renato Rosaldo, Pedro Pedraza, and Rosa Torruellas. 1988. Draft concept paper on cultural citizenship. Inter-University Program for Latino Research Cultural Studies Work Group.

Bernstein, Harry. 1996. Hotel needs to deal straight with workers. *Los Angeles Times,* Dec. 19.

Biederman, Patricia Ward. 1989. Why teach? *Los Angeles Times,* Nov. 26.

Block, A. G. 1986. March Fong Eu: A political career stalled near the top? *California Journal,* Nov.

Bonacich, Edna. 1972. A theory of ethnic antagonism: The split labor market. *American Sociological Review* 37(5): 547–59.

————. 1976. Advanced capitalism and black/white relations in the United States: A split labor market orientation. *American Sociological Review* 41(1): 34–51.

————. 1980. Class approaches to ethnicity and race. *Insurgent Sociologist* 10(2): 9–23.

Bonacich, Edna, and John Modell. 1980. *The economic basis of ethnic solidarity: Small business in the Japanese American community.* Berkeley: University of California Press.

Browning, Rufus P., Dale Rogers Marshall, and David H. Tabb. 1984. *Protest is not enough.* Berkeley: University of California Press.

————. 1990a. *Racial politics in American cities.* New York: Longman.

————. 1990b. Minority mobilization in ten cities: Failures and successes. In *Racial politics in American cities,* 8–30. Edited by Rufus P. Browning, Dale Rogers Marshall, and David H. Tabb. New York: Longman.

Cain, Bruce E. 1991. The contemporary context of ethnic and racial politics in California. In *Racial and ethnic politics in California,* 9–24. Edited by Byran O. Jackson and Michael B. Preston. Berkeley: IGS Press.

Cain, Bruce E., D. Roderick Kiewiet, and Carol J. Uhlaner. 1988. The evolution of partisanship among immigrants. Social Science Working Paper 687. Pasadena: Division of the Humanities and Social Sciences, California Institute of Technology.

Calderon, Jose Z. 1991. Mexican American politics in a multi-ethnic community: The case of Monterey Park: 1985–1990. Ph.D. dissertation, University of California, Los Angeles.

———. 1995. Multi-ethnic coalition building in a diverse school district. *Critical Sociologist* 21(1): 101–11.

Campbell, Angus, William Converse, Donald Stokes, and Warren Miller. 1960. *The American voter.* New York: John Wiley.

Carmichael, Stokely, and Charles V. Hamilton. 1967. *Black power: The politics of liberation in America.* New York: Random House.

Chan, Sucheng. 1986. *This bittersweet soil: The Chinese in California agriculture, 1860–1910.* Berkeley: University of California Press.

———. 1991. *Asian Americans: An interpretive history.* Boston: Twayne Publishers.

Chang, Edward T. 1993. Jewish and Korean merchants in African American perspective. *Amerasia Journal* 19(2): 5–21.

Chang, Irene. 1991. Anti-Asian hate crimes rise. *Los Angeles Times,* Jan. 27.

———. 1992. Council victors stressed community ties. *Los Angeles Times,* April 16.

Chinese American Parents and Teachers Association of Southern California [CAPTASC]. 1991. An open letter to Mrs. Rutherford and members of the board of education. April 1. Author's files.

Chow, Esther Ngan-Ling. 1987. The development of feminist consciousness among Asian American women. *Gender and Society* 1(3): 284–99.

Chu, Judy. 1989. Asian Pacific American women in mainstream politics. In *Making waves: An anthology of writings by and about Asian American women,* 405–21. Edited by Asian Women United of California. Boston: Beacon Press.

Chuman. Frank F. 1981. *The bamboo people: Japanese-Americans, their history and the law.* Chicago: Japanese American Research Project and Japanese American Citizens League.

Claremont McKenna College and *TradeWeek.* 1996. *CMC-TradeWeek 1995: Annual Regional Trade Report for the Los Angeles Customs District,* March 27.

Cohen, Lizabeth. 1990. *Making a new deal: Industrial workers in Chicago, 1919–1939.* New York: Cambridge University Press.

Cornell, Stephen. 1988. *The return of the native: American Indian political resurgence.* New York: Oxford University Press.

Curran, Ron. 1991. Politics. *Los Angeles Weekly,* April 19–25.

Czitrom, Daniel. 1991. Underworlds and underdogs: Big Tim Sullivan and metropolitan politics in New York, 1889–1913. *Journal of American History* 78(2): 536–58.

Dahl, Robert A. 1973. *Who governs? Democracy and power in an American city.* New Haven: Yale University Press.

Daniels, Roger. 1974. *The politics of prejudice.* New York: Atheneum.

———. 1986. *The decision to relocate the Japanese Americans.* Malabar, Fla.: Robert E. Krieger Publishing.

———. 1988. *Asian America: Chinese and Japanese in the United States since 1850.* Seattle: University of Washington Press.

Davidson, Chandler, ed. 1984. *Minority vote dilution.* Washington, D.C.: Howard University Press.

———. 1992. The Voting Rights Act: A brief history. In *Controversies in minority voting: The Voting Rights Act in perspective,* 7–51. Edited by Bernard Grofman and Chandler Davidson. Washington, D.C.: Brookings Institution.

Davidson, Chandler, and Bernard Grofman. 1994. *Quiet revolution in the South.* Princeton: Princeton University Press.

Del Olmo, Frank. 1997. Time at last to slay a giant cliché. *Los Angeles Times,* April 27.

de Tocqueville, Alexis. 1960. *Democracy in America.* New York: Knopf.

Di Leonardo, Micaela. 1984. *The varieties of ethnic experience: Kinship, class and gender among Italian Americans.* Ithaca: Cornell University Press.

Din, Grant. 1984. An analysis of Asian/Pacific American registration and voting patterns in San Francisco. M.A. thesis, Claremont Graduate School.

D'Souza, Dinesh. 1991. *Illiberal education: The politics of race and sex on campus.* New York: Free Press.

Ehrenreich, Barbara, and John Ehrenreich. 1979. The professional-managerial class. In *Between labor and capital,* 5–45. Edited by Pat Walker. Boston: South End Press.

Eisenger, Peter K. 1980. *The politics of displacement: Racial and ethnic transition in three American cities.* New York: Academic Press.

Eljera, Bert. 1996. Getting down to politics. *AsianWeek,* March 29.

———. 1997. California dreaming. *AsianWeek,* Jan. 17.

Emerson, Robert M. 1983. *Contemporary field research.* Prospect Heights: Waveland Press.

Enloe, Cynthia. 1981. The growth of the state and ethnic mobilization: The American experience. *Ethnic and Racial Studies* 4(2): 123–36.

Erie, Steven P. 1988. *Rainbow's end: Irish-Americans and the dilemmas of urban machine politics, 1840–1985.* Berkeley: University of California Press.

Erie, Steven P., and Harold Brackman. 1993. *Paths to political incorporation for Latinos and Asian Pacifics in California.* Berkeley: California Policy Seminar.

Espiritu, Yen L. 1992. *Asian American panethnicity: Bridging institutions and identities.* Philadelphia: Temple University Press.

———. 1997. *Asian American women and men: Labor, laws, and love.* Beverly Hills: Sage Publications.

Espiritu, Yen, and Paul Ong. 1994. Class constraints on racial solidarity among Asian Americans. In *The new Asian immigration in Los Angeles and global restructuring,* 295–321. Edited by Paul Ong, Edna Bonacich, and Lucie Cheng. Philadephia: Temple University Press.

Estrada, Leo F. 1991. Speech presented at the annual scholarship and community service awards banquet, San Gabriel Valley League of United Latin American Citizens Council, April 21.

Feagin, Joe. 1991. The continuing significance of race: Antiblack discrimination in public places. *American Sociological Review* 56(1): 101–16.

Feagin, Joe R., and Stella M. Capek. 1991. Grassroots movements in a class perspective. *Research in Political Sociology* 5: 27–53.

Feagin, Joe R., and Hernan Vera. 1995. *White Racism*. New York: Routledge.

Feng, Kathay, and Bonnie Tang. 1997. *1996 Southern California Asian Pacific American exit poll report*. Los Angles: Asian Pacific American Legal Center and National Asian Pacific American Legal Consortium.

Ferrell, David. 1991. Vote marks new era for First District. *Los Angeles Times*, Feb. 20.

Fisher, Robert. 1993. Grass-roots organizing worldwide: Common ground, historical roots, and the tension between democracy and the state. In *Mobilizing the community: Local politics in the era of the global city*, 3–27. Beverly Hills: Sage Publications.

Flanagan, James. 1994. Ethanol promoter understands economic engines. *Los Angeles Times*, July 10.

Fong, Timothy P. 1990. Interviews for the Oral History Program, Historical Society of Monterey Park and Monterey Park Historical Heritage Commission.

———. 1994. *The first suburban Chinatown*. Philadelphia: Temple University Press.

Frankenberg, Ruth. 1993. *The social construction of whiteness: White women, race matters*. Minneapolis: University of Minnesota Press.

Fuetsch, Michele. 1990. Big spender in Cerritos campaign draws criticism. *Los Angeles Times*, March 18.

Fugita, Stephen S., and David J. O'Brien. 1977. Economics, ideology, and ethnicity: The struggle between the United Farm Workers and the Nisei Farmers League. *Social Problems* 25(2): 146–56.

———. 1991. *Japanese American ethnicity: The persistence of community*. Seattle: University of Washington Press.

Gamson, William A. 1975. *The strategy of social protest*. Homewood, Ill.: Dorsey Press.

Gans, Herbert. 1962. *The urban villagers*. New York: Free Press.

———. 1979. Symbolic ethnicity: The future of ethnic groups and cultures in America. *Ethnic and Racial Studies* 2(1): 1–20.

———. 1994. Symbolic ethnicity and symbolic religiosity: Towards a comparison of ethnic and religious acculturation. *Ethnic and Racial Studies* 17(4): 577–92.

Garcia, Alma. 1989. The development of Chicana feminist discourse, 1790–1980. *Gender and Society* 3(2): 217–38.

Garcia, Mario T. 1989. *Mexican Americans: Leadership, ideology, and identity, 1930–1960*. New Haven: Yale University Press.

Geertz, Clifford. 1963. The integrative revolution: Primordial sentiments and civ-il politics in New States. In *Old societies and new states*, 105–57. Edited by Clifford Geertz. New York: Free Press of Glencoe.

Gerth, H. H., and C. Wright Mills. 1946. *From Max Weber: Essays in sociology*. New York: Oxford University Press.

Glazer, Nathan, and Daniel P. Moynihan. 1986. *Beyond the melting pot*. Cambridge: MIT Press.

Glenn, Evelyn Nakano. 1985. Racial ethnic women's labor: The intersection of race, gender and class oppression. *Review of Radical Political Economics* 17(3): 86–108.

Gomez-Quinones, Juan. 1990. *Chicano politics: Reality and promise, 1940–1990*. Albuquerque: University of New Mexico Press.

Gordon, Milton M. 1964. *Assimilation in American life*. New York: Oxford University Press.

Grebler, Leo, Joan W. Moore, and Ralph C. Guzman. 1970. *The Mexican-American people*. New York: Free Press.

Gregory, Steven. 1994. Race, rubbish, and resistance: Empowering difference in community politics. In *Race*, 366–91. Edited by Steven Gregory and Rojer Sanjek. New Brunswick: Rutgers University Press.

Griffith, Beatrice W. 1949. Viva Roybal—viva America. *Common Ground* 10(1): 61–70.

Grofman, Bernard, and Chandler Davidson, eds. 1992. *Controversies in minority voting: The Voting Rights Act in perspective*. Washington, D.C.: Brookings Institution.

Guinier, Lani. 1994. *The tyranny of the majority*. New York: Free Press.

Gutierrez, David. 1995. *Walls and mirrors: Mexican Americans, Mexican immigrants, and the politics of ethnicity*. Berkeley: University of California Press.

Ha, Julie. 1996. APAs voted overwhelmingly against Prop. 209. *Rafu Shimpo*, Nov. 8.

Hamilton, Denise. 1995. Builders go back to drawing board for comforts of home, Asian-style. *Los Angeles Times*, June 29.

Hannan, Michael T. 1979. The dynamics of ethnic boundaries in modern states. In *National development and the world system: Educational, economic, and political change, 1950–1970*, 253–75. Edited by John W. Meyer and Michael T. Hannan. Chicago: University of Chicago Press.

Harrison, Bennett, and Barry Bluestone. 1988. *The great u-turn: Corporate restructuring and the polarizing of America*. New York: Basic Books.

Hayes-Bautista, David, and Jorge Chapa. 1987. Latino terminology: Conceptual bases for standardized terminology. *American Journal of Public Health* 77(1): 61–68.

Hernandez, Antonia. 1995. President's message: In the midst of change we persevere. *Leading Hispanics* 8(1): 8.

Hero, Rodney E. 1992. *Latinos and the U.S. political system*. Philadelphia: Temple University Press.

Higham, John. 1984. *Send these to me: Immigrants in urban America.* Baltimore: Johns Hopkins University Press.

Hing, Bill Ong. 1993. *Making and remaking Asian America through immigration policy, 1850–1990.* Stanford: Stanford University Press.

Hing, Bill Ong, and Ronald Lee, eds. 1996. *The state of Asian Pacific America: Reframing the immigration debate.* Los Angeles: LEAP Asian Pacific American Public Policy Institute and Asian American Studies Center, University of California, Los Angeles.

Horton, John. 1988. Interview with Lily Chen, Los Angeles County, April 20.

———. 1989. The politics of ethnic change: Grass-roots responses to economic and demographic restructuring in Monterey Park, California. *Urban Geography* 10(6): 578–92.

———. 1992. The politics of diversity in Monterey Park. In *Structuring diversity: Ethnographic perspectives on the new immigration,* 215–46. Edited by Louise Lamphere. Chicago: University of Chicago Press.

———. 1995. *The politics of diversity: Immigration, resistance, and change in Monterey Park, California.* Philadelphia: Temple University Press.

Horton, John, and Jose Z. Calderon. 1992. Language struggles in a changing California community. In *Language loyalites: A source book on the official English controversy,* 186–94. Edited by James Crawford. Chicago: University of Chicago Press.

Horton, John, and Yen Fen Tseng. 1990. Voter's profile by ethnicity, city council election, Monterey Park, April 10, 1990 [unpublished table]. Author's files.

Horwitt, Sanford D. 1989. *Let them call me rebel: Saul Alinsky, his life and legacy.* New York: Knopf.

Hosokawa, Bill. 1969. *Nisei: The quiet Americans.* New York: William Morrow.

———. 1982. *JACL: In quest of justice.* New York: William Morrow.

How did everyone vote? 1996. *Wall Street Journal,* Nov. 7.

Huerta, Dolores. 1995. Selected questions and comments from the audience. *Critica* (Fall): 83–87.

Ichioka, Yuji. 1988. *The Issei: The world of the first generation Japanese immigrants, 1885–1924.* New York: Free Press.

Iritani, Evelyn. 1995a. L.A. surpasses New York City as top trade hub in 1994. *Los Angeles Times,* March 17.

———. 1996. Event feels effects of funds furor. *Los Angeles Times,* Oct. 21.

Irons, Peter. 1989. *Justice delayed: The record of the Japanese American internment cases.* Middleton: Wesleyan University Press.

Jackson, Kenneth T. 1985. *Crabgrass frontier: The suburbanization of the United States.* New York: Oxford University Press.

Jo, Yung-Hwan. 1980. *Political participation of Asian Americans: Problems and strategies.* Chicago: Pacific/Asian American Mental Health Research Center.

Johnston, Hank, Enrique Larana, and Joseph R. Gusfield. 1994. Identities, grievances and new social movements. In *New social movements: From ideology to identity,* 3–35. Edited by Enrique Larana, Hank Johnston, and Joseph R. Gusfield. Philadelphia: Temple University Press.

Johnston, Hank, and Bert Klandermans. 1995. *Social movements and culture.* Minneapolis: University of Minnesota Press.

Kang, Connie. 1993. Separate, distinct—and equal. *Los Angeles Times,* Aug. 20.

———. 1995. Building bridges to equality. *Los Angeles Times,* Jan. 7.

———. 1996. Asian gifts coverage called stereotyping. *Los Angeles Times,* Oct. 23.

Kaplan, Temma. 1982. Female consciousness and collective action: The case of Barcelona, 1910–1918. *Signs* 7(3): 545–66.

Kasinitz, Philip. 1992. *Caribbean New York: Black immigrants and the politics of race.* Ithaca: Cornell University Press.

Keohane, Nannerl O. 1981. Speaking from silence: Women and the science of politics. In *A feminist perspective in the academy: The difference it makes,* 86–100. Edited by Elizabeth Langland and Walter Gove. Chicago: University of Chicago Press.

Kim, Elaine, and Eui-Young Yu. 1996. *East to America: Korean American life stories.* New York: New Press.

Kim, Illsoo. 1981. *New urban immigrants: The Korean community in New York.* Princeton: Princeton University Press.

Kobashigawa, Ken. 1985–86. On the history of the Okinawans in North America. *Amerasia Journal* 12(2): 29–42.

Kotkin J., and Y. Kishimoto. 1988. *The third century.* New York: Crown Publishers.

Kuramoto, Ford H. 1980. Lessons learned in the federal funding game. In *Asian-Americans: Social and psychological perspectives,* 2:248–50. Edited by Russell Endo, Stanley Sue, and Nathaniel N. Wagner. Palo Alto: Science and Behavior Books.

Kwoh, Stewart, and Dale Minami. 1996. A question of fairness. *AsianWeek,* Oct. 18.

Kwong, Peter. 1996. *The new Chinatown.* New York: HarperCollins.

Lamphere, Louise. 1992. *Structuring diversity: Ethnographic perspectives on the new immigration.* Chicago: University of Chicago Press.

Lau, Don. 1991. State Democratic chair visits CADC and Wallenberg Clubs. *Asian-Week,* July 12.

LEAP. 1990. *LEAP Connections* 3(4).

Leonard, Karen I. 1992. *Making ethnic choices: California's Punjabi Mexican Americans.* Philadelphia: Temple University Press.

Lieberson, Stanley. 1980. *A piece of the pie: Blacks and white immigrants since 1880.* Berkeley: University of California Press.

Light, Ivan H. 1972. *Ethnic enterprise in America.* Berkeley: University of California Press.

Light, Ivan, and Edna Bonacich. 1988. *Immigrant entrepreneurs: Koreans in Los Angeles, 1965–1982.* Berkeley: University of California Press.

Lipsitz, George. 1988. *A life in the struggle: Ivory Perry and the culture of opposition*. Philadelphia: Temple University Press.

———. 1995. The possessive investment in whiteness: Racialized social democracy and the "white" problem in American studies. *American Quarterly* 47(3): 369–427.

Little Tokyo Anti-Eviction Force. 1976. Redevelopment in Los Angeles' Little Tokyo. In *Counterpoint*, 327–33. Edited by Emma Gee. Los Angeles: Asian American Studies Center, University of California, Los Angeles.

Lo, Clarence Y. H. 1990. *Small property versus big government: Social origins of the property tax revolt*. Berkeley: University of California Press.

Logan, John R., Richard D. Alba, and Shu-Yin Leung. 1996. Minority access to white suburbs: A multiregional comparison. *Social Forces* 74(3): 851–81.

Logan, John R., and Harvey L. Molotch. 1987. *Urban fortunes: The political economy of place*. Berkeley: University of California Press.

Lopez, David, and Yen Espiritu. 1990. Panethnicity in the United States: A theoretical framework. *Ethnic and Racial Studies* 13(2): 198–224.

Los Angeles County Commission on Human Relations. 1994. *Hate crime in Los Angeles County 1993: A report to the Los Angeles County Board of Supervisors*. Los Angeles: Commission on Human Relations.

Los Angeles Times. 1986. Election results. Nov. 6.

———. 1992. Redistricting in Los Angeles. Jan. 30.

———. 1995. Century 21 advertisement. July 9.

———. 1996. How DNC got caught in a donor dilemma. Dec. 23.

———. 1997a. Official to urge state agency to investigate election mailers. March 19.

———. 1997b. Election results. April 10.

Louie, Winnie, and Paul Ong. 1995. *Asian immigrant investors and the Immigration Act of 1990*. Berkeley: California Policy Seminar.

Lowe, Lisa. 1991. Heterogeneity, hybridity, multiplicity: Marking Asian American differences. *Diaspora* 1(1): 24–44.

———. 1996. *Immigrant acts: On Asian American cultural politics*. Durham: Duke University Press.

MALDEF. 1990–91. *Annual Report*. Los Angeles: MALDEF.

———. 1995–96. *Annual Report*. Los Angeles: MALDEF.

———. 1987. Newsletter. April.

Marquez, Benjamin. 1993. *LULAC: The evolution of a Mexican American political organization*. Austin: University of Texas Press.

Mason, William M., and John A. McKinstry. 1969. *The Japanese of Los Angeles, 1869–1929*. Los Angeles: Los Angeles County Museum of Natural History.

Massey, Douglas S., and Nancy A. Denton. 1993. *American apartheid*. Cambridge: Harvard University Press.

McAdam, Doug. 1982. *Political process and the development of black insurgency: 1930–1970*. Chicago: University of Chicago Press.

McCarthy, John D., and Mark Wolfson. 1997. Resource mobilization by local social movement organizations: Agency, strategy, and organization in the movement against drinking and driving. *American Sociological Review* 61(6): 1070–88.

McCarthy, John D., and Mayer N. Zald. 1979. *The dynamics of social movements: Resource mobilization, social control, and tactics.* Cambridge, Mass.: Winthrop.

McClain, Charles J. 1994. *In search of equality: The Chinese struggle against discrimination in nineteenth-century America.* Berkeley: University of California Press.

McCormick, Joseph, and Charles E. Jones. 1993. The conceptualization of deracialization: Thinking through the dilemma. In *Dilemmas of black politics: Issues of leadership and strategy,* 66–84. Edited by Georgia Persons. New York: HarperCollins.

McDonnell, Patrick. 1997. Immigrants warned of impending aid cuts. *Los Angeles Times,* Feb. 1.

McDonnell, Patrick, and Stuart Silverstein. 1997. AFL-CIO chief to press case in Japan. *Los Angeles Times,* Feb. 20.

Melucci, Alberto. 1989. *Nomads of the present: Social movements and individual needs in contemporary society.* Philadelphia: Temple University Press.

Merton, Robert. 1972. Insiders and outsiders: A chapter in the sociology of knowledge. *American Journal of Sociology* 78(1): 9–48.

Milbrath, Lester. 1965. *Political participation.* Chicago: Rand McNally.

Miller, Alan C. 1996. Democrats give back more disputed money. *Los Angeles Times,* Nov. 23.

Mizobe, Ruth. 1995. PSW-JACL apology to Fair Play Committee and WWI draft resisters of conscience. Speech presented at the Japanese American Cultural and Community Center, Los Angeles, Feb. 19.

Modell, John. 1977. *The economics and politics of racial accommodation: The Japanese of Los Angeles, 1900–1942.* Urbana: University of Illinois Press.

Monterey Park Planning Department. 1974. *Population and housing profile.* City of Monterey Park.

Monterey Park Seventy-fifth Anniversary Committee. 1991. *Reflections 1916–1991: Monterey Park's past, present and future.* Monterey Park: Historical Society and City.

Morris, Aldon D. 1984. *The origins of the civil rights movement.* New York: Free Press.

Morris, Aldon, D., and Carol McClurg Mueller. 1992. *Frontiers in social movement theory.* New Haven: Yale University Press.

Nagel, Joane. 1994. Constructing ethnicity: Creating and recreating ethnic identity and culture. *Social Problems* 41(1): 152–76.

———. 1996. *American Indian ethnic renewal: Red power and the resurgence of identity and culture.* New York: Oxford University Press.

Nagel, Joane, and Susan Olzak. 1982. Ethnic mobilization in new and old states: An extension of the competition model. *Social Problems* 30(2): 127–43.

Nakanishi, Don. 1985–86. Asian American politics: An agenda for research. *Amerasia Journal* 12(2): 1–27.

———. 1986. *The UCLA Asian Pacific American voter registration study.* Los Angeles: Asian Pacific Legal Center of Southern California.

———. 1989. A quota on excellence? The Asian American admissions debate. *Change*, Nov.-Dec.

———. 1991. The next swing vote? Asian Pacific Americans and California politics. In *Racial and ethnic politics in California,* 25–54. Edited by Byran O. Jackson and Michael B. Preston. Berkeley: IGS Press.

Nakanishi, Don, and J. D. Hokoyama. 1996. Preface. In *The state of Asian Pacific America,* vii–ix. Edited by Bill Ong Hing and Ronald Lee. Los Angeles: LEAP Asian Pacific American Public Policy Institute and Asian American Studies Center, University of California, Los Angeles.

Nakayama, Takeshi. 1990. Matsui meets supporters at L.A. fund-raiser reception. *Rafu Shimpo*, Dec. 10.

———. 1991. Nisei liberators reunited with Dachau survivors. *Rafu Shimpo*, Dec. 5.

National Asian Pacific American Legal Consortium [NAPALC]. 1994. *Audit of violence against Asian Pacific Americans: The consequences of intolerance in America.* Washington, D.C.: NAPALC.

National Committee against Discrimination in Housing, Inc. 1979. *Guide to fair housing law enforcement.* N.p.: Metro Fair Housing Centers and Other Local Fair Housing Groups.

Naylor, Nancy. 1991. Profile: Living her life with gusto. *UCLA Magazine*, Spring.

Newton, Edmund. 1990. San Gabriel Valley becomes the new power base of Latino voters. *Los Angeles Times,* Jan. 21.

———. 1995. This ship has come in: Long Beach steams past L.A. to become the nation's no. 1 port. *Los Angeles Times,* April 23.

Newton, Jim, and Matea Gold. 1997. Latino turnout a breakthrough. *Los Angeles Times,* April 10.

Nielsen, Francois. 1985. Toward a theory of ethnic solidarity in modern societies. *American Sociological Review* 50(2): 133–49.

Novak, Michael. 1996. *Unmeltable ethnics: Politics and culture in American life.* New Brunswick: Transaction.

Oberschall, Anthony. 1973. *Social conflict and social movements.* Englewood Cliffs: Prentice-Hall.

Okihiro, Gary Y. 1994. *Margins and mainstreams: Asians in American history and culture.* Seattle: University of Washington Press.

Okihiro, Gary Y., and Joan Myers. 1996. *Whispered silences: Japanese Americans and World War II.* Seattle: University of Washington Press.

Oliver, Melvin L., and Thomas M. Shapiro. 1995. *Black wealth/white wealth: A new perspective on racial inequality.* New York: Routledge.

Oliver, Melvin, and James H. Johnson, Jr. 1984. Inter-ethnic conflict in an urban ghetto: The case of blacks and Latinos in Los Angeles. *Research in Social Movements, Conflicts, and Change* 6: 57–94.

Oliver, Pamela E., and Gerald Marwell. 1992. Mobilizing technologies for collective action. In *Frontiers in social movement theory,* 251–72. Edited by Aldon D. Morris and Carol McClurg Mueller. New Haven: Yale University Press.

Olzak, Susan. 1983. Contemporary ethnic mobilization. *Annual Review of Sociology* 9: 355–74.

Olzak, Susan, and Joane Nagel. 1986. Introduction: Competitive ethnic relations, an overview. In *Competitive ethnic relations,* 1–14. Edited by Susan Olzak and Joane Nagel. New York: Academic Press.

Omatsu, Glenn. 1990a. Movement and process: Building campaigns for mass empowerment. *Amerasia Journal* 16(1): 63–80.

———. 1990b. Vietnamese workers in the UAW. *Gidra 1990.* Los Angeles: Gidra Staff.

Omi, Michael, and Howard Winant. 1986, 1994 (second ed.). *Racial formation in the United States.* New York: Routledge.

Ong, Aihwa. 1993. On the edge of empires: Flexible citizenship among Chinese in diaspora. *Positions* 1(3): 745–78.

Ong, Paul. 1989. *The widening divide: Income inequality and poverty in Los Angeles.* Los Angeles: Research Group on the Los Angeles Economy, School of Architecture and Urban Planning, University of California at Los Angeles.

———. 1991. *Asian Pacific islanders in California, 1990.* Los Angeles: Asian American Studies Center, University of California, Los Angeles.

———. 1993. *Beyond Asian American poverty: Community economic development policies and strategies.* Los Angeles: LEAP Asian Pacific American Public Policy Institute and Asian American Studies Center, University of California, Los Angeles.

———, ed. 1994. *The state of Asian Pacific America: Economic diversity, issues and policies.* Los Angeles: LEAP Asian Pacific American Public Policy Institute and Asian American Studies Center, University of California, Los Angeles.

Ong, Paul, and Don Nakanishi. 1996. Becoming citizens, becoming voters: The naturalization and political participation of Asian Pacific immigrants. In *Reframing the immigration debate,* 275–305. Edited by Bill Ong Hing and Ronald Lee. Los Angeles: LEAP Asian Pacific American Public Policy Institute and Asian American Studies Center, University of California, Los Angeles.

Ong, Paul, and John M. Liu. 1994. U.S. immigration policies and Asian migration. In *The new Asian immigration in Los Angeles and global restructuring,* 45–73. Edited by Paul Ong, Edna Bonacich, and Lucie Cheng. Philadelphia: Temple University Press.

Ong, Paul, and Suzanne Hee. 1993. *Losses in the Los Angeles civil unrest*. Los Angeles: Center for Pacific Rim Studies. University of California, Los Angeles.

Ong, Paul, and Shirley Hune, eds. 1993. *The state of Asian Pacific America: Policy issues to the year 2020*. Los Angeles: LEAP Asian Pacific American Public Policy Institute and Asian American Studies Center, University of California, Los Angeles.

Orozco, Cynthia E. 1992. The origins of the League of United Latin American Citizens (LULAC) and the Mexican American civil rights movement in Texas with an analysis of women's political participation in a gendered context, 1910–1929. Ph.D. dissertation, University of California, Los Angeles.

Pachon, Harry. 1991. U.S. citizenship and Latino participation in California politics. In *Racial and ethnic politics in California*, 71–88. Edited by Byran O. Jackson and Michael B. Preston. Berkeley: IGS Press.

Padilla, Felix M. 1985. *Latino ethnic consciousness*. Notre Dame: University of Notre Dame Press.

Pardo, Mary. 1990a. Identity and resistance: Mexican American women and grassroots activism in two Los Angeles communities. Ph.D. dissertation, University of California, Los Angeles.

———. 1990b. Mexican American grassroots community activists: Mothers of East Los Angeles. *Frontiers* 11(1): 1–7.

———. 1995. Doing it for the kids: Mexican American community activists, border feminists? In *Feminist organizations: Harvest of the new women's movement*, 356–71. Edited by Myra Marx Ferree and Patricia Yancey Martin. Philadelphia: Temple University Press.

Park, Edward J. W. 1996. Our L.A.? Korean Americans in Los Angeles after the civil unrest. In *Rethinking Los Angeles*, 153–68. Edited by Michael J. Dear, H. Eric Schockman, and Greg Hise. Beverly Hills: Sage Publications.

———. 1997. Between black and white: The formation of Korean American political consciousness. Paper presented at the University of California, San Diego Ethnic Studies Department seminar series, Nov. 6.

Park, Kyeyoung. 1995. The re-invention of affirmative action: Korean immigrants' changing conceptions of African Americans and Latin Americans. *Urban Anthropology* 24(1–2): 59–92.

———. 1996. Use and abuse of race and culture: Black-Korean tension in America. *American Anthropologist* 98(3): 492–99.

Portes, Alejandro. 1984. The rise of ethnicity: Determinants of ethnic perceptions among Cuban exiles in Miami. *American Sociological Review* 49(3): 383–97.

Portes, Alejandro, and Rafael Mozo. 1985. The political adaptation process of Cubans and other ethnic minorities in the United States: A preliminary analysis. *International Migration Review* 19(1): 35–61.

Portes, Alejandro, and Robert L. Bach. 1985. *Latin journey: Cuban and Mexican immigrants in the United States*. Berkeley: University of California Press.

Portes, Alejandro, and Ruben G. Rumbaut. 1990. *Immigrant America: A portrait.* Berkeley: University of California Press.

Proffitt, Steve. 1992. Antonia Hernandez. *Los Angeles Times,* Dec. 13.

Pulido, Laura. 1998. Development of the "people of color" identity in the environmental justice movement in the southwestern U.S. *Socialist Review* 96(4).

Rafu Shimpo. 1991. Alhambra City, Justice Department reach tentative agreement. June 8.

Rex, John. 1983. *Race relations in sociological theory.* London: Routledge and Kegan Paul.

Robnett, Belinda. 1997. *How long? How long? African American women in the struggles for civil rights.* New York: Oxford University Press.

Rodriguez, Richard. 1982. *Hunger of memory.* New York: Bantam Books.

Roediger, David. 1991. *The wages of whiteness: Race and the making of the American working class.* New York: Verso.

———. 1994. *Towards the abolition of whiteness.* New York: Verso.

Romo, Ricardo. 1983. *East Los Angeles: History of a barrio.* Austin: University of Texas Press.

Sacks, Karen Brodkin. 1988. Gender and grassroots leadership. In *Women and the politics of empowerment,* 77–94. Edited by Ann Bookman and Sandra Morgen. Philadelphia: Temple University Press.

Saito, Leland T. 1989. Japanese Americans and the new Chinese immigrants: The politics of adaptation. *California Sociologist* 12(2): 195–211.

———. 1993a. Contrasting patterns of adaptation: Japanese Americans and Chinese immigrants in Monterey Park. In *Bearing dreams, shaping visions: Asian Pacific American perspectives,* 33–43. Edited by Linda Revilla, Shawn Wong, and Gail Nomura. Pullman: Washington State University Press.

———. 1993b. Asian Americans and Latinos in San Gabriel Valley, California: Ethnic political cooperation and redistricting, 1990–91. *Amerasia Journal* 19(2): 55–68.

Saito, Leland T., and John Horton. 1994. The new Chinese immigration and the rise of Asian American politics in Monterey Park, California. In *The new Asian immigration in Los Angeles and global restructuring,* 233–63. Edited by Paul Ong, Edna Bonacich, and Lucie Cheng. Philadelphia: Temple University Press.

Santillan, Richard, and Federico A. Subervi-Velez. 1991. Latino participation in Republican Party politics in California. In *Racial and ethnic politics in California,* 285–319. Edited by Byran O. Jackson and Michael B. Preston. Berkeley: IGS Press.

Savage, David G. 1994. Minority-based gerrymandering facing backlash. *Los Angeles Times,* Oct. 8.

———. 1997. High court allows Prop. 209's repeal of affirmative action. *Los Angeles Times,* Nov. 4.

Saxton, Alexander. 1971. *The indispensable enemy.* Berkeley: University of California Press.

Scharlin, Craig, and Lilia V. Villanueva. 1992. *Philip Vera Cruz.* Los Angeles: Institute of Industrial Relations Labor Center and Asian American Studies Center, University of California, Los Angeles.

Schermerhorn, R. A. 1978. *Comparative ethnic relations: A framework for theory and research.* Chicago: University of Chicago Press.

Schlesinger, Arthur M., Jr. 1991. *The disuniting of America.* Pleasant Hills, Calif.: Whittle Direct Books.

Schiller, Nina Glick. 1994. *Nations unbound: Transnational projects, postcolonial predicaments, and deterritorialized nation-states.* Newark, N.J.: Gordon and Breach.

Schiller, Nina Glick, Linda Basch, and Cristina Blanc Szanton. 1992. Transnationalism: A new analytic framework for understanding migration. *Annals of the New York Academy of Sciences* 645:1–24.

Sedway Cooke Associates. 1987. *Monterey Park design.* Monterey Park: City of Monterey Park.

Seo, Diane. 1996. New voices in education. *Los Angeles Times,* Jan. 16.

Shinagawa, Larry Hajime. 1995. *Asian Pacific American electoral participation in the San Francisco Bay area.* San Francisco: Asian Law Caucus.

Simon, Richard. 1991. Molina wins historic contest for supervisor. *Los Angeles Times,* Feb. 20.

Soja, Edward W. 1989. *Postmodern geographies: The reassertion of space in critical social theory.* New York: Verso.

Soja, Edward W., and Allen J. Scott. 1996. Introduction to Los Angeles: City and region. In *The city: Los Angeles and urban theory at the end of the twentieth century,* 1–21. Edited by Allen J. Scott and Edward W. Soja. Berkeley: University of California Press.

Sonenshein, Raphael J. 1993. *Politics in black and white: Race and power in Los Angeles.* Princeton: Princeton University Press.

Song, Alfred H. 1980. The Asian-American in politics. In *Political participation of Asian Americans: Problems and strategies,* 16–20. Edited by Yung-Hwan Jo. Chicago: Pacific/Asian American Mental Health Research Center.

Southest Voter Registration Education Project [SVREP]. 1995. *Latino Vote '95.* Annual Conference Program, July 14–16.

———. 1997. *Latino Vote Reporter* 2(1): 1.

Special Masters on Reapportionment. 1991. Report and recommendations of special masters on reapportionment. Filed in the Supreme Court of the State of California, Nov. 29.

Steele, Shelby. 1990. *The content of our character: A new vision of race in America.* New York: St. Martin's Press.

Swidler, Ann. 1986. Culture in action: Symbols and strategies. *American Sociological Review* 51(2): 273–86.

Tachibana, Judy. 1986. California's Asians: Power from a growing population. *California Journal,* Nov., 535–43.

Takagi, Dana. 1993. *The retreat from race: Asian American admissions and racial politics*. New Brunswick: Rutgers University Press.

Takahashi, Jere. 1982. Japanese American responses to race relations: The formation of Nisei perspectives. *Amerasia Journal* 9(1): 29–57.

Takaki, Ronald. 1989. *Strangers from a different shore: A history of Asian Americans*. New York: Penguin Books.

Takash, Paula Cruz. 1993. Breaking barriers to representation: Chicana/Latina elected officials in California. *Urban Anthropology* 22(3–4): 325–60.

Tamayo, William, Robin Toma, and Stewart Kwoh. 1991. *The voting rights of Asian Pacific Americans*. Public Policy Project. Los Angeles: Asian American Studies Center, University of California, Los Angeles.

Thernstrom, Abigail M. 1987. *Whose votes count? Affirmative action and minority voting rights*. Cambridge: Harvard University Press.

Thompson, Richard H. 1979. Ethnicity versus class: An analysis of conflict in a North American Chinese community. *Ethnicity* 6(4): 306–26.

Tobar, Hector. 1993. The politics of anger. *Los Angeles Times Magazine,* Jan. 3.

Toma, Robin, Stewart Kwoh, and William Tamayo. 1991. Testimony of the coalition of Asian Pacific Americans for fair reapportionment before the California Assembly Committee on Elections, Reapportionment and Constitutional Amendments. April 23. Author's files.

Trottier, Richard. 1981. Charters of panethnic identity: Indigenous Americans and immigrant Asian Americans. In *Ethnic change,* 271–305. Edited by Charles Keyes. Seattle: University of Washington Press.

Tseng, Yen Fen. 1994a. Suburban ethnic economy: Chinese business communities in Los Angeles. Ph.D. dissertation, University of California, Los Angeles.

———. 1994b. Chinese ethnic economy: San Gabriel Valley, Los Angeles County. *Journal of Urban Affairs* 16(2): 169–89.

Uhlaner, Carole J. 1991. Perceived discrimination and prejudice and the coalition prospects of blacks, Latinos, and Asian Americans. In *Racial and ethnic politics in California,* 339–71. Edited by Byran O. Jackson and Michael B. Preston. Berkeley: IGS Press.

Underwood, Katherine. 1992. Process and politics: Multiracial electoral coalition building and representation in Los Angeles' Ninth District, 1949–1962. Ph.D. dissertation, University of California, San Diego.

———. 1995. Ethnicity is not enough: Latino-led multiracial coalitions in Los Angeles. Paper delivered at 1995 annual meeting of the American Political Science Association.

U.S. Bureau of the Census. 1983. *1980 census of population*. Vol. 1: *Characteristics of the population*. Washington, D.C.: U.S. Government Printing Office.

———. 1990a. C90STF3A: Hispanic origin by race. Washington, D.C.: U.S. Government Priting Office.

———. 1990b. Census of population and housing summary tape file 1A. Washington, D.C.: U.S. Government Printing Office.

———. 1990c. Census of population and housing summary tape file 3A. Washington, D.C.: U.S. Government Printing Office.

———. 1990d. Census of population and housing summary tape file 3C. Washington, D.C.: U.S. Government Printing Office.

———. 1996. Current population reports: P25–1130, population projections of the United States by age, sex, race, and Hispanic origin: 1995 to 2050. Washington, D.C.: U.S. Government Printing Office.

U.S. Commission on Civil Rights. 1973. *Understanding fair housing.* Washington, D.C.: U.S. Government Printing Office.

———. 1975. *Twenty years after* Brown: *Equal opportunity in housing.* Washington, D.C.: U.S. Government Printing Office.

———. 1992. *Civil rights issues facing Asian Americans in the 1990s.* Washington, D.C.: U.S. Government Printing Office.

van den Berghe, Pierre. 1967. *Race and racism.* New York: John Wiley.

Vea, Alfredo. 1993. *La Maravilla.* New York: Dutton.

Verba, Sidney, and Norman Nie. 1972. *Participation in America.* New York: Harper and Row.

Vigil, Maurilio. 1990. The ethnic organization as an instrument of political and social change: MALDEF, a case study. *Journal of Ethnic Studies* 18(1): 15–31.

Waldinger, Roger, and Mehdi Bozorgmehr. 1996. The making of a multicultural metropolis. In *Ethnic Los Angeles,* 3–37. Edited by Roger Waldinger and Mehdi Bozorgmehr. New York: Russell Sage Foundation.

Waldinger, Roger, and Yen Fen Tseng. 1992. Divergent diasporas: The Chinese communities of New York and Los Angeles compared. *Revue Europene des Migrations Internationales.* 8(3): 91–115.

Wang, Ling-Chi. 1996. Foreign money is no friend of ours. *AsianWeek,* Nov. 8.

Ward, Mike. 1986. Bolstered by Prop. 63 vote, foe of non-English signs renews attack. *Los Angeles Times,* Nov. 9.

Watanabe, Teresa. 1989. Taiwanese "brains" leave U.S. *Los Angeles Times,* Dec. 29.

Waters, Mary. 1990. *Ethnic options: Choosing identities in America.* Berkeley: University of California Press.

Weintraub, Daniel M. 1991. Incumbents come first in redistricting, speaker says. *Los Angeles Times,* Aug. 30.

Wollenberg, Charles. 1972. Race and class in rural California: The El Monte berry strike of 1933. *California Historical Quarterly* 51(2): 155–64.

———. 1978. *All deliberate speed: Segregation and exclusion in California schools, 1855–1975.* Berkeley: University of California Press.

Wu, Frank. 1996. Damage control. *AsianWeek,* Nov. 15.

Yancey, William L, Eugene P. Ericksen, and Richard N. Juliani. 1976. Emergent ethnicity: A review and reformulation. *American Sociological Review* 41(3): 391–403.

Yip, Alethea. 1996a. Dueling data. *AsianWeek,* Nov. 15.

———. 1996b. Asian votes shift to the left. *AsianWeek*, Nov. 15.

Yokota, Ryan Masaaki. 1994. "The people united, will never be defeated": Inter-ethnic solidarity between Asian Pacific islanders and Latina/os. *Rafu Shimpo*, Nov. 22.

Yoneda, Karl G. 1983. *Ganbatte: Sixty-year struggle of a Kibei worker*. Los Angeles: Asian American Studies Center, University of California, Los Angeles.

Yoon, In-Jin. 1991. The changing significance of ethnic and class resources in immigrant businesses: The case of Korean immigrant businesses in Chicago. *International Migration Review* 35(2): 303–31.

Zavella, Patricia. 1987. *Women's work and Chicano families: Cannery workers of the Santa Clara Valley*. Ithaca: Cornell University Press.

Zhou, Min. 1992. *Chinatown: The socioeconomic potential of an urban enclave*. Philadelphia: Temple University Press.

Zinn, Maxine. 1975. Political familism: Toward sex role equality in Chicano families. *Aztlan* 6(1): 13–25.

———. 1979. Field research in minority communities: Ethnic, methodological and political observations by an insider. *Social Problems* 27(2): 209–19.

INDEX

ABC (American-born Chinese), 9

Affirmative action. *See* Proposition 209

AFL-CIO, 156–57

African Americans: and civil rights movement, 3, 63, 75; and discrimination, 13–14, 32; disputes settled, 68; professional class, 63; in World War II, 25–26

Agricultural Labor Relations Act (California), 132

Agricultural Workers Organizing Committee (AWOC), 130

Alba, Richard, 39–40

Alhambra, Calif.: and employment discrimination, 162–63

Alhambra Redevelopment Agency, 119

Alhambra School Board and District, 107, 108, 109, 189, 190, 196; links diverse population, 24–25; and school violence, 150–53. *See also* Multi-Cultural Community Association

Alien Land Laws, 27, 133, 157

Alliance of Asian Pacific Labor, 159

Almada, David, 37, 58, 94, 95, 96, 147, 193

Alonso, Francisco, 84, 94

Amaya, Abel, 148

Amerasia Journal, 66

American: defined, 1; and "good immigrant," 59

American Civil Liberties Union (ACLU), 139, 173

American culture: Chinese perception of, 51

American Federation of Labor (AFL): and Japanese, 129, 153

American Legion: incident of discrimination, 13–14

Americanness: and Anglo culture, 41; under attack, 52; equated with whiteness, 39, 56, 145; and Japanese compliance, 145; Latinos and, 50, 153–54

Ammeian, Lucy, 44

Analytic factors, 197

Angelides, Phil, 119

Anglo culture, 41, 53

Anti-Asian incidents, 13, 170. *See also* Epithets; Hate crimes

Anti-immigrant views, 37, 111

APALC. *See* Asian Pacific American Legal Center

Aranjo, Roland, 68

Arax, Mark, 59

Architectural style: and symbolic ethnicity, 41, 47–48, 52, 53

Arroyo Group, 40, 41

Asian American Legal Defense and Education Fund (New York City), 69, 97

Asian American San Gabriel Valley group, 169

Asian American voting patterns, 97–102

Asian Americans: cultural construction and panethnicity, 2; economic power and employment, 36, 63; ethnic alliances developed, 8, 9, 31, 55–56, 61–63; identity construction, 55–63, 86; interethnic tensions, 38, 58; as laborers, 126, 128–33; and naturalization, 70; and panethnicity and political contributions, 89, 83, 96; political networks forged, 63–64, 76,

LELAND T. SAITO is an assistant professor of ethnic studies and affiliated with the Urban Studies and Planning Program at the University of California, San Diego. He holds a master's degree and Ph.D. in sociology from the University of California, Los Angeles.

THE ASIAN AMERICAN EXPERIENCE